How to Fly

An Educational Book

By

Christian Rühenbeck

Bibliographical Information of the Deutsche Nationalbibliothek
This publication is listed in the Deutsche Nationalbibliographie
of the Deutsche Nationalbibliothek; detailed bibliographical
information can be accessed under http://dnb.d-nb.de

Printing and Production: BoD – Books on Demand Norderstedt
Germany

ISBN: 978-3-7597-4499-9

It took several years to compile the content of this book, to conduct the experiments, and to formulate the texts. My family has been asked for a lot of patience during this process.

My gratitude for the intense support of my daughter Andrea Rühenbeck in translating my German textbook "Wie geht Fliegen?" cannot be expressed enough.

1894 - The American physicist Robert W. Wood reported on an impression during a visit to the Lilienthal's in Berlin-Lichterfelde:

"When the apparatus lay before me in the grass, with its large white wings shining brightly in the sunlight, I had the sensation as if the era of flying had truly begun. Here was an aircraft not just assembled by a fool to be shown at a fair for ten pennies or merely to provide material for articles on aviation. No: constructed by a capable engineer, this aircraft embodied the results of eight years of successful experiments. A machine that was made not just for observation but for flying."

(from "Der Traum vom Fliegen zwischen Mythos und Technik" by Wolfgang Behringer and Constance Ott-Koptschalijski, S. Fischer 1991, p. 388)

Table of Contents

Appendix

On the Airplane

We stand at the beginning of the runway. Impatiently, we wait for the plane to take off. Now the engines roar. They push the fully loaded aircraft forward. With an unexpectedly great force, we are pressed back into our seats. The Airbus accelerates like a race car! My gaze falls upon the many passengers seated tightly in rows of six before me, filled with an anxious calmness. Will the plane lift off? Through the small side window, I see how the wing looks different: several flaps at the trailing edge of the wing are angled downward. I wonder why. Suddenly, the plane takes off, creating a sensation similar to being in a moving elevator. Then, it is done, we are flying. Astonishing and hard to comprehend: A heavy aircraft carrying nearly 200 people and their luggage is suspended in the air, despite the fact that it supposedly lacks any visible support bars! Long before reaching cruising altitude, the wing reverts to its normal appearance. Monitors display the current speed, altitude, and outside temperature. We continue to accelerate. At an altitude of about 10 km (above sea level), we are flying towards our destination at over 850 km/h, with an outside temperature below minus 50 degrees Celsius.

Boredom in the next three hours? Not for me. I imagine that even the ancient Greeks Icarus and Daedalus, occasionally mentioned in stories, are sitting on this plane. I wonder what would be going through their minds. Or Leonardo da Vinci, who pondered the possibility of flying during the 15th and early 16th centuries. Yet, like many others after him, he could not unravel the true secret of flying, which is why his experiments and those of his successors failed. Even Otto Lilienthal, arguably the first to achieve human-piloted gliding flight, could only lift one end of the veil that conceals the actual secret of flying. However, like many other aviation pioneers, he discovered the initial principles and configurations required for gliding in the air. He conducted the first systematic observations on flying, shaped the appearance of a glider, and figured out how it should be "adjusted." I recall the numerous accidents in the early days of aviation. At the beginning of human-piloted flight, properly configuring a flying device was more a matter of trial and error than understanding the secret of flying. And what about this secret? I have often tried to figure it out but have not found the answer. Nowadays, there are many writings that claim to explain how flying works. However, much of it is contradictory, and some of it is utterly false. I have realized that, despite 125 years of successful aeronautics, there are ten explanations for flying in ten selected books about flying, but apparently none of them is universally accepted by all authors! I think that is a peculiar matter that should be explored! We call our age the age of knowledge. As a science journalist recently wrote: Modern science's X-ray vision leaves nothing hidden. Just as I am about to be annoyed that this might not hold true for flying, the descent begins. Once again, the wing flaps are extended below, followed by the landing gear. Occasionally, the plane is shaken by light turbulence, but the pilot smoothly touches down on the runway. The passengers spontaneously applaud. Why might that be? Well, everyone feels a sense of unease when flying, no matter how perfect the technology may be and how commonplace flying in modern aircraft has become. It is this combination of uneasy feelings and questions about the mystery of flying that continues to linger long afterwards.

Finally, I sat down and began to think about flying.

A Controversy

Instead of delving into the bewildering world of explanations about flying, I would rather present a controversy that reflects the current state of experts on the subject of flying. At the end of 2001, an article titled "Why Can an Airplane Fly?" was published in the science section of the national German newspaper "Die Zeit" and was also made available online on December 31, 2001. The complete text of this article can be found on page 163 and should be read before continuing.

You are surprised? So am I. Anyone interested in an explanation of flying will be left wondering after studying this article: What is going on? Why can't aeronautics experts agree on such an explanation that can be presented to a school textbook author or a NASA employee? Let us set aside the NASA employee for a moment. Then, explicitly, the textbook author is accused of using an explanation of flying that is clearly labeled as foolish by the two American professors Anderson and Eberhardt.[1] I think the textbook author should be protected. Instead, the question should be asked: Where did he get such "foolishness" from? Did he get it from experts who cannot convey their knowledge in an understandable way? And what knowledge are we even talking about?

Let us name, at this point, one of the explanations circulating in aviation, which has also been addressed by Anderson and Eberhardt. The so-called path length concept refers to the idea of the longer distance traveled by air parcels along the upper surface of the wing compared to air parcels on the lower surface. It is believed that these parcels, arriving at the trailing edge of the wing simultaneously, should therefore be traveling faster on the upper surface. As Anderson and Eberhardt rightly point out, this is "nonsense." However, one may question whether their alternative explanation is more convincing. Let us consider, for example, the so-called Coanda effect mentioned by them, an effect that is not found in the existing aeronautics literature, see page 245. According to this

---

[1] Anderson, D. F., Eberhardt, S. (2001). *Understanding Flight*. Second Chapter: How Airplanes Fly. New York: McGraw-Hill.

effect, the air flowing over the curved upper surface of a wing should be drawn towards the surface and, as the expert says, "adhere" to it (and in this way, some believe, generate lift). If one has paid attention in school, one should, however, wonder whether free air parcels (like gases in general) can be subjected to tensile forces and thus be drawn in. If this famous "suction" does not exist, then the adherence of the flowing air parcels to curved surfaces must have another reason. Aviation research is rather reserved in providing information on the cause of this flow adherence to curved surfaces. At this point, I would like to raise an important question regarding the clarification of flying: Why can air flows adhere to a cambered wing? This question is not the only one that arises when contemplating the ability to fly. It cannot be answered at this stage; we need to know more, as discussed in the chapter "What Keeps the Flow Attached?"

Anderson and Eberhardt, however, attribute the actual cause of aerodynamic lift to the pitch angle of the wing against the free flow of air. As their argument goes, this would push air masses downward, resulting in the creation of lift that keeps the aircraft in the air. However, with their motto "forget Bernoulli and use Newton's laws," they go against the widely held view of other aeronautics experts, who firmly believe that in an (ideal) flow around the wing, air parcels are not pushed downward anywhere. Instead, lift during flight is generated by the creation of a pressure difference above and below the wing. As someone with a scientific interest in aviation but lacking expertise, I encounter a fundamental problem here: Two quite different explanations exist for the same phenomenon ("... but equations don't explain why aerodynamic lift occurs... both theories are incomplete explanations... still, no consensus exists...").[2] Who is right in this case? Since such a

---

[2] Regis, E. (February 2020). *The Enigma of Aerodynamic Lift*. Scientific American, 322 (2), 44-51.

question can only be answered through observations, I have searched for flow patterns around the wing of a freely flying aircraft. However, such observations are hard to come by: Unlike observations in wind tunnels, observations of freely flying aircraft are quite rare. Therefore, answering the question of who is right is not so straightforward.

Although it may seem so, the disagreement reflected in the newspaper article is not solely an American invention. Similar alternative explanations for aerodynamic lift as a prerequisite for flying have also been the subject of many publications in Germany since 1985, primarily in specialized physics journals for schools.[3] The perspective on the cause of flying advocated by Anderson and Eberhardt has gained many followers and found its way into textbooks in Germany, as this explanation easily connects to the treatment of Newton's laws. It is astonishing that experts in aeronautics research have been reluctant to oppose this view, and if they do, they do so in a manner far less diplomatic than Professor Voit-Nitschmann, quoted in the "Zeit" article (see the caption for Figure 40). The reason for this restraint probably lies not only in experts' aversion to delving into the depths of school physics and clearing up a few misconceptions there but also in the fact that the traditional explanation of flying in aviation has several "gaps", which will be discussed in this book and have likely given rise to alternative ideas about flying.

Upon examining numerous recent publications in physics education about flying, authored by individuals with extensive experience in constructing and test-flying model aircraft, a particular suspicion arises: Have the authors made the effort to genuinely understand

---

[3] Weltner, K. (1985). *Rückstoßprinzip oder Bernoullisches Gesetz, physikalische und didaktische Analyse der Erklärungen des aerodynamischen Auftriebs.* München: Tagungsberichte der DPG 1985, FA Didaktik

the "recipes" by which one can make a model glider fly? Or even what these recipes might have to do with generating lift? One tends to read about observations and experiments conducted on fixed wings in the air flow, which, for understandable reasons, support Anderson and Eberhardt's view of the actual cause of lift generation. In this book, therefore, I intend to proceed as follows: Only those who truly experiment with freely movable simple gliders and thereby study how to make them glide properly, only those who then possess certain insights into flying mechanics, will find the door that leads to the secret laboratory of aerodynamic lift as the basis of flying.

When Scott Eberhardt, quoted in the "Zeit" article, laments that his students, despite having excellent mathematical training, cannot develop a genuine understanding of flight physics, it is also related to the origin and significance of the Bernoulli equation, which is considered essential for the generation of aerodynamic lift in classical aeronautics literature. The truth is this equation is indeed not understandable. On the other hand, its application is so successful that it must contain a kernel of truth. But what is that "kernel"? The fact that we achieve success with an equation that is not fully understood needs to be investigated. This is addressed in the chapters "Hydrodynamic Paradox, What is It?" and "Bernoulli Equations".

It is undisputed that due to the extraordinary complexity of the air flow around wings, only the mentioned wind tunnel evaluations in the "Zeit" article can provide more precise information about the magnitude of lift. Therefore, the opinion, fueled by Professor Voit-Nitschmann, also quoted in the article, is often expressed that without a wind tunnel, a true understanding of the cause(s) of lift generation is not possible. If that were true, the author of this book could stop writing, and as an interested reader, you could stop reading further. Because then, the secret of flying would have to be sought in modern wind tunnels, the depths of modern supercomputers, and artificial intelligence (AI). Currently, even the most powerful computers need to be fed with existing knowledge to perform meaningful data processing.

I am concerned with the existing knowledge. Thankfully, it has not been fully exhausted. It becomes evident that neither a wind tunnel nor a supercomputer is necessary to achieve a basic understanding of lift generation. On the contrary, a wing (or wing segment) that is not adequately free to move in a wind tunnel hinders significant insights into understanding lift generation and instead promotes some of the ideas that have led to alternative explanations of lift that fundamentally differ from those of aeronautics. To make this point clear, we must delve deep into the beginnings again, into observations of the behavior of flat and curved plates in the air flow. Please refer to the chapters "How Does Sinking Work?", "What Does Lilienthal Tell Us?", "How Does Gliding Work?", and "The Purpose of Airfoils" for a more detailed exploration of these topics.

As you continue reading the book, you will find that the author is "caught between two stools," not fully endorsing either Anderson and Eberhardt or the aeronautics experts in every aspect. While this may be uncomfortable, it frees the mind to approach the mystery of flying from entirely different angles. And that can be quite exciting. However, before delving into that, let us address a fundamental remark regarding the last sentence of the aforementioned "Zeit" article. The belief that physics has unraveled all secrets is also a fallacy and should be thoroughly dispelled. In fact, upon closer examination, nature and physics, as one aspect of describing nature, are practically composed of mysteries! Einstein once said something along the lines of: "The more I understand the world, the more I realize how little I know about it." Those who engage in research discover that every seemingly solved problem brings forth many new problems. Therefore, it is to be expected that every presumed answer to the question of "How does flying work?" will raise a multitude of new questions, whose answers will either confirm existing assumptions or lead to a new and different understanding.

Why so Much Physics and Mathematics?

"How to fly" that is the title of my book about one of humanity's oldest dreams: the dream of flying. This dream has been a reality for over 125 years. Flying is now a common experience in our daily lives, but it still does not happen without a racing heart. Watching a paper plane crash is not particularly exciting. It is even worse to see a meticulously assembled model aircraft shatter on the ground. We dare not even imagine the thought of a large airplane, carrying ourselves or others, on the verge of crashing. Because these incidents still occur, it is evident that flying, and therefore understanding flying, is not a simple or straightforward matter.

However, there are writings that claim flying is easy to explain. I wonder what the authors were thinking. Have they completely overlooked the constant evolution of so-called secure knowledge throughout the development of natural sciences? Anyone interested in the natural sciences has repeatedly experienced that there are no easily explainable natural phenomena. This becomes apparent to anyone who has ever truly pondered something that seemed simple. Need a brief example? Everyone knows that a stone falls. Some people know how a stone falls. No one knows why a stone falls. Or do they? One should approach someone who claims to know with skepticism. On page 165, you will find a fascinating story about asking "why" questions ("Mia asks"). Scientists cannot answer why a stone falls. They address how a stone falls, down to the smallest details. To do so, they rely not only on physics (formulas) but also on a significant amount of mathematics (calculations).

The healthiest working hypothesis has proven to be to assume, in principle, that no natural phenomenon is easy to explain, and that bird flight is among the particularly complex natural phenomena. This means that anyone seeking to understand how flying works will have to face several difficulties. Physics and mathematics, as tools, contribute to these difficulties in a distinct way. And here lies a problem for both the author and the reader: except for a few exceptions, nobody enjoys reading books filled with physical formulas and mathematical derivations. But what can be done? Talking about flying or, more precisely, discussing the conditions of flying without using formulas is like going on a beach vacation without water. As an author, what can I do to minimize disruption to the reader's experience? Mathematical descriptions and derivations are relegated to an appendix, while the underlying physics behind each observation of flying still needs to be discussed in the text.

In the field of physics education, there have been recent developments that also have implications for our topic of flying. The question arises regarding which emphasis of natural description is more important or accurate. Are many processes better described as dynamic, such as through flows, energy flows (i.e., power transfer or absorption), entropy flows (i.e., heat transfer), or momentum flows (i.e., force interactions)?[4] Or can nature be more accurately captured through the assessment of a sequence of static snapshots? Is natural description more aligned with process variables or with more easily measurable state variables? For some, this may seem like an argument about trivialities. However, caution is advised: Explanations of flying have also become part of this discussion!

---

[4] Falk, G., Hermann, F. (1979). *Ein moderner Physikkurs für Anfänger und seine Begründung. Klassische Mechanik in moderner Darstellung.* Konzepte eines zeitgemäßen Physikunterrichts. Hildesheim: Schroedel, 3, 80.

In the early days of aviation, it quickly became apparent that reasonable simplifications of flow assessment were needed. Two methods were available: tracking the fate of individual fluid particles (Lagrangian) or examining the space through which the fluid particles flow (Eulerian). Due to the complexity and difficulty of the first method, focus was placed on the second method, which has become the foundation of modern aeronautics research.[5] However, some researchers eventually returned to the first method.

Since the emergence of alternative descriptions of physical processes, a similar discussion has unfolded in the explanation of flying: Some believe that when it comes to the cause of dynamic lift, Newton's principles should be followed, and they give credence to the idea of finding a specific impulse current (i.e., the fate of individual fluid particles). They believe they have discovered this impulse current through the deflection of air parcels by the wing during flight (see the article from the science section of "Die Zeit" on Page 163). This viewpoint contrasts with the description of flying by classical aerodynamics as a quasi-steady state, resulting from the creation of a sustained pressure difference above and below a wing (i.e., altering the space through which the fluid particles flow). The curious reader is perplexed and wonders which is true. Is it "to" or "fro?" It is not easy to weigh the options and contribute to a decision! This book is an attempt to address this issue.

Unfortunately, since the early days of aeronautics, there have been remarkably diverse opinions circulating about the explanation of flying, including many that are hardly worth considering. This raises the fundamental question: Has flying been sufficiently understood at all? Is the working hypothesis that flying is by no means fully understood too bold? Can a more comprehensive understanding of

---

[5] Schlichting, H., Truckenbrodt, E. (1967). *Aerodynamik des Flugzeuges, Erster Band*. Berlin, Heidelberg, New York: Springer, 22.

flying be achieved by first clarifying basic observations, and then forming one's own opinion as the complexities of the subject increase, thereby potentially gaining a better understanding of how flying works? What result awaits the curious reader? Will all questions be answered? The author of this book does not want to be exposed to criticism for delivering yet another example of annoying trivial literature on the subject of "how to fly." The reader will be confronted with many contradictions and inconsistencies regarding flying and attempts to clarify them. In the end, you will indeed know how to properly adjust a functioning aircraft and understand why it needs to be done that way using physics and mathematics. However, caution should be exercised when it comes to the question of how flying works, as it is necessary to approach it with a mindset of "this could be how it is." Because the wisdom still holds true, as a young person once aptly expressed in the face of ever-changing perspectives on natural phenomena: **In truth, reality is quite different**.

Who could benefit from the content of this book? The present book, according to the author's hope, will fill some of the gaps left by aeronautics research and address the causes of misconceptions and alternative ideas regarding the true origin of aerodynamic lift. It may also bridge the knowledge gap between a high school graduate and the offerings of university studies, thus eliminating deficiencies in understanding flight physics. Because flying cannot be accomplished solely with excellent mathematical knowledge or fancy computer programs; flying can only be experienced. Insights from the theory and practice of simple model gliders will therefore play a significant role in this book. After all, how can one explain the flight of an aircraft if they cannot even explain the gliding of a model aircraft? While aviation experts may argue that aircraft fly at different Reynolds numbers, they may be correct, but they have not yet explained anything.

Part I: Am I Flying?

What Does Archimedes Tell Us?

Whether the Greek mathematician Archimedes knew anything about his fellow countrymen Icarus and Daedalus and their ideas about flying is not known. It is also not known if he ever contemplated the topic of flying, although he did delve into the concept of lift. However, not the kind of lift required for flying. Nevertheless, it is worth starting with the traces left by Archimedes when discussing the subject of flying.

Archimedes is known to have marveled and wondered why his weight seemed to disappear every time he took his weekly bath. Allegedly, he exclaimed, "Eureka!" which roughly translates to "I have found it!"

The phenomenon that prompted Archimedes' exclamation is known today as lift, specifically static lift. Everyone is familiar with what it means. When I lie in a full bathtub, I no longer have to support my weight. Where did my weight go? The answer that Archimedes came up with is now known as Archimedes' principle: the lift experienced by an object is equal to the weight of the fluid (water or air) displaced by the submerged object. Thus, my weight is compensated for by this lift. While this is obviously true, it does not explain where this lift comes from! At this point, we encounter a type of explanation that is often provided. We "experts" tend to evade the question by "explaining" the disappearance of our weight in the water with a principle. However, upon closer examination, a principle is not an explanation but rather a clever disguise of the fact that the observation described by the principle is not actually explained. Is

Archimedes' principle merely a placebo? As a hopefully appreciative reader, you may say: "Oh my goodness, we're already stuck before anything about flying can be discussed!" If Archimedes' principle suffices for your understanding of static lift, then there is no need for you to further study this book. Because for the similar problem of weight compensation in flying, you can simply come up with a similar principle, a principle of Daedalus, where the weight of the aircraft is ultimately compensated for by something called dynamic lift. I suspect that now it becomes clearer that this has nothing to do with an explanation. It would be advisable to continue studying this book just to be cautious.

While principles are indispensable for human interactions, they are not sufficient in the field of natural sciences, as they are merely experiences encapsulated in working hypotheses. So, we find ourselves stuck. Such a situation always piques the interest of a scientist because they want to know precisely and comprehensively where and why they are stuck. However, one thing already seems clear: in both cases, static lift - which refers to weight compensation in a bathtub - and dynamic lift - which refers to weight compensation in flying - we are dealing with the same effect. But is the cause comparable as well? We need to examine this more closely.

In contrast to dynamic lift, static lift is considered relatively easy to understand. However, static lift provides a negligible contribution to the overall lift of an aircraft, as it operates in the air rather than in water. Does that mean we do not need to further understand it? Since we aim to contribute more than just a principle of Daedalus to the understanding of dynamic lift, it is important to initially focus on understanding static lift. By doing so, we can better contextualize the issues and conditions related to dynamic lift.

Let us first examine what can be observed in static lift. Take a small balloon, fill it with a quarter liter of water, and hang it on a spring balance (force meter). The balance shows the weight (or mass), as seen in Figure 1. Then, submerge the water-filled balloon, while still hanging on the spring balance, into a glass container filled with water. Behold: The weight reading disappears, a nod to Archimedes! Place the water-filled container on a digital scale with the tare function, and then submerge the water-filled balloon hanging on the spring balance. The weight reappears. Ah, no magic trick, the weight did not disappear. Upon closer observation, one will notice that the water level in the container has risen after the immersion, precisely by the volume of the submerged balloon. Therefore, it is said that a submerged body (assuming it is heavy enough) displaces an amount of water equal to its volume, and its weight is reduced by the weight of the displaced water. So, where does the weight go? It is contained within the displaced water, which is now lifted. When I go swimming in the Baltic Sea, my weight is spread out over a large area because the water level of the Baltic Sea rises by a tiny fraction.

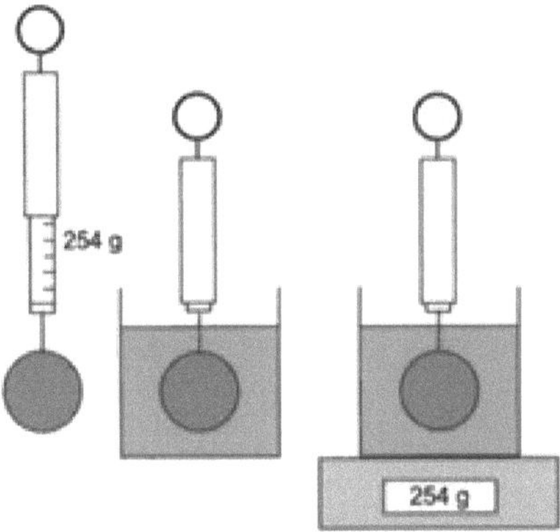

Figure 1

What we have so far is a good observation of static lift, but not a complete explanation. If the experiment described in Figure 1 is conducted in the International Space Station (ISS), which is in orbit around the Earth, one will not be able to observe what is seen on the

Earth's surface. This indicates that something is still missing in explaining static lift. It is not only the fluid (water or air) in which lift is observed that matters, but also the location where the observation takes place. So, what is special about the Earth's surface? To express this uniqueness in a physics context: Gravitation (gravity) exists there, and one is within a gravitational field. At this location, all objects have not only their mass, which they have everywhere, but also a weight proportional to their mass (for quantities and units, refer to page 1699). This weight is thus one of the causes of lift. The question now is whether we can make use of this fact to come closer to an explanation of lift.

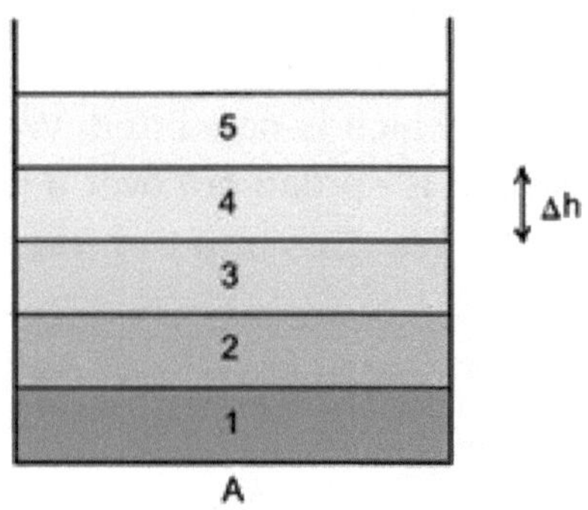

Figure 2

In Figure 2, five equally thick portions of water are depicted layered above a bottom or cross-sectional area A. Each of these water portions has a volume, mass, and weight. Page 172 provides a compilation of how the hydrostatic pressure and thus the hydrostatic basic equation arise from these measurements. With each additional portion of water, an additional weight is exerted on the bottom surface area or individual cross-sectional areas. The term "pressure" has been coined for the weight exerted on a bottom or cross-sectional area (the issue of the concept of pressure will be further explained shortly). Since the same pressure prevails everywhere within a cross-sectional area ("equipotential surface"), it is also referred to as hydrostatic or isotropic pressure. This pressure acts in all directions due to the easily movable particles that constitute the fluid, particularly upwards on the underside of a body immersed in the fluid (!).

What does this mean now? As you dive deeper, the isotropic pressure within the gravitational field of the Earth increases. Alternatively, if a body is immersed in a fluid, the pressure on its upper side is lower than on its lower side. This fact can now be utilized for understanding lift! When the weight of a submerged body becomes smaller or even disappears, this reduction in weight is caused by the pressure difference acting above and below the body (this logically applies to a body floating on the water surface as well). Such an "explanation" of static lift is applicable to the immersion of a body in water (e.g., a submarine) as well as in air (e.g., a hot air balloon). Since each practical application yields something verifiably true, one is inclined to consider this "explanation" as sufficient (in terms of completeness).

Can one speak of a theory in this explanation of lift? Probably not, because there are ambiguities in the ordinary understanding of pressure (i.e., a change in space). With the usual definition of pressure as the quotient of the acting force and the area, we encounter the following problem: Using a directed quantity force (a vector), acting on an area element, the undirected or omnidirectional quantity of pressure (a scalar) has been defined. This is obviously inconvenient for a physical theory. When we consider a force, we understand it as a physical construct that we assume acts from a specific direction on a point (the point of application), and not on an area. To fix this, we can imagine the area as a fixed wall and replace the application of pressure on the entire area with the application of an orthogonally oriented equivalent force at the so-called pressure point, which is a specific point on the area. In doing so, we bypass the mathematically and physically challenging understanding of pressure as a tensor and specifically of hydrostatic pressure as an isotropic tensor. The method of replacing pressure on a wall with the application of orthogonal equivalent forces on area elements of that wall will help us in many instances later on. The question of the significance of the internal structure of a fluid in its ability to exert pressure on a wall will also occupy us later on.

It is this "vague" image that makes pressure an unknown entity for many, capable of anything that cannot be understood. In this book, therefore, it is important to pay attention to using the term "pressure" as clearly as possible, stating precisely what is meant by it and specifying all the conditions under which the concept of pressure is significant and helpful (see also the chapter "What Keeps the Flow Attached?").

There is no shortage of attempts to avoid the aforementioned problems with understanding pressure or pressure differences, which are static concepts resulting in a force called lift. Due to the definition of force as a change in momentum and the concept of current derived from electrical theory, some people would like to replace the static force application described earlier with the application of a dynamic impulse current. In the case of lift, such an impulse current would be responsible for (partially) compensating for the weight. One could envision this as illustrated in Figure 3: An impulse current flows from the Earth's surface into the lifted body, passes through it, and then returns to the Earth's surface through the surrounding fluid. In such an image, the problem arises of finding a mechanism for this impulse current, both for static lift and later for dynamic lift.

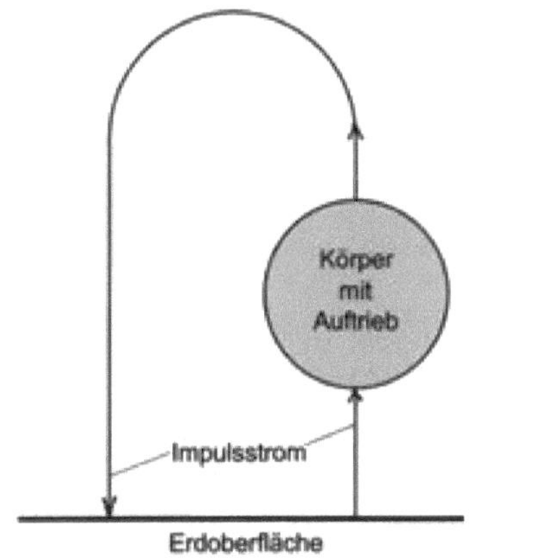

Figure 3

"Körper mit Auftrieb:"
Body with lift

"Impulsstrom:"
Momentum current

"Erdoberfläche:"
Earth's surface

Assuming that a mechanism for this impulse current can be identified, what has been achieved? While it allows us to avoid the problems with pressure phenomena at the location of the body, it is difficult to obtain quantitative information about lift. Why is that? By approaching the lift problem globally, local information is lost. We will encounter this difficulty in greater detail when it comes to dynamic lift. The same problem arises there: local information with comprehension issues regarding pressure versus always correct global impulse current physics without local information. In both cases, static and dynamic lift, the goal is the same: to explain the compensation of the weight of the affected body. In the case of a hot air balloon or an airplane, it holds true: **Air may not have bars, but it works, nonetheless.**

How Does Sinking Work?

There is a motion in the air where the weight of the moving body is completely compensated: sinking. Sinking is different from falling, specifically free-falling. If a stone is dropped from a great height, it initially undergoes free fall, meaning the stone's falling speed increases in a certain way. However, within a period of about 20 seconds after the start of the fall, the falling stone transitions into sinking: the stone no longer accelerates, but rather sinks at a constant, albeit considerably high, speed. Where does this come from?

When you hold your hand out of the open window of a fast-moving vehicle, you feel a force exerted by the air flow. The hand experiences so-called aerodynamic forces, including drag and a noticeable dynamic lift when the palm of the hand is facing in the right direction. Considering the tangible force experienced here, one can imagine that a similar force occurs when an object sinks in the air—a force capable of compensating for the object's weight. This is intriguing because flying also involves compensating for the weight of the aircraft. However, what does flying have to do with sinking? Flying is predominantly a horizontal motion, while sinking is vertical. Can understanding sinking bring us closer to understanding flying?

Observation reveals that all bodies with a (average) density greater than that of air sink when released—some faster, others slower. This leads us to the first question: What does this depend on? Upon closer inspection, a surprising discovery is made: thin, flat bodies (such as leaves) prefer to orient themselves horizontally during sinking, thus allowing them to sink as slowly as possible. This raises the second question: What is the reason behind this behavior?

Let us first address the second question. When leaves fall from trees in autumn, peculiar observations can be made. Many leaves sway irregularly back and forth while rotating, while others sink quite evenly without any swaying motion. Some leaves rotate during their descent like a rolling object, and a few even perform something akin to gliding. The latter can be observed, for example, in maple leaves that fall with their stems (this will be described in more detail in the chapter "Forward Sinking — What is It?"). If one tries to replicate similar movement patterns using sinking sheets of paper, so-called modeling, one will encounter difficulties. "Difficulties" here refers to stabilization issues that will only become understandable after further study of this book.

However, the most striking observation about the behavior of these leaves is that they prefer to sink in a transverse orientation, i.e., with the greatest air resistance. One could imagine that they would instead prefer to sink in the direction of minimal resistance, a perpendicular direction. To clarify this observation, we conduct a simple experiment, as shown in Figure 4. It is an experiment that astonishes the uninformed observer and prompts the informed observer to contemplate further.

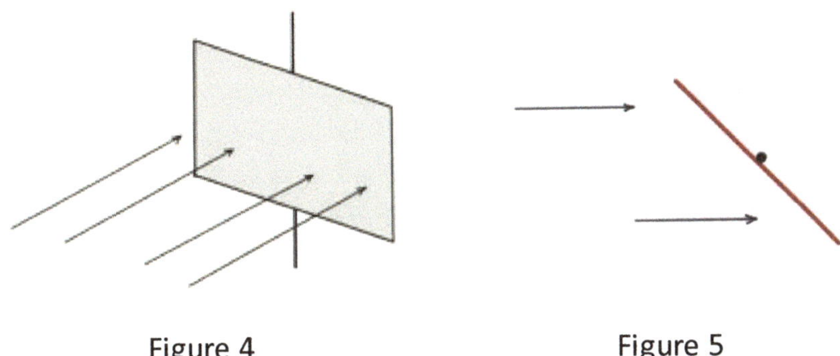

Figure 4   Figure 5

A postcard is attached in the middle of a knitting needle, which is held between two fingers at its ends in the air flow of a hairdryer. One will be amazed because no matter what one tries, the postcard always aligns itself transversally, i.e., with maximum resistance to the air flow! Although this simple observation, as we will see, is one of the prerequisites for a mechanical understanding of flying, it has not been found in the literature on flying so far. This is likely not only because it is considered insignificant but also because it is not easy to comprehend. In Figure 5, a top-down view is taken of a postcard initially positioned at an angle to the air flow from Figure 4. One can imagine that the air parcels arriving from the left (at the top in Figure 5) experience a significantly greater change in momentum when overcoming the left (upper) edge compared to the air parcels arriving from the right around the right (lower) edge. Assuming the central position of the knitting needle and a swirling of the air, the left half of the postcard thus creates a higher resistance than the right half, resulting in an unbalanced torque. The resistances of the two halves of the postcard and, therefore, the moments causing clockwise or counterclockwise rotation are equal in magnitude only when the postcard is perfectly aligned perpendicularly to the direction of the air flow.

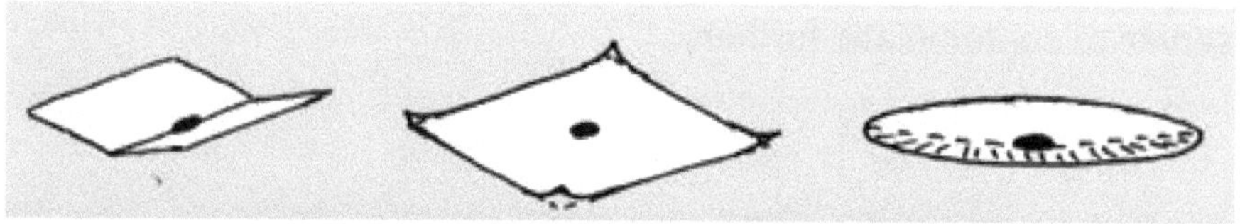

Figure 6

In Figure 4, the postcard is stabilized in the air flow by being threaded through a knitting needle. The situation can be rotated by 90 degrees: one simply lets a postcard sink, and the airflow occurs automatically. Unfortunately, the sinking process is not observed to be uniform; the postcard oscillates back and forth similar to the autumn leaves described earlier. If we want to study the sinking process more closely, it needs to be stabilized. The necessary stabilization techniques are similar to those required for stable flight later on. Three of them are outlined in Figure 6. Either the postcard is lightly folded into a shallow V-shape, or the four corners are bent upward. Alternatively, a circular plane that is pressed down like a flat cone can be used. In each case, a variable ballast piece (e.g., made of lead) is attached in the middle, allowing for different sink rates to be achieved.

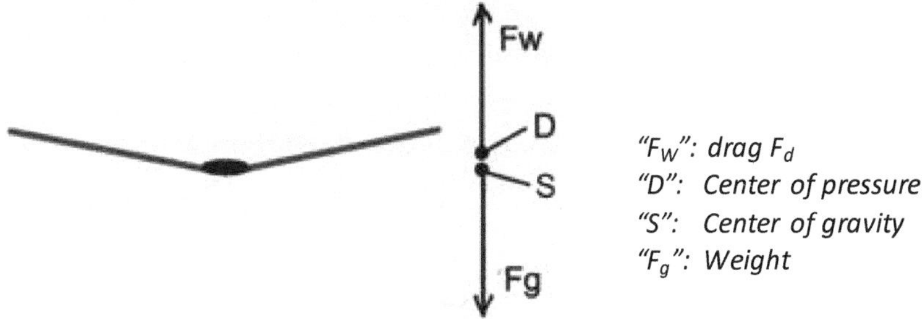

Figure 7

In Figure 7, the nature of stabilization can be characterized, using the example of the postcard from Figure 6, which is folded into a slight V-shape. The center of gravity, denoted as S (which in Earth's gravitational field is the same as the center of mass), where the weight force F_g acts, is located slightly below the center of pressure, denoted as D, where the air force (in this case, the drag force F_d) acts. Both forces are directed in opposite directions and are equal in magnitude during uniform sinking (the apparent question of why a sinking process can occur at all is one of the questions in kinematics that can be confusing). The terms center of gravity and center of pressure may seem casually mentioned here, but they will be of central importance for the ability to fly later on. Therefore, a brief "definition" of these points is provided. Since Newton's time, there has been an axiom (a postulate) for extended bodies, which states the following: All ("elementary") parts of an arbitrarily shaped body experience an attraction, known as weight, in the Earth's gravitational field. The effect of all these partial weights can be combined into a total weight, denoted as F_g in Figure 7, which acts at a particular point called the center of gravity, denoted as S. If a body is supported or suspended at its center of gravity, it experiences no resulting torque. The center of pressure can be understood in an equivalent way: All ("elementary") parts of an arbitrarily shaped body experience a force called drag (resistance) when in a continuous air flow. The effect of all these partial resistances or drags can be combined into a total drag, denoted as F_d in Figure 7, which acts at a particular point called the center of pressure, denoted as D. If a body in an air flow is "supported" (i.e., fixed in a way that allows rotation) at its center of pressure, it experiences no resulting torque (as observed in Figure 4). Now it is easy to understand when a body can sink stably in the Earth's gravitational field: when its center of gravity is located a certain distance below its center of pressure.

The simple fact depicted in Figure 7 alone is sufficient to dispel a widely held misconception about flying, as shown in Figure 8 (the image is taken from a course on flying authored by a university professor intended for school education).[6] In this image, during horizontal flight, it is assumed that the air force, which compensates for the weight F_g, comes from lift generated by the wing and the horizontal tailplane, with the center of gravity S positioned in between. The author had in mind an equilibrium of torques, as indicated by the labeled distances l_1 and l_2, meaning that the resultant center of pressure from the points of application of F_{P1} and F_{P2} lies directly above the center of gravity. However, in accordance with Figure 7, such a configuration does <u>not</u> result in horizontal flight but rather to vertical sinking (or a forward sinking, as discussed in the next chapter) in that flight attitude! A model aircraft enthusiast would say: The aircraft behaves similar to a model airplane with activated thermal brake. In order to fly, the positions of the center of gravity and center of pressure of the aircraft must indeed be different! It will be revealed that specific positions of the center of gravity and center of pressure are crucial for flying.

---

[6] Luchner, K. (1990). *Fliegen – angewandte Physik*. Praxis Schriftenreihe Physik. Köln: Aulis, 48, 95.

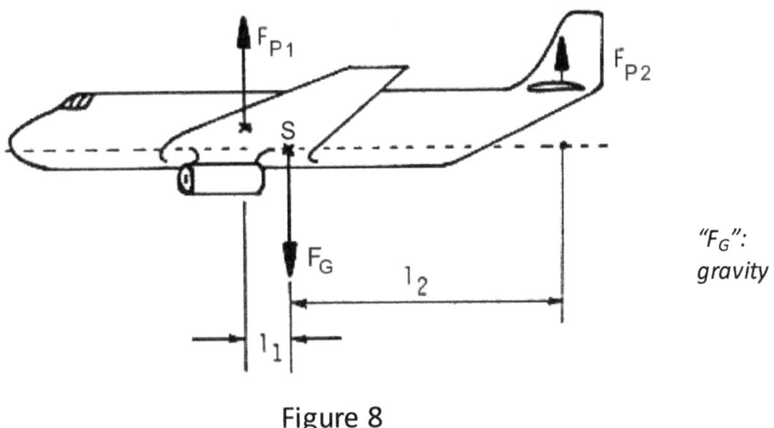

Figure 8

Now we can turn our attention to answering the first question: What can be observed during uniform sinking experiments according to Figure 6? As a reminder, uniform descent occurs only after a certain "run-up distance," which needs to be considered in descent measurements. When using paper cards of equal surface areas, a close proportionality between weight and the square of the vertical sink rate is found. If cards of different surface areas are used, a proportionality between weight and the surface area A can be assumed, but there are deviations that are related to the shape of the surface, which need to be explained.

If a knife is slowly drawn through honey in a direction perpendicular to the knife's surface, one can observe a flow pattern on its surface similar to the one on the left in Figure 9 (laminar flow). However, if a board is rapidly moved through water in a direction perpendicular to its surface, one can observe a flow pattern on the water's surface similar to the one on the right in Figure 9 (turbulent flow). When a flat body moves through air, as shown in Figure 6, only a flow pattern similar to the one on the right in Figure 9 is observed, which involves the formation of vortices behind the object. We can assume that the majority of the resistance encountered in this case is caused by these vortices or turbulence. Resistance (caused by turbulence e.g.) is called "drag" in aerodynamics. The magnitude of the drag can be measured more accurately, as detailed on Page 172.

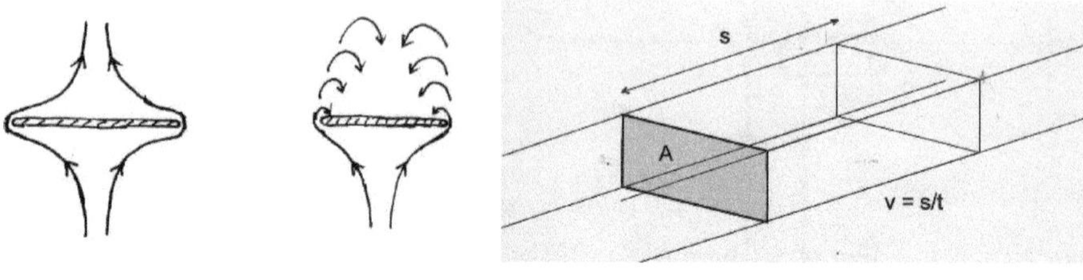

Figure 9   Figure 10

Starting from Figure 10, let us first consider a plate with the surface area A that is moving through the air with a velocity v in the direction of the surface normal. Within a time interval t, a volume of air V is being accelerated by this motion. To accomplish this, work must be done to accelerate the air. Factoring in the density of the air and the concept of "energy density" (which is a complex concept), we arrive at the intuitive notion of dynamic pressure generated by the motion of the plate. However, equating energy density and pressure can be problematic, as will become apparent in the chapter on the "Hydrodynamic Paradox, What is It?"

Since we do not know whether a volume $V = As$ is actually being swirled behind plate A in Figure 10 during the time interval t, or whether it is larger or smaller, a dimensionless factor c_d should be introduced. This factor, called the "drag coefficient," encompasses all the unknowns that can only be determined experimentally. With this coefficient, we can establish an equation for the aerodynamic drag, applicable to all bodies with a maximum cross-sectional area A moving through the air with a velocity v that is neither too small nor too high, assuming a density ρ of the air. According to Figure 7, since the magnitude of the drag force F_d is equal to the magnitude of the weight force F_g during uniform sinking, the drag coefficient of bodies can be easily determined by measuring the vertical sink rate. For sharp-edged square surfaces, drag coefficients c_d around 1.23 are found, for elongated rectangular surfaces up to 2, for circular surfaces around 1.17, for table tennis balls around 0.31, and for Styrofoam balls around 0.26. Where no measured values are known, the approximate value of 1 is usually used. This demonstrates the level of uncertainty that can exist when it comes to the more or less turbulent flow around a body.

Now let us describe in more detail a specific sinking process that is of particular importance for flying. We will focus on the vertical sinking velocity of an aircraft in its normal flight attitude, which corresponds to the sinking process depicted in the force and moment distribution of Figure 8. This state is achieved in uncontrolled free-flight model gliders using a technique known as thermal braking. For such a model glider, with the following data: wing loading $F_g/A = 12 \ N/m^2$, air density $\rho = 1.25 \ kg/m^3$ (standard density), and a drag coefficient $c_d \approx 1$, using the equation provided on page 172, the vertical sink rate can be calculated to be approximately $v_\perp \approx 4{,}4 \ \frac{m}{s}$. Now, an astonishing fact emerges that is not described anywhere in the aeronautics literature: This value is approximately equal to the speed at which this glider normally flies! Further calculations confirm that this observation holds true for all aircraft. This fact will gain significant importance in explaining how flying works.

Another problem is the determination of the drag of an aircraft during flight, specifically during horizontal motion. The precise determination of the corresponding drag coefficient during flight is crucial if we want to understand why aeronautics research primarily focuses on it. However, the question of where the dynamic lift comes from and how it compensates for the weight during flight is largely unrelated to the issue of drag. That is why the lift problem is often treated separately from drag questions. Nevertheless, drag is significant when it comes to the efficiency of flight, such as determining how long a glider can stay airborne without propulsion, as discussed in the chapter "Quality of Flight".

Forward Sinking, What is It?

Undoubtedly, wind tunnels play a significant role in conducting precise measurements in aeronautics research. However, the readers of this book usually do not have access to such research facilities and their measurement instruments. Therefore, one might feel a bit envious of the opportunities available to those researchers who can make observations and conduct investigations in wind tunnels. Does this mean that further research to understand flying should be abandoned? It may sound surprising, but there is no need to mourn the absence of a wind tunnel. In fact, there are still many things that have not been done in a wind tunnel that can be easily accomplished at the "kitchen table!" To illustrate this point, let us consider a simple example. When a flat plate is placed in a wind tunnel, it is usually fixed at some angle (known as the "angle of attack") relative to the direction of air flow. Longitudinal and transversal forces are then measured directly or indirectly using distant axes and torque measurements. However, a fixed plate no longer has the degree of freedom for rotational motion around a nearby axis, and observations such as those shown in Figure 4 and later in Figures 12 and 13 cannot be made!

In contrast, in a wind tunnel, the observation depicted in Figure 11 is typically made. Can we trust such observations regarding the magnitudes of the determined forces? In this case, an inclined flat plate is mounted, and two forces are observed: a longitudinal force and a transversal force, which are (initially without hesitation) interpreted as drag and lift, respectively. But are these forces truly observed correctly? How does the torque described in Figure 5, which is suppressed by the rigid fixation of the plate, affect the observed forces? The torque wants to rotate the plate precisely perpendicular to the direction of flow. However, it cannot do so... —??—I have no idea what complex consequences such forced flow patterns may have. However, how wonderful it is that we do not need observations in a wind tunnel and can still make progress in a way that may be simple and even accurate in addressing the subject of flying.

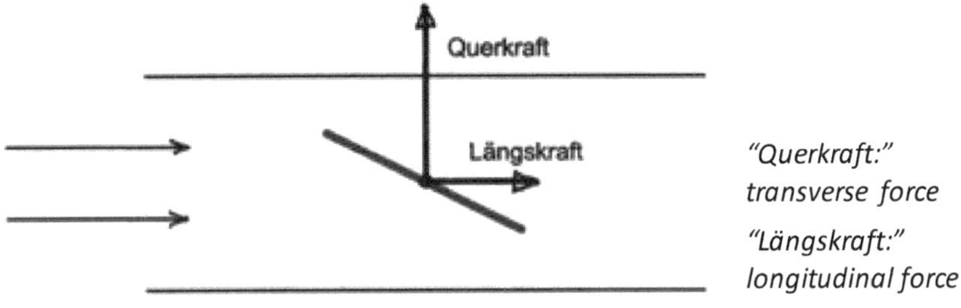

Figure 11

A tilt of the flat plate in the air flow with the angle of attack α can be achieved without any rigid fixation by shifting the knitting needle away from the axis of symmetry, as shown in Figure 4, seen in Figure 12 from above. Now, depending on the position of the axis, the flow around the flat plate can rotate into a moment-free position, and the observable longitudinal and transversal forces are more closely related to drag and lift.

To make a significant discovery that is essential for flying, the following observations need to be conducted in a more systematic manner. For this purpose, a flat plate, for example, made of two thin layers of cardboard, is prepared with drinking straws placed inside as depicted in Figure 13, through which the knitting needle can be inserted. Using the air flow from a hairdryer, the following observations can be made: In position 1 (axis of symmetry), the plate assumes the familiar transverse position with an angle $\alpha = 90°$; in position 2, a slight inclination with $\alpha < 90°$; in position 3, the inclination shown in Figure 13 with $\alpha \approx 45°$; in position 4, a similar inclination to Figure 12; in position 5, a fluctuating inclination around $\alpha \approx 0°$; and in position 6 and any further forward position, the plate stabilizes like a flag in the wind. By "forward," we now refer to the leading edge of a plate, which is first encountered by the air flow.

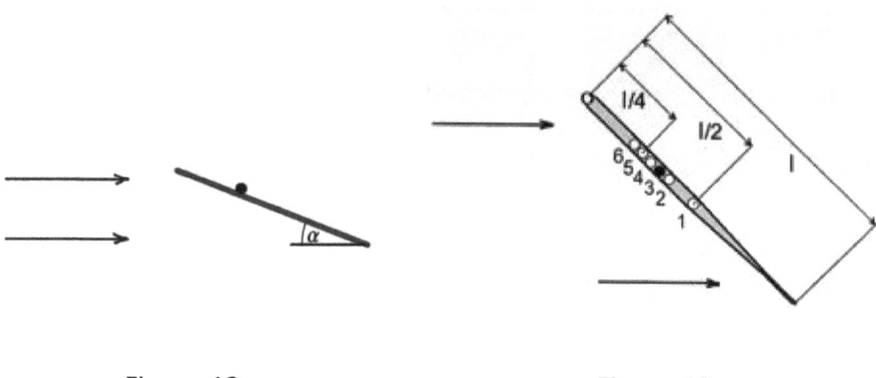

Figure 12   Figure 13

In addition to position 1 at $x = l / 2$, where l is the length of the flat plate's surface being overlapped by the air flow, position 5 at $x = l / 4$ proves to be quite interesting. There seems to be an indifferent equilibrium state at that position, where neither a stable alignment like a flag in the wind nor a stable inclination of the flat plate in the air flow occurs. It appears to be a "neutral" point where neither a transverse force nor, in ideal flow conditions, a longitudinal force occurs. The line located at $x = l / 4$ from the leading edge of the flat plate is referred to as the "quarter-chord line," later of a wing, and the point on this quarter-chord line lying on the symmetry axis of the plate is called the "neutral point." Where technically feasible, depending on the inclination of the flat plate in Figure 13, one can observe the forces mentioned in Figure 11: longitudinal forces and transverse forces. However, these forces now appear in their pure form because, unlike the conventional observation in the wind tunnel with a rigidly fixed plate, they are observed only after the moment equilibrium has been established.

As described in the previous chapter, the experimental setup can also be rotated by 90 degrees, with the force applied through the knitting needle being replaced by weight. This will result in sinking processes. How do they occur? Let us first look at nature and examine the behavior of a maple leaf with its stem, which was mentioned earlier. If something like forward sinking is observed in the fall, it can now be explained, as shown in Figure 14.

Figure 14

The two characteristic lines of Figure 13 run through the surface of the maple leaf at $l/2$ and $l/4$. When the leaf stem is removed, the stabilized leaf sinks vertically because its center of gravity is located at $l/2$. However, when the stem is present, the center of gravity (like the axis in Figure 13) is shifted further to the left near the quarter-chord line at $l/4$. As a result, the leaf with the stem does not sink vertically but obliquely or forward. This resembles a form of gliding, albeit a poor one. What can we imagine here? The guidance of a plate by a knitting needle (Figure 12) has been replaced by the effect of the weight at the center of gravity of the plate. In relation to the direction of the incoming air, the leaf thus assumes a position like that in Figure 12.

Figure 15 juxtaposes the two cases: a postcard in the air flow (left) and the maple leaf during forward sinking or the model of Figure 16 during forward sinking (right). The axis position A corresponds to the position of the center of gravity S, the force acting on the axis F_S corresponds to the weight F_g, transverse force F_t corresponds to lift F_l. The counterforce to the weight is the air force F_L acting at the pressure point D, which is the vector sum of lift F_l and the longitudinal force of resistance F_d (drag).

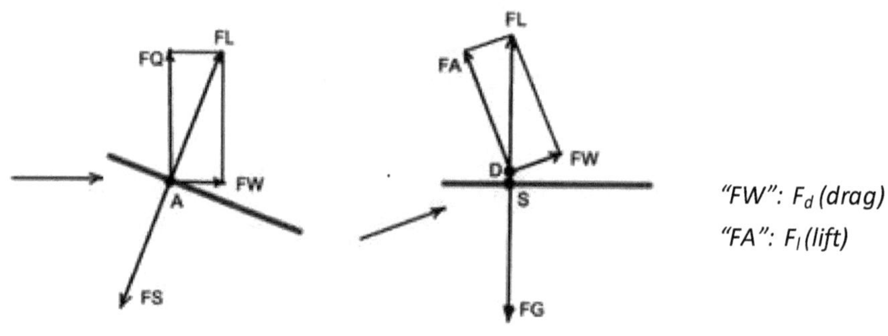

Figure 15

The depictions in Figure 15 are, of course, idealized, but necessary for the beginning. The lack of understanding of the complex reality of the flow around finite surfaces cannot play a decisive role in the understanding from the start. Therefore, we consider such incomplete representations to be quite meaningful as long as they are not fundamentally incorrect or contradict the observations. When comparing Figures 7 and 15, right subfigure, a similar distribution of forces to compensate for the weight is noticeable, but with a changed

"Anströmung" (German, which can be translated as "approach flow"), which means a different direction of movement. It would be interesting, albeit difficult, to simulate something like this in a wind tunnel.

An additional note regarding the term "lift" introduced for the first time in Figure 15 is necessary. For now, this lift, as a component of the aerodynamic force, is nothing more than a renamed transverse force. The origin of this force does not need to be explained at this point, as it is not straightforward. The transverse force in Figure 11 is referred to as lift in Figure 15 because, together with drag, it contributes to the compensation of weight similar to static lift.

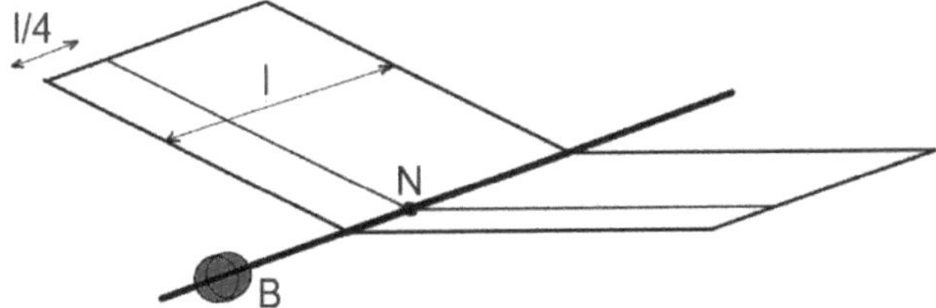

Figure 16

One can model the forward sinking of a postcard: Figure 16 depicts a possible design of such a model: a cardboard surface in a shallow V-shape (10 degrees on each side) with a knitting needle or preferably a thin wooden rod attached at the center of the fold line. A movable ballast piece B can be attached to it. The previously described neutral point N, located at the intersection of the quarter line and the symmetry axis, is marked. Without ballast B, this surface will sink vertically. By attaching a suitable ballast piece, increasingly forward sinking can be achieved, which approaches gliding when the center of gravity is just behind the neutral point. However, it is not true gliding yet: it sinks at a steeper angle than observed in actual gliders, it is not particularly stable, and there is a recurring "pitching" motion. The glide ratio described on page 173 is relatively small for forward sinking. To achieve stable and, above all, improved gliding, another idea will be necessary (see the chapter "How Does Gliding Work?".

What has been described in this chapter cannot be found anywhere in the existing literature on flying. Such findings will encounter us frequently throughout this book. It is astonishing, considering how simple, obvious, and easily executable all of this is. Apparently, the creation of forward sinking as a first approximation to gliding has been regarded as too "primitive" or unimportant to be acknowledged so far.

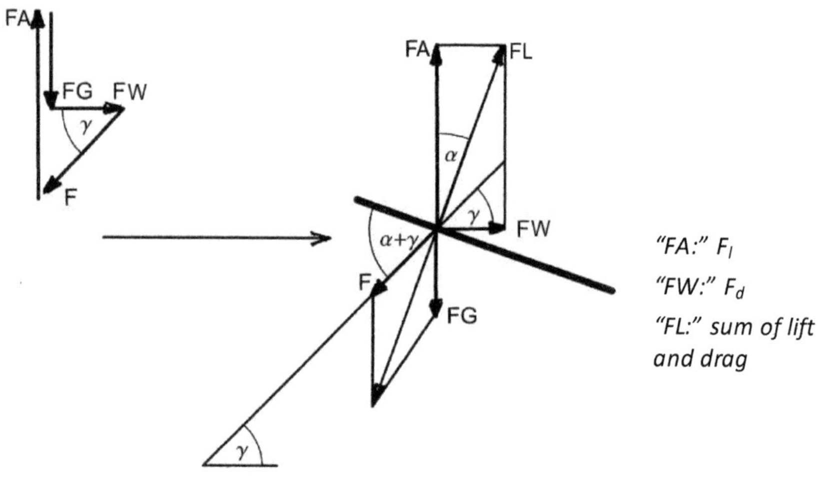

Figure 17

There are three application areas to highlight based on our current knowledge. The case depicted in Figure 15 represents the aeronautics' dreaded "stall," which occurs when the air flow over the wing separates. A second application is the ascent of a kite, as shown in Figure 17. In this case, we can include the pulling force F in the string and the ascent angle γ. Figure 17 can be used for further considerations (the "kite equation"), although we will not delve into it here. The third application area pertains to paragliding (see Figure 79). Despite employing aerodynamic tricks that result in better glide ratios than those of forward sinking, the fundamental principle behind paragliding is essentially forward sinking.

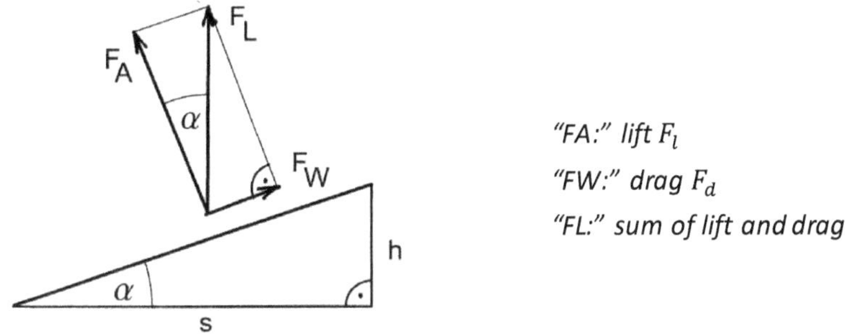

"FA:" lift F_l

"FW:" drag F_d

"FL:" sum of lift and drag

Figure 18

The quality of the "glide" behavior of forward sinking can be described in a way that is also relevant for understanding the behavior of real gliders and airplanes, as shown on page 173. When viewed from the side, the forward sinking occurs as depicted in Figure 18: Starting from a height h, with a glide angle α formed against the horizontal, the ground is reached after covering a distance s. The ratio of distance to height difference is called the glide ratio ε. A glide ratio of 3 means that the flying object has descended one meter after covering a horizontal distance of three meters. Such glide ratios are achievable in the case of forward sinking according to Figure 16, at best. With the aforementioned paragliders, glide ratios of more than double that value can be achieved, while modern high-performance gliders achieve glide ratios more than fifteen times higher. Understanding where this improvement comes from and how it can be achieved is one of the objectives of this book. Caution: The technical term *"sink rate"* undergoes a change in meaning. Now, in contrast to vertical sinking, it refers to the measure of descent during gliding, which can be obtained from the ratio of the height difference to the duration. Glide ratio and sink rate are quality indicators that appear, for example, in data sheets of gliders, but with completely different numerical values than those seen with forward sinking here.

It is natural to believe that the two performance indicators, glide ratio and sink rate, are related in a simple way, and it would not be necessary to mention both in data sheets. However, this is not the case. On page 173, it is described how these two performance indicators are related, referring to Figure 18. The important approximation for sink rate mentioned there applies with a deviation of less than 5% for glide ratios above 3, including best forward sinking. However, to predict sink rate, one must know the flying speed. We will address the topic of flying speed later in the chapter "Quality of Flight".

What Does Lilienthal Tell Us?

In the late 19th century, aviation pioneer Otto Lilienthal expressed the view, as the quintessence of his extensive research on flying, that flying is primarily a matter of drag.[7] While he did not explicitly mention the concept of forward sinking, he may have implied it with the statement "everything is drag." The transverse force F_t that occurs when a flat plate is inclined in the air flow, as shown in Figure 15 (left image), is a component of an "aerodynamic force" F_L generated by the turbulence of the air flow. This force is necessary to compensate for the weight F_g during forward sinking shown in Figure 15 (right image). This aerodynamic force consists of the components transverse force (or lift) and longitudinal force, which is considered the actual drag according to current understanding. With

---

[7] Lilienthal, O. (1996). *Der Vogelflug als Grundlage der Fliegekunst*. München: Oldenbourg Wissenschaftsverlag.

a known angle α, the magnitudes of the longitudinal and transverse forces can be determined. This conclusion seems reasonable, although it must be honestly admitted that by equating transverse force with lift, something that has not been fully thought through has been stated. Above all, flying is not solely a matter of drag.

With Figure 7, we learned that the weight of a flat body sinking vertically in the air (or water) is compensated by the drag, as described on page 174. If this were not the case, the body would be in free fall. With Figure 15, we learned that the shifting of the center of gravity leads to forward sinking, and it is worth questioning whether the weight is also compensated by drag in this case and whether Lilienthal would approve of this approach. Let us examine forward sinking more closely from this perspective.

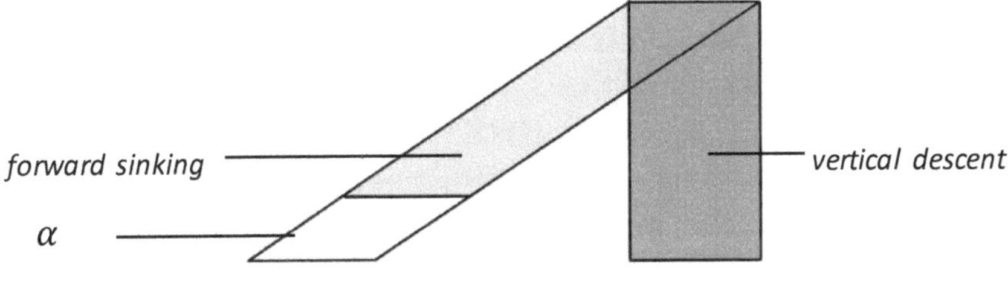

Figure 19

Assuming a horizontal position, during forward sinking, the effective area for generating the aerodynamic force, as shown in Figure 12, decreases due to the sine of the angle of attack α. Consequently, the magnitude of the aerodynamic force also decreases. Figure 19 illustrates the mathematical principle of Cavalieri: the surface area of equal-height sections remains the same when the sections are sheared. Therefore, during forward sinking, approximately the same volume of air is being swirled within the same time interval as during vertical sinking to generate the required resistance for weight compensation. However, the forward sinking flat body has to cover a longer distance in the same time period. To maintain the same amount of work (turbulence of air) performed during forward sinking, its velocity v in the direction of the forward sinking must increase. When the motion speed in the air changes, the resistance also changes, as indicated by the drag equation on page 172. Hence, we know that as the motion speed increases, the magnitude of the aerodynamic force, which compensates for the weight, also increases. Therefore, two opposing effects alter the magnitude of the aerodynamic force during forward sinking: a reduction in the effective surface area of the sinking body and an increase in its motion speed. The aerodynamic force that occurs during forward sinking is determined by the weight F_g of the body that needs to be compensated. These relationships are mathematically captured on Page 174.

Subsequently, as the angle of attack α decreases, the sink rate during forward sinking decreases. This is indicated in Figure 19 by the shading: during the time interval in which vertical sinking occurs (dark shading), the forward sinking plate is positioned slightly above (lighter shading). It is possible that this observation led Otto Lilienthal to the concept of "reduction of lift work" during forward sinking. He described how flat sinking with a small angle of attack α would be equivalent to a correspondingly small "lift work."

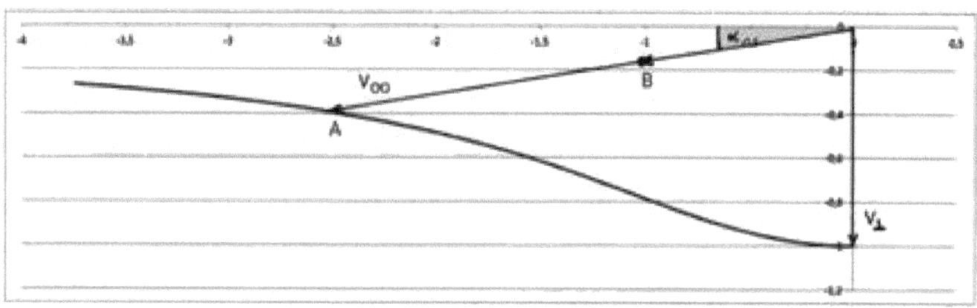

Figure 20

We can attempt to illustrate such an interpretation of Lilienthal's considerations using modern means, as shown in Figure 20. The velocity vectors v_∞, necessary to achieve weight compensation solely through the aforementioned resistance, terminate at points along the curve. The curve points have coordinates $(x|y)$, which are provided on Page 174. In Figure 20, the magnitude of $v_\perp$ is set to 1, so for $\alpha = 90°$, i.e., for vertical sinking, v_∞ has the same magnitude as $v_\perp$. As α decreases and the forward sinking happens at a steeper angle, v_∞ increases in magnitude, initially slowly and then progressively faster. Figure 20 is designed to allow for the determination of the corresponding magnitude and direction of the motion velocity v_∞ for specific angles α.

The points A and B in the diagram of Figure 20 represent the data of a glider, which will be described in the next chapter, capable of flying with a glide angle α of approximately 7.5°. According to Lilienthal's hypothesis of resistance, this glider should require a flight velocity v_∞, solely from its resistance, that exceeds the magnitude of the vertical sink rate by more than double (point A). However, what is observed? The gliding occurs at a much lower flight velocity, with a magnitude roughly equal to that of the vertical sink rate $v_\perp$ (point B in Figure 20). **Thus, it appears that the concept of resistance is not suitable for describing flight.**

How Does Gliding Work?

However, it is not only the failure of the resistance concept that has been described, which is why gliding cannot be achieved through forward sinking alone. More significant is the observation that reducing the angle of attack α of a flat plate against the direction of free flow, which, according to Figures 13 and 15, could be achieved by bringing the center of gravity closer to the neutral point (the center of gravity lies behind the neutral point when viewed in the direction of flight), leads to decreasing stability in forward sinking. In practice, when dealing with glide ratios ε of slightly more than 3, corresponding to angles of attack α of about 20 degrees, one has reached the limit; going further is not feasible. To achieve higher glide ratios, a stabilization of the angle of attack of the flat plate at lower angles is required. Although the idea for achieving this is not too far-fetched, it has not been found in the literature on flying in the context of stabilizing flat gliding.

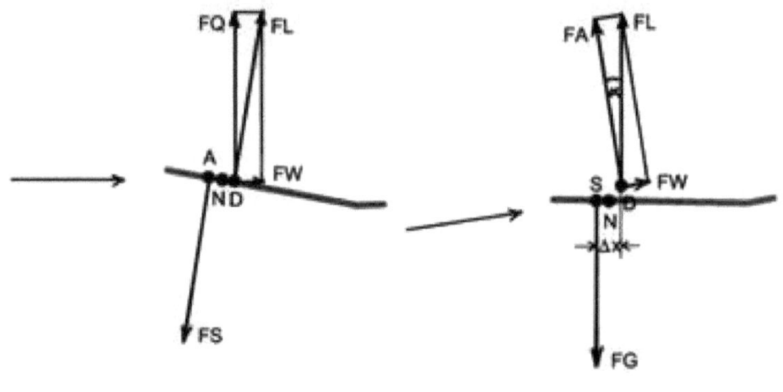

Figure 21

"N:" neutral point; "D:" center of pressure; "S:" center of gravity; "F_A": lift F_l; "F_W": drag F_d; α angle of attack; Δx: distance SD, see chapter "Truly Symmetrical?"

With the prepared flat plate shown in Figure 13, we use position 6 to thread the knitting needle. In the air flow, the plate will behave like a flag. Now, when the trailing edge of the plate is slightly bent, similar to Figure 21, and after being blown by a hairdryer, as shown in the left part of the image, we observe that this bending, depending on the size of the involved area and the magnitude of the bending angle, leads to a more or less slight but stable inclination of the plate. Aha: Pre-positioning the axis of the knitting needle, point A in the left part of Figure 21, in front of the neutral point, point N, together with a slight bending of the trailing edge, results in the desired small angle of attack against the air flow while maintaining sufficient stability. This should also work for the forward sinking shown in Figure 16. And behold: When ensuring that the center of gravity, point S in the right part of Figure 21, is in the "right" position, just in front of the neutral point, and at the same time, the trailing edge is slightly curved upward, a genuine and stable gliding with glide ratios up to 8 is observed, in contrast to the frequently pitching forward sinker with a best glide ratio of around 3! This glider's flight path leads to point B in Figure 20.

In addition to new questions, Figure 21 contains remarkable information that seems to be of central importance for achieving stable gliding as a prerequisite for flying, but it has not appeared in the specialized literature in this context so far. When adjusting a flyer (such as in instructions for setting up model aircraft), significant importance is indeed given to the "right" position of the center of gravity, but it is not explained why. We will see that determining the "right" position of the center of gravity does not have to be a matter of trial and error or a secret recipe known only to experts. As Figure 21 shows, finding the "right" position of the center of gravity is relatively easy in the case of a flat plate used as a wing (and likewise for a wing whose cross-section has a symmetrical airfoil that is not too thick). It remains to be explained why the center of gravity is of paramount importance for achieving a flight state that not only differs significantly from forward sinking but also embodies what is understood as flying and the generation of that force known as aerodynamic lift. The perceptive reader may already sense that, along the path we have embarked on to understand flying, there are further hurdles yet to come, requiring patience on our part. It can be predicted that in the end, there will be no simple explanation and there may still be unresolved questions—and a sense of wonder at how nature has managed to create such magnificent gliders as birds of prey, which have no idea what they are capable of.

Let us summarize some of the intriguing aspects of Figure 21. The pressure point D, which is the point of application for the aerodynamic force F_L, consisting of the transverse force F_t and the longitudinal force F_d, can only be located behind the neutral point N, which lies on the quarter-chord line of the plate. We have seen this in the chapter "Forward Sinking, What is It?" Moving the position of the knitting needle to a point A just in front of of the neutral point, along with a slight bending of the trailing edge, results in stable orientations of the flat plate with small angles of attack and transverse forces that, when compared to the drags, prove to be surprisingly large if one has a measuring device for such forces. Otherwise, it is known that the transverse force must be significantly greater in magnitude than the longitudinal force, otherwise, they would not be able to compensate for the weight, as shown in Figure 21. In the case of the glider, the role of the knitting needle position A is taken over by the center of gravity S, where the weight F_G acts.

Indeed, the arrangement described is likely to astonish and even perplex physicists. It involves two opposing forces, F_g and F_L, of equal magnitude whose points of application are not aligned, as in the case of the forward sinker in Figure 15 (right subfigure), but are offset by a distance Δx in the flight direction (thus lying on different lines of action). This creates a torque, in this case, a nose-heavy moment (pitching moment) that would cause the glider to rotate into a vertical nosedive. However, that is not what happens! If there is no rotation into a vertical nosedive, a counter-torque moment must occur during gliding to balance out this nose-heavy moment.

Now we can delve into the discussion of where this counter-torque moment comes from. At first glance, the bent end of the flat plate is suspected of altering the flow pattern and acting like a "rudder."

Most readers at this point, given our current knowledge, would probably agree with such a view. However, it might be puzzling that this "rudder" does not result in what rudders usually cause, namely sustained turning, or in our case, a looping maneuver. As we continue our deliberations, it becomes evident that another mechanism exists, one that provides an appropriate counter-torque moment and is directly related to the generation of dynamic lift. In fact, a demonstration of this mechanism can be provided immediately.

The distance Δx by which the points of application of the aerodynamic force and the weight force (or their lines of action) are separated in the direction of flight, as seen in Figure 21, is by no means unknown in the technical literature. This phenomenon is referred to as the stability measure (we will have to consider questions of flight stabilization more thoroughly later, see the chapter "Truly Symmetrical?"). It is well-known that the disappearance of this stability measure (e.g., through the notorious repositioning of the center of gravity to reduce drag and increase performance) is synonymous with the loss of sufficient lift capacity of the wing, i.e., the disappearance of dynamic lift. However, this apparent fact, namely the relationship between stability measure and the generation of dynamic lift, and thus the significance of this stability measure for the generation of dynamic lift, is practically not discussed in the technical literature. However, this relationship becomes a central concern in clarifying the question: How to fly.

A glider like the one shown in Figure 16, which consists of just a wing, is referred to as a "flying wing" (German Nurflügel) or a pure-wing. In nature, there are several types of flying seeds that exhibit such pure-wing characteristics, with the most famous one being the Zanonia seed, as depicted in Figure 22. The actual seed is located at the center of the leading edge of a thin leaf-like structure that is slightly bent at the back. Due to its weight, it determines the necessary center of gravity for gliding. The maple seed has a similar structure, but the asymmetric position of the seed leads to rotation of the seed leaf during descent (similar to the principle of an autogyro).

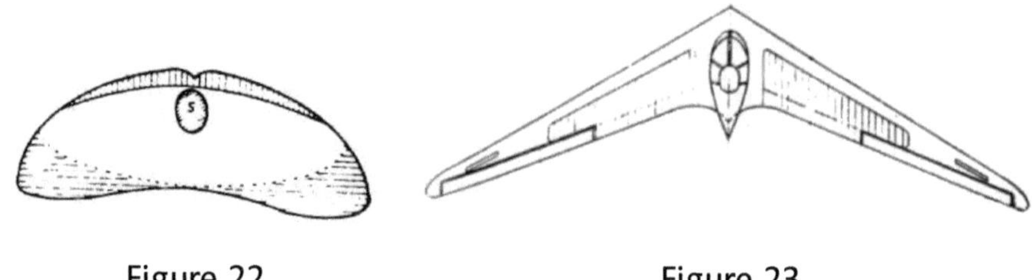

Figure 22   Figure 23

The Zanonia seed was frequently used as a model in the early days of aviation, and it served as an inspiration for the wing shape of Lilienthal's glider, for example. The final stage of human-piloted flight with performance-oriented flying wings was represented by the Horten flying wings, designed and successfully flown by the Horten brothers until 1960. An example is shown in Figure 23.[8] However, this mature technology did not prevail in the field of high-performance sailplane construction, as no modern high-performance glider is a flying wing. The reason for this is quite understandable: The control surface, or "rudder," necessary for longitudinal stability and lift generation, as shown in Figure 21, can only be integrated into the wing itself, near the wing's neutral point. As a result, it acts at a shorter lever arm compared to a corresponding "rudder," known as a horizontal tailplane or stabilizer, which is located separately from the wing and farther from the wing's neutral point.

The aircraft configurations depicted in top view in Figures 24 and 25 are considered typical gliders today. Figure 24 shows a simple homemade glider, while Figure 25 represents a high-performance

---

[8] Horten, R., Seliger, P. (1987). *Die Geschichte der Horten-Flugzeuge 1933-1960*. Graz: Weishaupt.

sailplane (ASW 17).[9] In these designs, the horizontal tailplane is set to a slightly negative angle of incidence relative to the wing, typically around -2 degrees. This important aspect of flying will be discussed in more detail later.

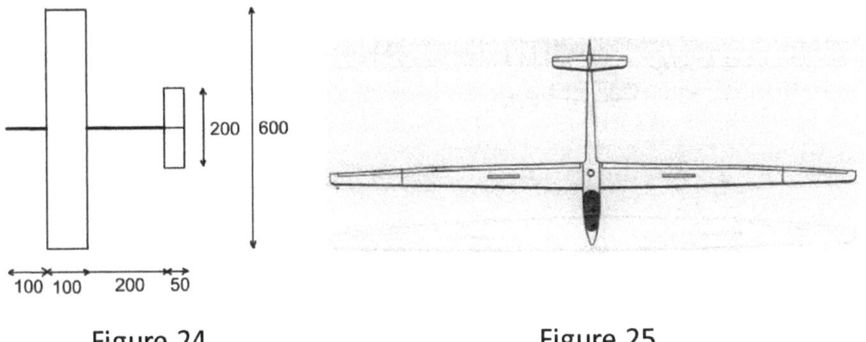

Figure 24Figure 25

The homemade glider depicted in Figure 24, with a flat board made of thin balsa wood as its wing, is capable of even better gliding performance than the converted forward sinking glider shown in Figure 16. It can achieve glide ratios of up to 12. However, the high-performance sailplane shown in Figure 25 can glide much more efficiently, with glide ratios exceeding 45. We will delve into the various improvements that can be made to achieve such performance later.

Now it is possible to provide an initial interim assessment. We know the flight mechanical conditions that must be fulfilled to achieve stable gliding: a larger board as the wing with a slight V-shape, a significantly smaller board as the horizontal tailplane positioned slightly behind and below the wing with a slightly negative angle of incidence, a careful adjustment of the center of gravity located in front of the wing's neutral point, a fuselage rod for securely

---

[9] Buch, H. (1980). *Segelfliegen*. Berlin: transpress VEB, 185.

connecting the wing and stabilizer with a fin at the end (vertical stabilizer).

However, we still have no clue as to why such an arrangement generates aerodynamic lift. Furthermore, we are yet to understand the nature of this lift. In the following chapters, we will gradually delve into this matter. But first, let us make a few remarks regarding the question of which wing property makes gliders more successful.

The Purpose of Airfoils

Illustrated by the glide ratio described in the chapter "Forward Sinking — What is It?" and on page 174, the development of our flying objects so far looks as follows: The vertically sinking flat plate moves with a glide ratio of 0; the forward sinking flat plate moves with a best glide ratio of around 3; the pure-wing glider with the flat plate as the wing surface moves with a best glide ratio of 8; the regular glider, as shown in Figure 24, with a flat plate as the wing moves with a best glide ratio of 12. And what is next? Good model gliders fly with glide ratios around 20. High-performance gliders achieve best glide ratios of over 45. There has been further development towards better gliding (which may have reached a limit now). But what is the decisive reason for this development? If we observe bird wings, like Otto Lilienthal did in the past, besides many still unknown or unexplored properties, they possess one characteristic that appears to be essential: Their cross-section is not flat like a plate but rather curved (cambered) to varying degrees, and they are not uniformly thick throughout but thicker in the front section of the cross-section than in the rear section. In Figure 26, the two wing cross-sections are depicted, showing the profile of a flat plate (left) and a bird-like wing (right). What could be the reason for these changes developed by nature millions of years ago?

Figure 26

To better understand this, let us revisit an observation described in Figure 9. When a flat plate is vertically sinking in the air, a vortex forms at the edge of the plate due to the separation of air flow around a sharp corner, creating an inward-directed vortex. The generation of such vortices requires the performance of work, which is obtained from the sinking process, i.e., a decrease in the potential energy of the sinking body. We do not need to delve into the appearance or the specific mechanisms of these vortices right now. It is sufficient to represent this vortex formation at an edge using an appropriate graphic, as shown in Figure 9. However, when we transition to forward sinking, as depicted in Figure 27 where the plate is moving to the left during sinking, the question arises: How does the inward-directed vortex at the left, front edge behave in this case?

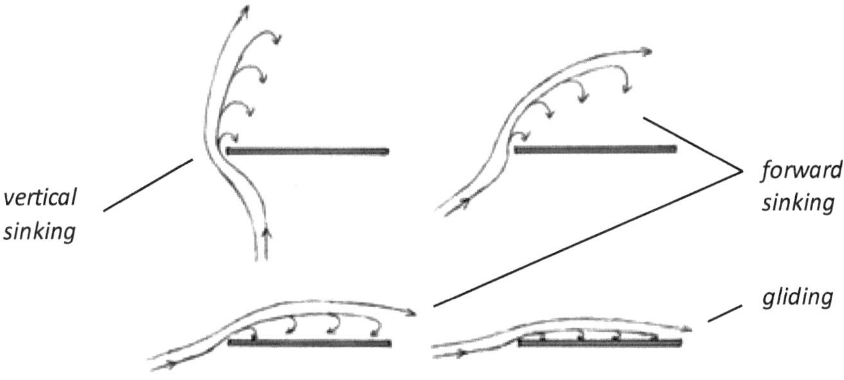

Figure 27

Figure 27 illustrates a possible sequence of these vortex formations, with the movement to the left and the decreasing angle of attack against the direction of air flow. In a preliminary analysis, one could say that the vortex zone formed at the left (front) edge gradually aligns itself more with the upper surface of the flat plate as the angle of attack decreases. As simplistic as this observation may initially seem, the conclusions drawn regarding the need for a more favorable profile that reduces vortices are obvious.

Figure 28

Looking at the flow pattern depicted in the last sub-image of Figure 27, with a small angle of attack, one could come up with the following idea: If the wing is appropriately curved, the last remaining vortices above the wing could be reduced, perhaps even prevented. Figure 28, left sub-image, illustrates a presumed flow pattern in the case of a cambered plate. However, this can give rise to a new problem, namely vortex formation on the underside of the wing. To mitigate this vortex formation as well, the airfoil can be thickened by partially filling it on the underside, as shown in Figure 28, right sub-image. A similar airfoil is successfully used in model aircraft construction ("Jedelsky" profile). The thickening in the front part of the airfoil also offers a significant advantage, namely providing more space for the internal construction of a stable and torsional rigid wing.

The path to a rudimentary understanding of the shape of modern airfoils in aeronautics is now not far off, as shown in Figure 29. To suppress as many vortex formations as possible, in addition to the basic structure depicted in Figure 28, one must ensure slightly curved surfaces, a "sharp" termination of the profile at the wing trailing edge, and a rounded shape at the wing leading edge (nose) that allows the incoming air parcels to glide past smoothly. We will delve into the specific profile parameters and their significance in more detail, as discussed on page 193.

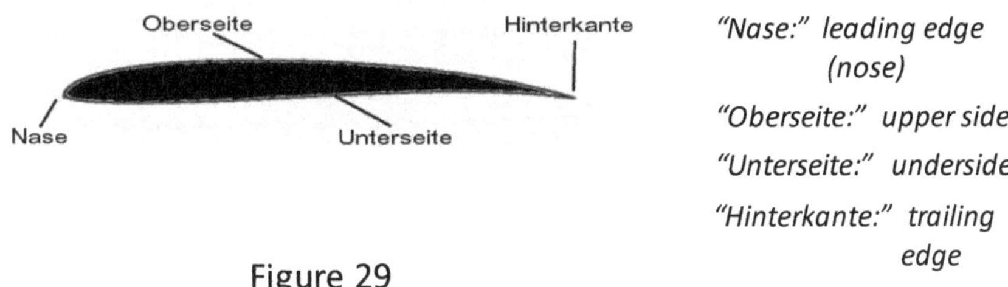

"Nase:" leading edge (nose)

"Oberseite:" upper side

"Unterseite:" underside

"Hinterkante:" trailing edge

Figure 29

Now a problem arises, which is not uncommon in aeronautics literature. Many believe that only this type of profiling creates what is known as aerodynamic lift. As we progress through this book, it will become clear that this is a misconception that needs to be addressed right away. The shape of an airfoil, such as the one shown in Figure 29, does not create aerodynamic lift, or to put it differently, **the generation of aerodynamic lift is <u>not</u> determined by the design of the airfoil**. Instead, airfoils are intended to minimize the formation of local vortices and thereby reduce resistance as much as possible. However, these local vortex zones on the wing surfaces (referred to as "bubbles" in the technical literature) will also affect the lift generated by other means. For the performance or quality of an aircraft, the ratio of lift to drag (which is the same as the glide ratio, see Figure 18) is significant. These two properties can be described independently in principle, but in practice, they are not independent of each other. This ambivalent relationship not only makes flying a complex matter but also complicates the explanation of flight. To make progress in explaining the matter, the following chapters will initially describe lift and drag as separate entities. Later, a synthesis will be achieved, leading to a more complete description of flight characteristics, as discussed in the chapter "Quality of Flight".

Part II: Why?

Aerodynamic Lift

After the failure of the resistance concept to explain aerodynamic lift, as described in the chapter "What Does Lilienthal Tell Us?", finding a satisfactory answer becomes challenging. What mechanism is responsible for the existence of lift? In the field of aeronautics, this question is considered sufficiently answered, and we will discuss it later. However, some scientists, aiming for an explanation of flying based on not only easily understandable but also supposedly "more correct" physics (see page 163), provide a completely different explanation. In popular science writings (and unfortunately not only there), there are explanations that should not be taken seriously. As a small example, the notion that there is a "suction" above the wing that keeps the aircraft in the air may sound convincing to many, but it raises questions about where this suction comes from. Moreover, it fails to address whether the surrounding air is capable of exerting suction in the first place. We know that the surrounding air cannot do that: a volume of air can and will fill any space provided to it, and there are no tensile forces present in that space (although there are, as we will see later, pressure forces). Therefore, there is no higher being above the wing preventing the aircraft from falling by means of suction...

Those scientists who aim for an explanation of aerodynamic lift based on easily understandable and teachable physics (referred to as "elementalization") rely on a mechanism that resembles the one outlined in Figure 3: an impulse current. Since an impulse current corresponds to a commonly understood force in physics, such a mechanism is not fundamentally incorrect for describing dynamic lift. The difficulty arises when one seeks a specific impulse current carried by matter (such as the air flow through a helicopter rotor) to justify the lift force as a reaction force. It did not take long to find such a search: Immediately behind a wing inclined against the flow of air on an aircraft generating lift, the air flow exiting at the wing's trailing edge has a downward component $v_\perp$, as shown in Figure 30. It is postulated that the wing generates an overall downward air flow during flight, which is supposed to support the aircraft in an equivalent manner to how a rapidly rotating rotor carries a helicopter.[10]

Figure 30

Indeed, having a mechanism that involves the reaction force of downward-directed air flow to compensate for the weight of the aircraft appears so convincing that questions about whether this mechanism is sufficient to explain all aspects related to the gliding of an aircraft are no longer asked. It is not even necessary to inquire, for example, whether such a mechanism allows for glide ratios of magnitude 50 in high-performance gliders (as the significant amount of resistance resulting from redirecting substantial air flow to compensate for the weight prevents this, see also page 235). It suffices to consider the observations described in the chapters "How

---

[10] Weltner, K. (1990). *Fliegen und Flugzeuge.* Unterricht Physik. Stuttgart: Velber und Klett, 4, 4 ff.

Does Sinking Work?" and "What Does Lilienthal Tell Us?": **Both the uniform vertical sinking of an aircraft in level flight and the nearly horizontal gliding of the aircraft without propulsion occur at approximately the same speeds**. Due to the need for weight compensation, this means that during horizontal flight, the wing of an aircraft would have to accelerate downward approximately the same amount of air mass per unit time as is being induced by the vertical sinking. Given the high glide ratios, these two requirements appear completely incompatible. Therefore, it seems that any further considerations regarding the concept of that specific impulse current consisting of air masses accelerated downward by the wing become unnecessary.

This leaves us with the question of the cause of the aerodynamic lift that is discussed in aeronautics research. In the search for an answer to this question, it is noticeable that there is considerably less interest compared to the question of where drag comes from and how to minimize it. One gets the impression that lift somehow exists (as mentioned in Prof. Voit-Nitschmann's response in the "Zeit" article, page 163), its magnitude can be accurately determined, and any calculations based on it yield verifiably correct results. However, there are still unanswered questions, including those related to fundamental physics, as hinted at in the preceding chapters. It is these remaining open questions that the aforementioned scientists refer to when they seek to justify their alternative mechanism for dynamic lift. In this and the following chapters, an attempt is made to provide answers to these outstanding questions.

In aeronautics research, the phenomenon of lift is treated separately from the phenomenon of drag. This is a strong idealization because, in practice, both are aerodynamic forces of the same nature, whose vector sum compensates for the weight of the aircraft. Additionally, the lift phenomenon cannot be represented in its pure form, i.e., without the presence of some associated phenomena that can be attributed to drag. However, since it will be revealed that the causes of lift and drag can be well separated from each other, we now follow such an idealization and examine whether it can bring us closer to understanding the lift phenomenon.

The initial steps towards this idealization have already been taken through observations presented in the preceding chapters. Forward sinking, as shown in Figures 15 and 16, moves with a glide ratio of around 3. Why? Because significant drag is generated during this motion. A flying wing glider, as shown in Figure 21, moves with a glide ratio of up to 8. Why? Because this glider experiences a lower amount of drag. A conventional glider with a flat plate as its wing, as depicted in Figure 24, moves with a glide ratio of up to 12. The sailplane in Figure 25 moves with a glide ratio of just under 50. Why? Because the drag, including the airfoil similar to the one in Figure 29, could be significantly reduced. What can we expect from an ideal glider then? It should have an infinite glide ratio, meaning it does not descend as long as there is no more drag. Throughout various discussions, we will see that this ideal state will fundamentally never be attainable (see the chapter "Where Does Drag Come From?"). However, it will still be useful, not only for the sake of pure theory but also to uncover the actual reason for the generation of aerodynamic lift, to assume such an ideal state. Aerodynamic lift, as demonstrated by the glide ratios of modern high-performance gliders that come quite close to the ideal aircraft, must be explainable independently of drag.

Now it gets interesting: No descent without drag, despite the weight still being present? What does that remind us of? Of course, it reminds us of static lift, as discussed in the chapter "What Does Archimedes Tell Us?". There, we could justify the (partial) compensation of weight with a pressure difference in a gravitational field. Is a pressure difference in a gravitational field also responsible for aerodynamic lift? The question of the necessity of a gravitational field is quickly resolved. Without a gravitational field, there is no weight, and without weight, there is no lift, as Newton would put it. Observations in the weightlessness of a space station like the ISS or during so-called parabolic flights could provide important insights here. Certainly, observations conducted in a wind tunnel with wing segments attached would yield similar results (transverse forces, longitudinal forces) as those on the Earth's surface within a gravitational field. However, in the conventional sense, gliders do not fly up there! Care to bet? The depiction of interplanetary space fighters chasing each other in science fiction movies does not function as portrayed and therefore does not serve as suitable reference material.

Now, let us consider the matter of pressure difference. It does exist: Pressure measurements on wing surfaces during flight have provided a fairly accurate measurement of the average pressure difference between the upper and lower surfaces of the wing, which corresponds to the wing loading F_g/A . In aircraft terminology, wing loading refers to the ratio of weight F_g to the (effective) wing area A, a ratio that has the unit of pressure. This leads us to the first question: Is the pressure difference required for flying significantly large or not?

It is important to realize how remarkably small this pressure difference needs to be to compensate for the weight of an aircraft. Let us take the Airbus A380 as an example, which is a large and heavy aircraft. It has a takeoff weight of about 500 tons and a wing area of approximately 800 square meters. Therefore, the wing loading F_g/A is 0.625 tons/square meter or 6,250 N/m^2, which is slightly more than 6.2% of the average atmospheric pressure near the Earth's surface. Is that a lot or a little? Our intuition tells us that if such a pressure difference is supposed to lift an A380, then it must be significant. However, when comparing it to the magnitude of atmospheric pressure in our surrounding air (approximately 100,000 N/m^2 near the Earth's surface), it is actually quite small. To put it into perspective, consider that a stranded A380 next to a runway can be lifted using air cushions placed under the wings, and the pressure of these cushions can be generated by the force of a person's lungs (it's relatively easy to create a 62 cm water column by blowing into a water-filled thin U-tube). In the case of the sailplane shown in Figure 25, with a surface load of about 330 N/m^2, the average pressure difference is just slightly more than 0.3% of the average atmospheric pressure (equivalent to 3 cm water column). For a model glider with a wing loading of approximately 20 N/m^2, it is even lower at around 0.02% (equivalent to 2 mm water column). Therefore, the generation of such small pressure differences to lift aircraft appears to be entirely feasible.

The possibility of creating such pressure differences should be supported by a physical examination, as detailed on page 174. The data from the ASW 17 sailplane shown in Figure 25 were used for this analysis. During flight, a certain amount of work is extracted from the potential energy reserve as the sailplane descends. This work can be used to create a volume of air with altered pressure (the work required to overcome certain resistances is initially neglected, as we are considering idealized gliding). The area swept by the wing per second can be calculated from the wingspan of this sailplane, which is 20 m, and the flight velocity of 23 m/s. As will be explained later, this air layer aligns quite well with the corresponding air layer immediately above the wing surfaces, which is formed for a completely different reason (boundary layer, as discussed in the chapter "Where Does Drag Come From?").

It appears that, similar to static lift, the measurement of the magnitude of aerodynamic lift is possible using pressure differences.

Does this also provide an explanation for its cause? In addressing this question, aeronautics research relies on the successful application of the Bernoulli equation.[11] While the formal derivation of the Bernoulli equation is possible (see the chapter "Bernoulli Equations"), one may still seek a justification for its deeper physical origin. In the literature, one occasionally encounters a mention of a peculiar observation called the hydrodynamic paradox, but the explanation provided for it relies on the Bernoulli equation. This creates a classic circular argument: the hydrodynamic paradox is explained using the Bernoulli equation, while the Bernoulli equation itself is an effect of the hydrodynamic paradox, as we will see. How can we break free from this circular argument? As strange as it may sound, clarifying the fluid mechanics observation known as the hydrodynamic paradox, which seems to be completely insignificant in traditional aviation, will provide us with the crucial insight to progress in our understanding of the Bernoulli equation.

Hydrodynamic Paradox, What is It?

The hydrodynamic paradox! What connection does it have with aerodynamic lift? That might be the question some ask when they are accustomed to the explanations provided by aeronautics research regarding the generation of aerodynamic lift. In those explanations, this paradox is either not mentioned at all or only briefly discussed in relation to the application of the Bernoulli equation. However, there is another way to view it. Let us be open to surprises!

In Figure 31, left panel, an occurrence of the well-known hydrostatic paradox is illustrated: In an inner shallow vessel with an upright tube,

---

¹¹ Schlichting, H., Truckenbrodt, E. (1967). Aerodynamik des Flugzeuges, Erster Band. Berlin, Heidelberg, New York: Springer, 38 ff.

after filling it with water (indicated in black), the pressure at the bottom is the same as when the vessel is removed, and the gray portion of the large vessel is filled with water. The paradox lies in the fact that it appears as if non-existent water generates the same bottom pressure as existing water, as long as there is a (tiny) upright tube with the same water level. This reminds us of the bursting of a wine barrel that is filled from a great height through a hose connection. A manifestation of the much less-known hydrodynamic paradox is depicted in Figure 31, right panel: Below a plate A with a central pipe through which air is blown, there is another plate B, completely unattached or suspended. Despite vigorous blowing of air, the lower plate B "sticks" to the upper plate A with a small gap. The paradox lies in the fact that neither the weight of the lower plate, nor a perceived excess pressure, nor the impulse changes exerted by the incoming air can cause the lower plate to detach from the upper plate!

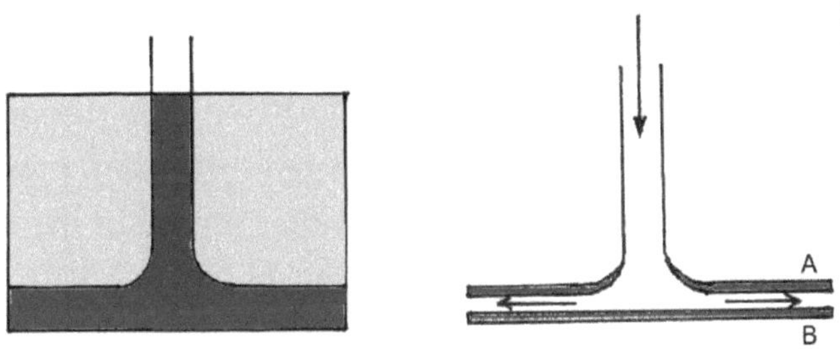

Figure 31

The hydrodynamic paradox can be demonstrated impressively in a simple experiment, as shown in Figure 32. A well-fitting cardboard cone cannot be blown out of a glass funnel, no matter how forcefully one blows into it. Similarly, a ping pong ball or, as captured in the right panel, a (weighted) Styrofoam ball cannot be blown out of a funnel. It is truly astonishing to witness!

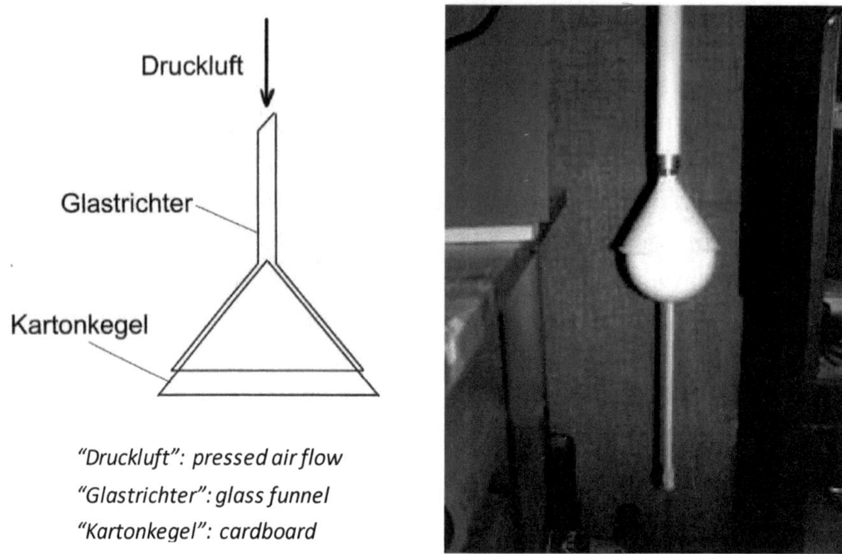

"Druckluft": pressed air flow
"Glastrichter": glass funnel
"Kartonkegel": cardboard

Figure 31

Physically speaking, the phenomenon observed in the hydrodynamic paradox can be attributed to a different effect rather than the force resulting from changes in the momentum of flowing matter and associated pressures, which is typically considered in the context of impulse current physics. While this physics is present, its influence is much weaker compared to another effect at play. In the search for an explanatory idea, one comes across the ambient air pressure in which these observations are made: in a vacuum, the phenomena observed in Figure 32, for example, do not occur at all. If there is no miraculous explanation enabling observations of the hydrodynamic paradox, then the pressure in the air gap between plates A and B in Figure 31, or between the cardboard cone or Styrofoam ball and the walls of the funnel in Figure 32, must be lower (!) than the surrounding air pressure in such a way that a corresponding "lift" prevents the falling of plate B or the cardboard cone or Styrofoam ball.

Indeed, the question of how such reduced pressure can occur in the air gap, despite blowing into it with an excess pressure, is intriguing. In the scarce literature on the hydrodynamic paradox, the "explanation" often refers to the Bernoulli equation, which will be further explored. However, it is peculiar that the understanding of the conventional Bernoulli equation itself relies on observations of cases of the hydrodynamic paradox, as mentioned earlier. Thus, one phenomenon is explained by the other, and vice versa, leading to a circular argument that explains nothing. Is it possible to break free from this circular reasoning? It is indeed possible if one succeeds in explaining the hydrodynamic paradox in another way.

In a later chapter, we will discuss the effects of air pressure and their descriptions in more detail (see the chapter "What Keeps the Flow Attached?"). For now, it is time to address the question of where air pressure comes from. Air is a mixture of gases and, like all gases, has an internal structure that can be described as follows: Invisible particles of air (molecules) fly seemingly on their own and independently of each other in an incredibly large number, crisscrossing and colliding with each other, as well as with any walls they encounter. When there is less air (or "less" air compared to the other side) behind a wall, these collisions with the wall manifest as what we call pressure (or pressure difference). In an idealized analysis, assuming elastic collisions between air particles themselves and with limiting walls, the magnitude of hydrostatic pressure can be determined in a straightforward manner (kinetic theory of gases). In the air surrounding us, regardless of the type and internal structure of the particles, the average velocity of air particles at 20° Celsius is approximately 400 m/s, as indicated on page 176.

There are observations suggesting that the collision between two air particles can be considered elastic, but not the collision with a wall. Two phenomena are mentioned in this context: the radiometer effect and the formation of a boundary layer in aeronautics (see the chapter "Where Does Drag Come From?"). One can imagine that an air particle, upon colliding with a wall, is briefly held in place (adhesion), during which it "forgets" its original momentum and is subsequently emitted with some other momentum. However, due to the constant temperature, the magnitudes of these momenta, on average, remain the same. If a large number of air particles participate in such local processes, it has no effect on the global manifestation of pressure, which requires summing up numerous changes in momentum. Therefore, it is not a mistake to assume, in the initial derivation of pressure in the kinetic theory of gases, that the collision with the wall is also elastic. Now, the crucial question arises: What happens when the wall and a larger portion of air move relative to each other, meaning that there is air flow along the wall or, equivalently, a wall is moved perpendicular to its surface normal, as in the case of an aircraft wing surface being traversed by an air flow?

When a wall is moved in the air or when air flows over a wall, the statistical manifestation of pressure will be different since all air particles colliding with the wall, as a result of adhesion, carry a transverse momentum imparted by the wall. Let us simplify the explanation using Figure 33 and the "A Basic Bernoulli Equation", see page 175. Initially, let us focus on particles that collide perpendicularly with the wall (or, more generally, on the components of momentum orthogonal to the wall). After emission, the magnitude of the momentum of the reflected particle remains the same, on average, due to the assumed constant temperature, but its direction changes. By using the Pythagorean theorem and the factor $1/2\,\rho$, where ρ is the density of the air, we can derive a first simple Bernoulli equation, up to a factor ≤ 1. Does this result change significantly when we consider all possible directions of individual momenta? No, a reduction in pressure just above the wall due to the transverse momentum acquired during the collision will always occur. We can omit quantitative details at this point. The conventional derivation of the Bernoulli equation used in aeronautics will be discussed later in the chapter "Bernoulli Equations".

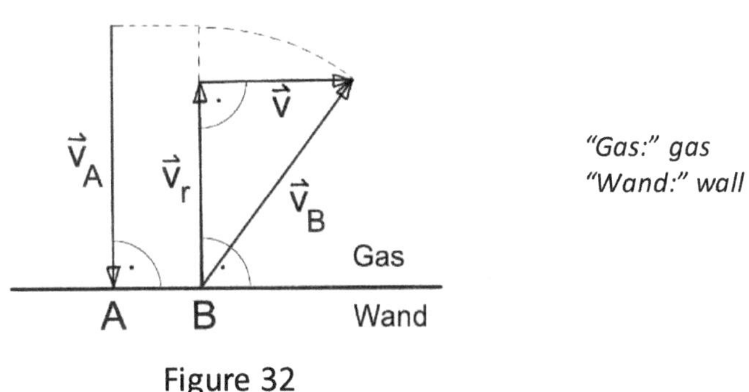

"Gas:" gas
"Wand:" wall

Figure 32

One may distrust this simple derivation. It is reassuring that the aforementioned average particle velocity is obtained. Is the Bernoulli equation mentioned on page 176 credible enough? With its help, one can directly indicate the measure of pressure reduction above an overflowing wall in relation to the flow velocity. In the case of the Airbus A380 mentioned in the chapter "Aerodynamic Lift", the generation of a (mean) pressure difference of about $6.250 \, \frac{N}{m^2}$ is required to keep the aircraft in the air. Using the Bernoulli equation mentioned on page 175, an average flow velocity of $v = \sqrt{\dfrac{2\left(p(0)-p(v)\right)}{\rho}} \approx \sqrt{\dfrac{2 \cdot 6.250 \; N/m^2}{\rho}} = 100 \, \frac{m}{s} = 360 \, \frac{km}{h}$ is required for that. This is an approximation that is only slightly above the takeoff or generation of a (mean) pressure difference of about $6.250\,\frac{N}{m^2}$ is required to keep the aircraft in the air. Using the Bernoulli equation mentioned on page 175, an average flow velocity of $v = \sqrt{\frac{2\,(p(0)-p(v))}{\rho}} \approx \sqrt{\frac{2\cdot6.250\ N/m^2}{\rho}} = 100\,\frac{m}{s} = 360\,\frac{km}{h}$ is required for that. This is an approximation that is only slightly above the takeoff or

landing speed of this aircraft, as also described in the chapter "Parameters of Practical Gliding".

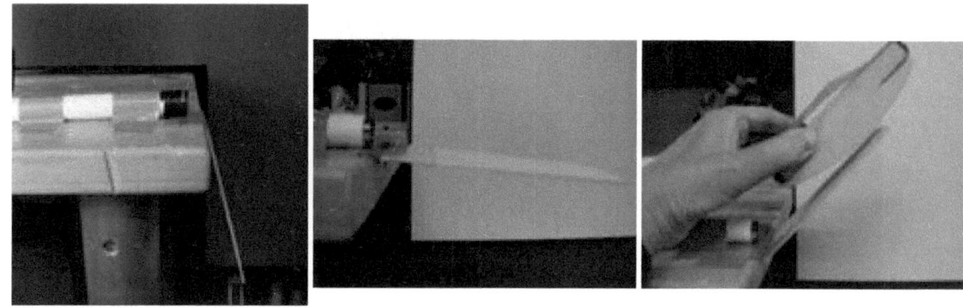

Figure 33

Using a sufficiently strong blower (a hairdryer will not do), the pressure reduction above a flowing flat surface can be made visible, as shown in Figure 34. A thin balsa board, about 15 cm long, is attached movably to the edge of a table using adhesive tape. In the left panel, the blower is turned off, while in the middle panel, it is turned on. The board needs to be slightly lifted to allow the air flow from the nozzle to catch it, but it remains in the position shown. The observed lifting of the board can only be explained by a reduction in pressure directly above the board.

In the right panel, the effect of narrowing the air flow above the board is demonstrated (a 'bottleneck'). It should be noted that the steeply rising board is still being blown horizontally by the blower—hydrodynamic paradox! One can only marvel at this effect, as it contradicts the conventional understanding of impulse current physics...

It appears that the hydrodynamic paradox can be understood by considering the particle nature of air and evaluating the pressure conditions in the flowing air gap compared to the ambient pressure. The simple Bernoulli equation provided on page 175 can be used for quantitative assessments. With this understanding, it becomes possible to make statements about pressure reductions directly above flowing surfaces and thus explain the generation of aerodynamic lift.

Bernoulli Equations

The interested reader is kindly asked to understand that we will now delve deeper into the realm of aeronautics experts. There are two reasons for this. Firstly, the utilization of the Bernoulli equation continues to be the backbone of modern aeronautics research on the generation of aerodynamic lift. This equation provides verifiable results, making it an indispensable tool. Secondly, we should discuss the areas and reasons for criticism regarding the derivation of this equation as used in aeronautics, as it can be challenging to comprehend. However, this discussion requires a certain level of mathematical physics. If it disrupts the flow of our reasoning, feel free to skip this chapter and the beginning of the next. In this chapter, we will address problems and seek an understanding of the Bernoulli equation as applied in aeronautics, as the magnitude of aerodynamic lift can only be quantitatively assessed through wind tunnel experiments. With the simple equation provided on page 175, we have a version of this equation that allows us to continue our thinking without delving into profound physics and mathematics. However, it is worth noting that the derivation of the Bernoulli equation used in the aeronautics literature differs significantly, and it is important for us to explore this. Additionally, it should be noted that the Bernoulli equation used in the aeronautics literature is an approximation, albeit a particularly good one for flow velocities that are not too high.

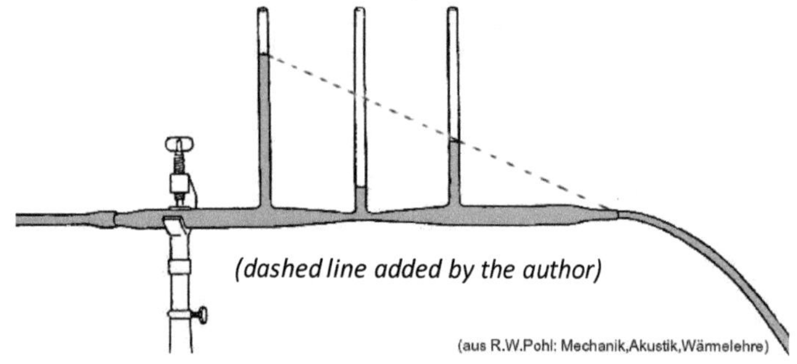

Figure 34

To introduce the effect that is supposed to lead to the Bernoulli equation in college, the observation depicted in Figure 35 is commonly used.[12] In a constricted section of a water-filled conduit, a reduction in pressure occurs. Along the length of the pipe, there is a pressure drop due to flow resistance, but in the narrowing of the cross-section, a significant reduction in pressure is also observed. With the chapter "Hydrodynamic Paradox, What is It?" we can assume that this effect is a version of this paradox, although the

---

[12] Pohl, R. W. (1953). *Mechanik, Akustik, Wärmelehre.* Berlin, Göttingen, Heidelberg: Springer, 145.

properties of water that lead to this effect are still largely unknown, unlike those of air.

We start from the hydrostatic basic equation, see page 170. For the sake of simplicity and to facilitate understanding, all subsequent equations are written without vector notation. While this approach is not without its problems, it is meaningful when the field direction (running coordinate r) as well as the directions of forces such as weight and air force are always parallel to the same line. In the form mentioned in the appendix, the equation represents a local equilibrium between a so-called volume force and a force referred to as pressure force (understanding of hydrostatic lift, see the chapter "What Does Archimedes Tell Us?").

The transition from the hydrostatic to the hydrodynamic basic equation can be accomplished using a correction term (acceleration).[13] However, with this correction, a different directional dependence, a different "field direction," comes into play, where only inertial forces or their components in the direction of flow play a role. Unfortunately, this aspect is often not emphasized. The dynamic pressure on page 172 provides an example of this.

Since most practically relevant flow processes, such as those involved in flying, are stationary, time-dependent quantities can be replaced (see page 176). Let us focus on the case of (ideal) flying, where the component of gravity parallel to an equipotential surface in the Earth's gravitational field is zero. In this case, the hydrodynamic basic equation takes on a relatively simple form. While mathematically correct, this equation no longer reveals the underlying physical interpretation. This has led to a justified question raised by critics, in terms of the chicken and the egg dilemma: What is causative — a

---

[13] Joos, G. (1959). *Lehrbuch der theoretischen Physik*. Leipzig: Geest & Portig, 182.

pressure change resulting in a velocity change or a velocity change resulting in a pressure change? Therefore, on page 176, we take a step back and can now see that in the case of dv/dr < 0, i.e., a velocity decrease along a streamline, dp/dr must be > 0, indicating an increase in pressure in that direction, and vice versa. Together with the continuity equation, which is not addressed in this book because it is not required, this provides an answer to the assignment of cause and effect: an increase in velocity along a streamline leads to a decrease in pressure. This conclusion may appear paradoxical because an increase in flow velocity in a pipe with a constant cross-section is usually achieved with an increase in pressure. However, this paradox bears no resemblance to the hydrodynamic paradox described above. Furthermore, it is not necessarily true that the pressure change along a streamline can be equated so easily with a change in hydrostatic pressure, which includes pressure acting perpendicular to the direction of the streamline. This equivalence is required if one wants to achieve a decrease in pressure over a flow-over surface. Thus, there is still a need for clarification, not only in terms of the information on pressure in the chapter "What Does Archimedes Tell Us?".

The derivation of the Bernoulli equation described on page 176 contains a point that should be highlighted. The d'Alembert correction term of acceleration, as an addition to the hydrostatic basic equation, was introduced with a negative sign. The reason behind this choice is often not apparent. If a positive sign were used instead, the desired Bernoulli equation would not be obtained!

By using the hydrodynamic basic equation, it is possible to derive various forms of the Bernoulli equation. These different forms arise from more detailed considerations regarding the meaning of density ρ. If this density is assumed to be practically constant (model of an incompressible fluid), the integration of this equation leads to the form of the Bernoulli equation mentioned on page 178, which is commonly used in the literature. It describes a decrease in pressure along a streamline as the flow velocity v increases. However, it can only be approximately correct for flow velocities $v < v_0$ because exceeding a reference velocity v_0 would result in negative pressures, which is physically impossible. The significance of this reference velocity needs to be clarified in the specific application case, which we will discuss next.

The assumption of constant density is reasonable and accurate for the fluid water. Therefore, an assessment of the observation depicted in Figure 35 can be made using the Bernoulli equation from page 176, provided that the reference velocity v_0 is known. For example, if the water in the experimental setup of Figure 35 is supplied with a pressure of p(0) = 2 atm (corresponding to an overpressure of 1 atm), the reference velocity v_0 can be calculated as $v_0 = \sqrt{2p(0)/\rho} \approx 14$ m/s, which is significantly higher than the flow velocities typically achievable in thin pipes for water. If a pressure reduction of 0.2 m of water column is observed at the constriction, using the Bernoulli equation yields v $\approx$ 0.14 v_0. As can be seen later, this value is still below the validity range of the equation, $< v_0/4$.

The assumption of constant density is arbitrary and contradicts statements in aerodynamics that dynamic lift is attributed to the generation of local pressure differences on the wing, causing local densities to vary. In the case of gases, therefore, a density that varies with pressure is used in a first step, as shown on Appendix Page 178. It is assumed that even in an open gas flow with local density fluctuations, Boyle's law can be applied. After adjusting the hydrodynamic basic equation, a first alternative Bernoulli equation is derived. The reference velocity v_0, that appears here is significantly larger for gases than for water. In the case of air, it is $v_0 = \sqrt{2p(0)/\rho}$ $\approx$ 400 m/s as shown on page 177.

In addition to pressure, the density of a gas also depends on temperature. Therefore, in a second step, a density that varies with both pressure and temperature is considered for the gas. For this purpose, the general gas equation must be used. If the continuity equation holds for a gas flow, the density can be expressed as a function of other variables, as shown on page 178. This leads to another adjusted hydrodynamic basic equation, which can be integrated if the meaning of $T(v)$ is known.

By considering the inelastic collisions of air particles with a wall described in the chapter "Hydrodynamic Paradox, what is it?", an energy analysis can be conducted. For simplicity, let us first focus on particles that collide perpendicularly with the wall, as shown in Figure 33, and denote the particle energy after emission and absorption of a transverse impulse. This information can be found on page 178. Then, the contribution of the scalar product $\vec{v}_B \vec{v}$ averaged over a large number of particles colliding with the wall is determined to be zero. Consequently, there are particles in a certain layer above the impinged wall with increased kinetic energy. By interpreting pV as energy using the general gas equation, this is associated with a temperature T. The observation of a potentially significant increase in wall temperature due to the "friction" of a flow is particularly made in spaceflight after reentering the Earth's atmosphere. However, let us continue with the aforementioned approximation of a sufficiently small temperature change, specifically for the wall itself. In this case, the ratio $\frac{T_0}{T(v)}$ at the wall can be directly replaced by the ratio $\frac{\epsilon_A}{\epsilon_r}$. Integrating the further adjusted hydro-dynamic basic equation leads to a second alternative Bernoulli equation, as shown on page 178.

Now we assume that this equation approximately represents the pressure conditions in the boundary layer (as described in the chapter "Where Does Drag Come From?"), that is, directly at the surfaces of the wing. With this second alternative Bernoulli equation, the question of whether a pressure change occurring along a streamline can also be understood as a hydrostatic pressure acting perpendicular to it becomes unnecessary. This equation is based on the (omnidirectional) gas kinetic pressure on an overflown surface.

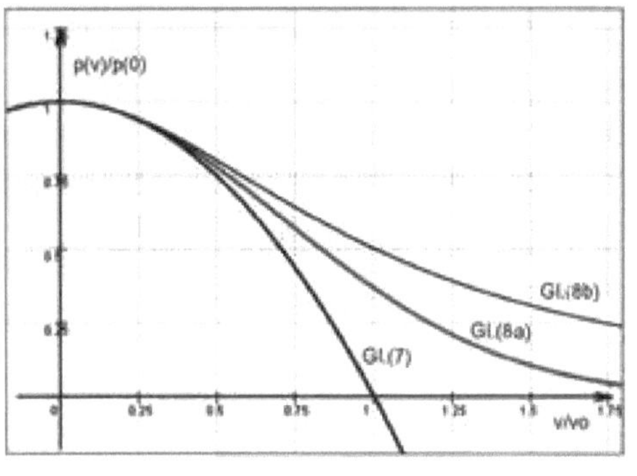

"Gl." (Gleichung) denotes "equation"

Figure 35

In Figure 36, the three versions of the Bernoulli equation mentioned on pages 175 to 178 are graphically represented. All three equations have in common that in the range of velocities $v < \frac{v_0}{4}$, the deviations between them are so small that the use of the simple equation on page 175, assuming constant density, does not cause any significant errors. Therefore, all flight movements in the air with a velocity of $v_\infty < \frac{v_0}{4} = 100\,\frac{m}{s} = 360\,\frac{km}{h}$ can be described using this equation. This velocity range includes all birds, all model and glider aircraft, as well as many motorized aircraft. Thus, the Bernoulli basic equation on page 175, assuming constant density, is sufficiently accurate and useful for the aerodynamics of this velocity range.

The Lift Equation

One more dose of mathematics, and we will have completed the line of reasoning of aeronautics experts. The concept of line integral and the resulting concept of circulation lead to the lift equation, as described on page 180.

The total resulting change in velocity is composed of numerous infinitesimal changes, dv, along the path, where l represents the length of the surface being flown over, such as the wing depth or the length of the airfoil (as shown in Figure 29), and ds represents infinitesimal pieces of the path (here, we must not neglect vectors). Referring to Figure 37, we circulate around the entire cross-section of the wing, so to speak. What is being summed up in this process is called circulation, which refers to the product of summing up all velocity contributions and their corresponding path increments over the entire length of the closed path.

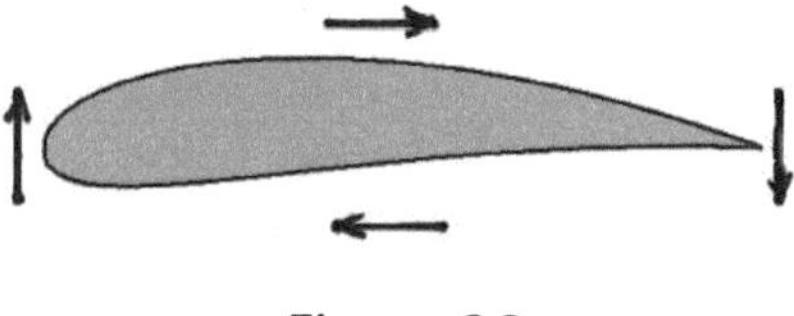

Figure 36

The term circulation, in a literal sense, refers to the act of going around the airfoil. During this process, all encountered (positive and negative) infinitesimal changes in velocity, ds, are accumulated. Initially, such an endeavor seems utterly hopeless because the details of the flow around the wing, specifically the magnitudes of individual velocity changes immediately at the surface, are unknown. However, the mathematics of fluid dynamics provides a solution: When one goes around a vortex center on any closed path and collects all velocity changes encountered, the resulting magnitude is always the same. This magnitude is called the vortex strength or circulation, denoted as Γ, and it represents the "line integral of velocities along a closed path." It is important to consider vectors in this context, particularly the scalar products of local velocity changes and local path increments (as described on page 180).

For a readily apparent reason, we choose a circle as the closed path around the airfoil, touching the profile at the leading edge and trailing edge (see Figure 38). Why this circle? While there may be a chaotic distribution of velocity contributions in different directions around the airfoil, we focus on the specific location of the wing's trailing edge. There, a measurable velocity $\vec{v}_\perp$ exists, as depicted in Figure 30. This is because $v_\perp = v_\infty \sin\alpha$, deduced from the smooth flow (the "Kutta condition") observed at the trailing edge of an ideal as well as a properly streamlined real wing (as described in the chapter "Where Does Drag Come From?"), along with the trailing wake caused by the boundary layer. Only this one known point is sufficient to determine the circulation (as explained on page 180). It leads to the equation for the magnitude of the aerodynamic lift force $F_l = \frac{1}{2}\rho A v_\infty^2 c_l$, which we will utilize in the following chapters due to its remarkable accuracy in reproducing observations of a properly streamlined wing. However, it should be noted that determining the magnitude of circulation is a mathematically specialized flow problem that cannot be discussed here.

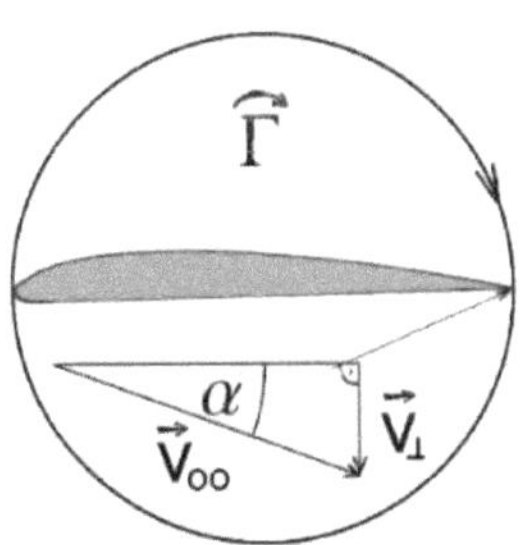

Figure 37

During flight, we encounter small angles α between the direction of the flow and the wing's trailing edge. As shown in Figure 39, the lift coefficient c_l increases almost linearly with α, due to the sinusoidal relationship. In practical aviation, for uncontrolled gliders, the lift coefficient typically has a value just below 1. Therefore, the calculated aerodynamic lift is approximately equal to the resistance encountered during vertical descent (as discussed in the chapter "How Does Sinking Work?"). This provides a satisfying confirmation of the observations described in that chapter, supported by the theory. However, we will still need to explore the angle of attack, referred to as α here, further in other chapters, including "What Else Is of Significance?"

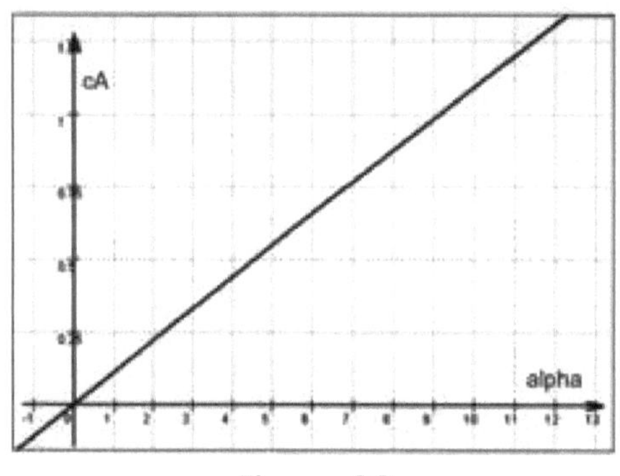

"cA:" lift coefficient c_l
"alpha:" angle of attack

Figure 38

Circulation: More Than Just a Mathematical Trick?

Does the circulation flow around a wing with lift have any significance beyond being a mathematical trick to describe the (ideal) flow around a wing in its immediate vicinity, or does it involve physics as well? In Figure 40, the aerospace research community envisions an ideal flow around a lifting wing. It should be noted that this flow pattern is not an observation but rather a somewhat complex calculation. The deviation from undisturbed horizontal flow in the immediate vicinity of the wing's cross-section is a result of the superposition of a localized or stationary vortex that moves with the wing, as indicated by the direction of rotation depicted in Figure 37.

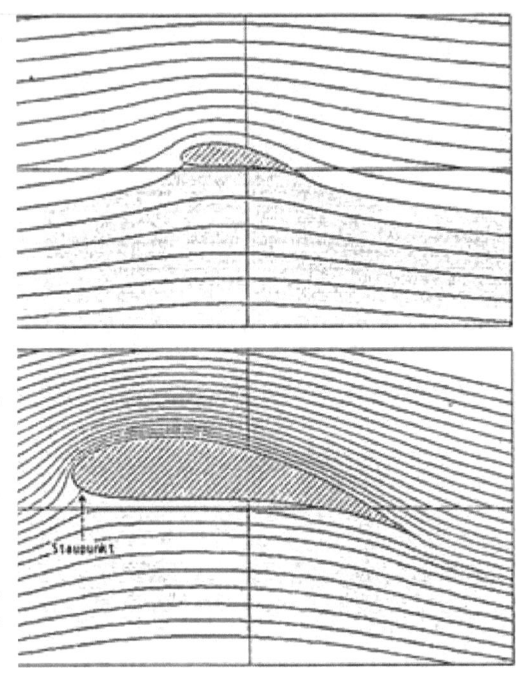

Exactly calculated flow around an airfoil as perceived by the accompanying observer.

The limiting case of an infinitely large wingspan and vanishing viscosity (more precisely: infinite Reynolds number).

There is no mention here of a diversion of the flow as the cause of lift; for as one moves farther away from the wing, the flow field becomes increasingly symmetric in front and behind the wing and eventually transitions uniformly into undisturbed horizontal flow.

Figure 39

This superposition of two flow fields is not unique to fluid dynamics. A similar concept exists in electromagnetism, where two magnetic fields are superimposed: an external homogeneous field (analogous to the horizontal air flow) and the local magnetic field generated by a current-carrying conductor (analogous to the circulation flow). In the case of electromagnetism, the appearance of a transverse force on the current-carrying conductor, due to its circular magnetic field interacting with the initially homogeneous external field, is observed as the Lorentz force, as shown in Figure 41. Similarly, the lift force $\vec{F}_l \propto \vec{b} \times \vec{v}_\infty$ can be understood as a vector product, with $\vec{b}$ pointing in the direction of the wing's spanwise axis, which is analogous to the vortex axis.

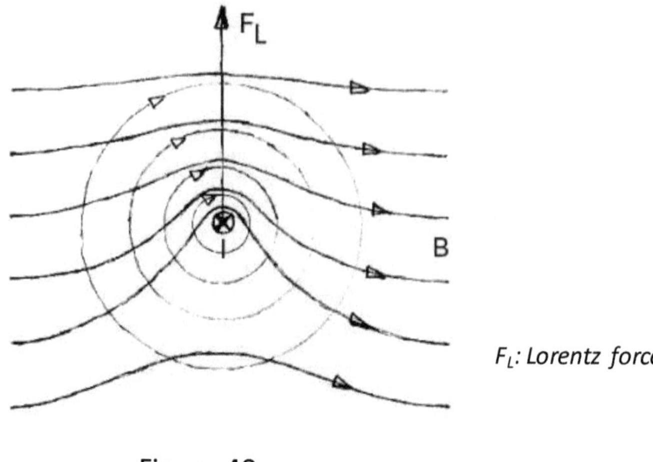

F_L: Lorentz force

Figure 40

Apart from theory, can a flow similar to the one depicted in Figure 40 around a wing generating lift be observed? This is the crucial question, as definitive observational results from freely flying aircraft are scarce in the scientific literature. This is not only because the calculated streamlines in Figure 40 are based on wing angles of attack that cannot be replicated in practice without causing flow separation (as discussed in the chapter "What Keeps the Flow Attached?"). Observations that approximate the ideal case can only be made on significantly lower angles of attack and with wing sections (airfoil profiles) that are much less curved or cambered. As a result, the streamlines are flatter and much more difficult to observe. Moreover, these few observations were conducted in wind tunnels, where unknown distortions can occur due to the suppression of moments, as described in the chapter "Forward Sinking — What is It?". In the chapter "What Are the Consequences of the Wing's Camber?, we will see that, unlike a flat wing, it is impossible to suspend a cambered wing freely in one axis without moments in order to replicate free flight for observational purposes.

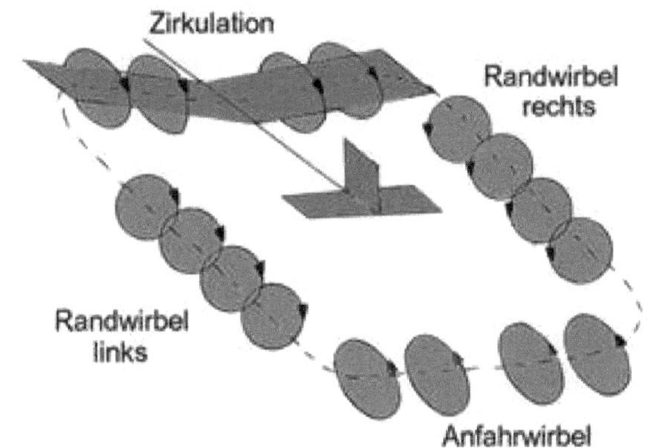

"Zirkulation": circulation

„Randwirbel links:" wing tip vortex left

„Randwirbel rechts:" wing tip vortex right

„Anfahrwirbel:" start-up vortex

Figure 41

In aeronautics research, the presence of a vortex that travels with the wing during flight, with a vortex strength Γ (henceforth referred to as circulation, although not entirely accurate, it is a concise term), is initially theoretically justified using the circulation theorem of fluid dynamics. According to this theorem, a vortex rotating around a vortex line (axis) cannot have an end: either the vortex is infinitely extended or the vortex line, along with the vortex, forms a closed loop like a bicycle inner tube (toroid). During flight, this closed vortex line consists of four segments that form a closed system, as shown in Figure 42: The departing aircraft carries the stationary circulation around the wing and leaves behind the counter-vortex, also known as the starting vortex. During flight, the two counter-rotating lift-induced vortices left by the wingtips represent the connection between these two vortices (we will address these lift-induced vortices further in the chapter "Where Does Drag Come From?"). If you will, the vortex system depicted in Figure 42 resembles an oversized, angular smoke ring.

So far, the circulation (or vortex) theorem in aerodynamics remains the sole explanation for the formation of a circulation flow around a wing generating lift. However, this explanation is not firmly grounded. Both the lift-induced vortices and, even more so, the starting vortex dissipate after a short time. It is not apparent how vortices that continually move away and quickly disappear can sustain a constant circulation around the wing. There is no concept presented to explain the nature or mechanism of the "long-range effect" within this vortex system. Such an explanation for the formation of a sustained circulation flow, which is necessary for generating aerodynamic lift, is therefore unsatisfactory. Instead, we need to search for a suitable mechanism capable of producing a persistent deformation of the flow field in the immediate vicinity of the wing during flight, resembling the flow pattern depicted in Figure 40 and thus interpreted as a superposition of the free stream with a circulation flow. Once again, finding a suitable explanation proves to be a challenging task.

Remarkable: The solution to this problem is not entirely unknown; it lies within our existing knowledge of flight mechanics! The direct relationship between the separation of the center of pressure and the center of gravity, resulting in a nose-heavy pitching moment, on the one hand, and the generation of aerodynamic lift on the other hand, is recognized in the literature but not extensively discussed. Following the circulation flow pattern, as shown in Figure 37, this flow creates a moment around the quarter-chord line of the wing that counteracts the pitching moment: it prevents the glider from descending steeply as described in the section "How does gliding work?" At this point, and only at this point, the significance of Newtonian mechanics in flight becomes apparent: similar to the axiom "force equals counterforce" (weight and lift), here we have the axiom "moment equals counter moment" (pitching moment and circulation moment). Consequently, it follows that establishing a pitching moment in the glider results in a circulation flow around the wing and, thus, generates aerodynamic lift. Those who may doubt this conclusion are invited to attempt to make a glider fly with no pitching moment, meaning the center of gravity and the center of pressure coincide or directly align vertically with each other.

At this point, it is necessary to take another interim assessment to clarify how flying works. In the initial assessment at the end of the chapter "How Does Gliding Work?, we had answers to questions about the basic design of a glider and how it should be configured for stable gliding flight. However, the next obvious question remained unanswered: what is the source of what we call aerodynamic lift. We now have that answer. It has become apparent that the correct positions of the center of gravity and the center of pressure are not only crucial for flight mechanics but also for generating aerodynamic lift. Determining the location of the center of pressure is straightforward when the wing is rectangular and consists of a flat plate or has a thinner symmetrical airfoil section. However, such wings can only achieve glide ratios that are much lower than those achieved by birds of prey or modern sailplanes. In the chapter "The Purpose of Airfoils?", we discussed how a specific type of wing cambering and airfoil design can contribute to significantly reduced drag during air flow. Therefore, when it comes to the efficiency of gliding, we need to address questions about the sources of drag. Since the pitching moment is so important for generating aerodynamic lift, and adjusting the position of the center of gravity in a glider is relatively simple, the next question to be answered is: where is the center of pressure located on a cambered wing?

What Are the Consequences of the Wing's Camber?

In the chapter "Forward Sinking — What is It?" we learned about the neutral point of a flat plate. It is located at the quarter chord of the plate. In the chapter "How Does Gliding Work?" we found the center of pressure of the flat plate when used as a wing for a glider: It is located just behind the neutral point when viewed in the direction of flight. For a glider with such a wing to fly, the center of gravity must be located slightly ahead of the neutral point. In the chapter "The Purpose of Airfoils" we saw the reason why wing cross-sections are better cambered. When a plate is not flat but curved, it is referred to as a cambered plate. Wings with thin cambered cross-sections (profiles) like many bird wings resemble cambered plates, as shown in Figure 26.

If the flat plate shown in Figure 13 is cambered and positioned in the air flow while being able to rotate around an axis, it is not possible to find a stable position with the generation of a usable transverse force (lift) as in the case of the flat plate. The reason for this lies in the pressure point migration, which depends on the angle of attack and the degree of camber. The stabilization of a cambered plate in the air flow with a small angle of attack is only possible with an upward curvature of the trailing edge of the wing, similar to Figure 21, or by setting the horizontal tailplane located behind the wing slightly negatively with respect to the chord line (see the chapter "How to Adjust a Glider").

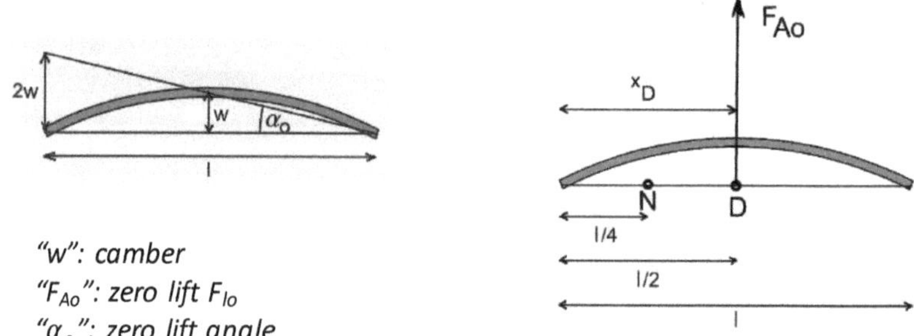

"w": camber
"F_{Ao}": zero lift F_{lo}
"α_o": zero lift angle

Figure 42

In Figure 43, important data of a cambered plate are noted. For now, it is sufficient to assume that the camber of the plate's cross-section follows a circular arc (later, other curvatures will also be described). In this case, the highest point of curvature, denoted as w, is located at $l/2$, where l is the depth of the wing. If it is possible to position such a cambered plate, which is rotatable around an axis passing through the middle of the wing at $l/2$ and stabilized by a horizontal tailplane located further away from the wing, into an air flow, one will observe a transverse force F_{l0}. Recalling the description in the previous chapter "Circulation: More Than Just a Mathematical Trick" and illustrated in Figure 44 using the example of a cambered plate, the air flow around it consists of undisturbed horizontal streamlines and a vortex. Due to symmetry, the point of attack of the aerodynamic force F_{l0}, the center of pressure D, will be located at $x_D = l/2$.

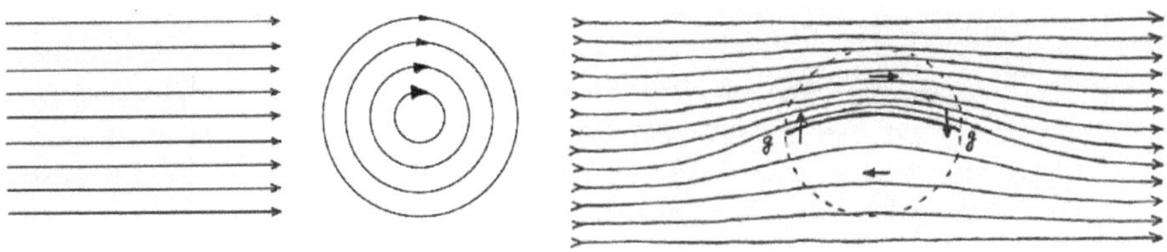

Horizontal flow plus circulation vortex result in the flow pattern for a cambered plate. The flow pattern for a cambered plate (right) is formed by the combination of horizontal flow and a circulation vortex.

Figure 43

One can observe that, provided the flow disturbances are relatively minimal, the observed transverse force on the cambered plate is approximately equal to that of a flat plate inclined at the angle α_0, as shown in Figure 43 on the left. Using the lift equation noted on page 180, this transverse force corresponds to the lift equation mentioned on the same page for the cambered plate not inclined against the free flow. The angle α_0 mentioned here is called the zero-lift angle because the lift becomes zero, if the cambered plate is inclined negatively at this angle against the flow. The magnitude of this zero-lift angle can be determined using Figure 43. A comparison of this approximation with data on this angle and the camber information of specific airfoils found in the literature shows a satisfactory agreement.

If the cambered plate is now inclined at an angle α against the flow, the lift of the non-inclined cambered plate is added to the lift of the inclined flat plate, see Page 180. To prevent any misunderstanding here: The camber of the plate is not crucial for generating a larger lift, as a flat plate inclined at an angle $\alpha + \alpha_0$ potentially generates the same lift. However, such a highly inclined flat plate is no longer adequately flowed around. The camber rather serves for a more streamlined flow, as described in the chapter "The Purpose of Airfoils". Thus, the camber of a wing is the long-discovered alternative to the highly inclined flat wing with poor flow characteristics that reduce lift and increase drag.

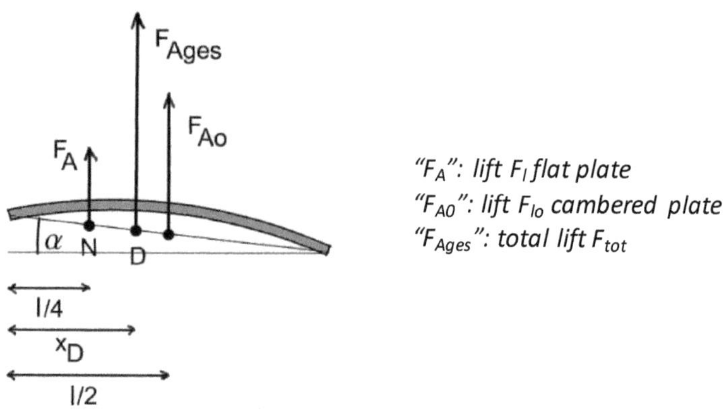

"F_A": lift F_l flat plate
"F_{AO}": lift F_{lo} cambered plate
"F_{Ages}": total lift F_{tot}

Figure 44

In Figure 45, it is illustrated how a new location of the pressure point is formed when the cambered plate is inclined. The pressure point of the flat plate is located close to the neutral point N, which is approximately at $\frac{l}{4}$, for small angles of attack α. The pressure point of the un-inclined cambered plate is at $\frac{l}{2}$. To find the point of application of the resultant force F_{tot}, i.e., the sought-after pressure point D of the inclined cambered plate, we use the equilibrium condition of the torque moments around the pressure point, as described on page 181. After rearranging the equation to $\frac{x_D}{l}$ and transitioning to the coefficients, we finally obtain the mentioned statement of the relative position of the pressure point of the inclined cambered plate. This result for the position of the pressure point of the inclined cambered plate is interesting in two respects. (1) If we determine the moment coefficient $c_{m0.25}$ around the neutral point N, we can see that this moment is (almost) constant. Thus, the neutral point located at $l/4$ has an additional significance beyond its geometric meaning described in the chapter "Forward Sinking — What is It?" In the English literature, it is therefore also called the aerodynamic center. And (2) on page 180 provides information about the pressure point migration with the angle of attack α based on the position of the pressure point.

A representation of this pressure point migration for the camber ratio $\frac{w}{l} = 4\%$ is illustrated in Figure 46, Curve 2, with the angle of attack α in degrees. Curve 1 corresponds to the camber ratio of zero, i.e., for the flat plate and symmetric airfoils of not too large thickness. In that case, no pressure point migration occurs when the angle of attack changes within the usual range, for example, due to a disturbance in the flight path. Therefore, it is said that thin symmetric airfoils are pressure point stable. However, with the cambered plate as well as cambered airfoils, the location of the pressure point changes significantly as the angle of attack varies against the flow, as shown by Curve 2.

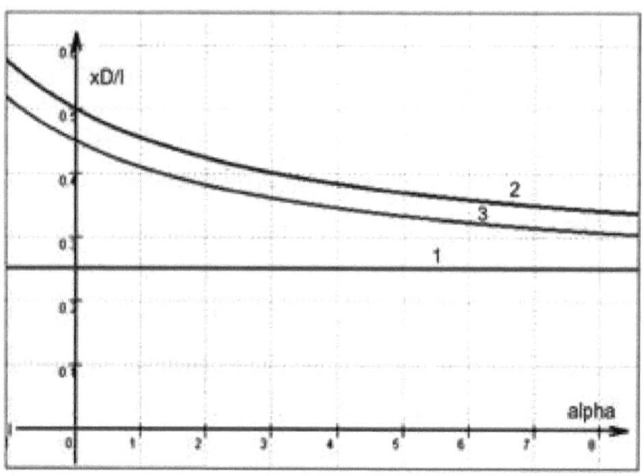

Figure 45

In Figure 46, Curve 3 is plotted, from which information about the center of gravity can be obtained. In the chapter "How Does Gliding Work?", the stability measure Δx, which represents the distance between the pressure point and the center of gravity, was mentioned. To achieve stable flight, the center of gravity must be located Δx ahead of the pressure point in the direction of flight. Curve 3 indicates the position of the center of gravity when a stability measure of $\frac{\Delta x}{l} = 5\%$ is required. With an airfoil camber of 4% and typical angles of attack, the center of gravity is located at approximately 1/3 of the reference wing depth. This center of gravity position aligns well with practical experience. The term "reference wing depth" will be clarified shortly.

Firstly, an important note regarding the angles α and α_0 mentioned in this book so far is necessary. The angle α was initially used to describe the inclination of the flat plate against the free stream during the Forward Sinking, as discussed in the chapter "Forward Sinking — What is It?" Later, it was used to describe the angle of attack of the flat plate during gliding, as explained in the chapter

"How Does Gliding Work?", assuming it is approximately correct. In Figure 30, it was first mentioned how the flow separates from the trailing edge of the wing, forming an angle α with respect to the direction of the free stream. For the inclined flat plate, it is immediately apparent that these two angles are the same, which was assumed there. In Figure 43, this outflow angle for the cambered plate is larger, nearly twice as large as the zero-lift angle of attack, α_0. When the cambered plate is inclined against the free stream during free flight, the "effective" angle of attack α approximately corresponds to the outflow angle α at the wing's trailing edge, which determines the magnitude of circulation and thus the aerodynamic lift. Due to this relationship, there was no need to differentiate between these angles with different designations. It should be noted that the equality of these angles is only approximate, which is why the quantitative results described in the following chapters should be used to verify this assumption. Further information about the angles that occur during flight can be found in the chapter "How to Adjust a Glider".

The neutral point can be immediately determined for a rectangular wing shape, but it becomes more challenging for other wing shapes. Since the neutral point has a special significance as an aerodynamic center, determining its location for non-rectangular wing shapes is important. The reference wing is a rectangular surrogate wing used to capture data that are essential for setting up a flight-capable state of the aircraft. When using a flat or cambered rectangular plate as a wing, the reference wing with all essential points such as the neutral point, pressure point, and center of gravity is immediately given, as shown in Figure 46. However, wings of ordinary aircraft as well as birds typically do not have a rectangular shape. This is sometimes for aesthetic reasons but more often for reasons related to reducing induced drag (see the following chapter "Where Does Drag Come From?") or adapting to higher flight velocities (swept wings). For a non-rectangular wing, the shape and position of a rectangular reference wing need to be determined, which replaces the wing in all essential characteristics, i.e., indicating its neutral point location and, depending on the airfoil camber, the pressure and center of gravity locations. For this purpose, a simple geometric method has proven successful.

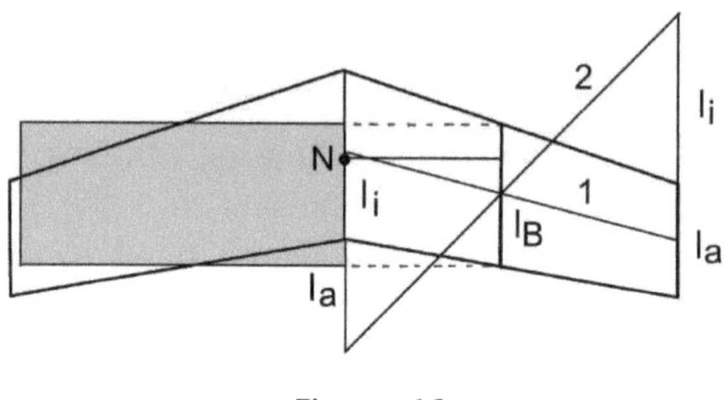

Figure 46

Any wing is first approximated by a trapezoidal wing, such as the one shown in Figure 47, to the best possible extent. This swept trapezoidal wing has a depth l_i at the symmetry axis (inner edge) and a depth l_a at the outer edge. Referring to one wing half, the reference wing depth l_B is obtained as the original wing depth at the intersection of the center of gravity lines 1 and 2 (center of gravity lines of one wing half). At the same time, the location of l_B also indicates the position of the reference wing relative to the original wing, with the left half of the reference wing shaded in gray in Figure 47. The point N located at $1/4$ of the reference wing depth on the symmetry axis is the neutral point of the reference wing, and it is also the neutral point of the original wing. With a representation similar to Figure 46, one can then determine the other important points, such as the pressure point and the center of gravity. Additionally, on starting from Page 226, there is an article discussing a specific issue related to the location of the center of gravity in a commercial aircraft.

Part III: Efficient Gliding?

In Part I: Am I Flying? and Part II: Why? it has been explained how flying is possible and where the necessary lift comes from. In this Part III, the focus is on describing what factors contribute to the quality of flight. What factors contribute to achieving the best possible gliding performance?

Where Does Drag Come From?

In the chapter "Aerodynamic Lift" an ideal condition of flying without sinking was described, where the only aerodynamic force is lift. However, in reality, this condition can only be approximated (as discussed in the following chapter "Quality of Flight"), as there are inevitable drags during flight. Overcoming these drags requires work, which is provided by the engines in powered aircraft or extracted from the glider's potential energy reserves. Therefore, even the best glider will always experience sinking.

In the chapter "How Does Sinking Work?" we introduced the concept of drag and on page 174, we learned about the magnitude of drag and the concept of drag coefficient. The drag coefficient can be significantly reduced through appropriate shaping and surface design of a body moving through a fluid. In nature, sharks, dolphins, and penguins exhibit drag coefficients below 0.01, and similar values are achieved in modern high-performance gliders.

In aeronautics, drags can be broadly classified into two categories: those that are fundamentally avoidable or could be avoided to the extent that they are minimized, and those that are fundamentally unavoidable. For fundamentally avoidable drags, the term "parasitic drag" is used, with the coefficient denoted as c_{d0}. Fundamentally unavoidable drags are also known as induced drag, with the coefficient denoted as c_{di}. The main representatives of these two types of drag will be described below.

Among the fundamentally avoidable drags, there are some that are not only fundamentally but also absolutely avoidable. These include all drags caused by protruding parts on the aircraft that do not contribute to lift generation, such as struts, tension wires, rivets, rough surfaces, or edges on the cockpit, as well as flaps or extended control surfaces and the resulting flow disturbances. We will now disregard such contributions to drag. Among the fundamentally avoidable drags, there is a type of drag that can be significantly reduced but not completely eliminated through wing profiling and the surface design of flow-exposed areas.

Nature shows us that a smooth surface does not always mean the lowest possible drag. This can be observed in the structured skin of sharks and dolphins, as well as in the feather patterns of penguins and birds of prey. How a surface should be structured to minimize drag depending on the type of motion in the fluid is one of the main subjects of modern aeronautics research. In this book on flying, only a rough overview of this topic can be provided.

With the clarification of the hydrodynamic paradox, as described in the chapter "Hydrodynamic Paradox, What is It?", it is known that particles coming from a gas space and striking a wall momentarily "stick" to it, causing them to come to a rest in the case of flow over a wall and hinder the progress of other particles in the subsequent emission from the wall, thus contributing to a certain flow resistance. What are the consequences?

Let us consider a smooth flat surface over which a flow with velocity $v > 0$ is present, or equivalently, it is moving perpendicular to the surface normal with a velocity $v > 0$ relative to a stationary fluid. As long as the flow velocity v is not too large, we observe that "nothing happens," and the described hindrance of the free flow particles by the particles emitted from the wall seems to have no significant effect apart from a small flow resistance. Only after exceeding a certain critical flow velocity, "something happens," and local vortices are formed directly at the surface. Somehow, the freely flowing fluid particles no longer interact well with the fluid particles decelerated (or accelerated) by the wall. With increasing velocity of the free flow, both these particles and immediately adjacent particles experience increasingly drastic changes in velocity, eventually leading to the formation of local vortices and an increase in resistance.

This phenomenon was first described by Osborne Reynolds in 1883 for pipe flows. In his honor, this transition from smooth (laminar) to turbulent flow is characterized by the critical Reynolds number, or simply the critical Re number. The Reynolds number itself is a dimensionless ratio of the work of acceleration to the work of friction and, in the case of air near the Earth's surface, is given by $Re = 73{,}500 \cdot l \cdot v_\infty$, where l is the length of the surface area being flowed over in meters and v_∞ is the velocity of the free flow in m/s. The factor of 73,500, with the unit s/m^2, arises from the ratio of ρ/η, which represents the density and viscosity of the air.[14]

The critical Reynolds numbers for bodies experiencing flow around them are difficult to predict accurately in theory. The fact that smooth polished spheres have a critical Reynolds number of approximately 300,000 means that, in practice, spheres cannot be uniformly surrounded by fluid (unless the flow is extremely slow). In normal conditions, separation occurs, which generates resistance due to vortex formation. The critical Reynolds number is reached at a flow velocity of approximately $v_\infty \approx \dfrac{300{,}000 \; m}{73{,}500 \; s} \approx 4\dfrac{m}{s}$ for a sphere with a

---

[14] Schlichting, H., Truckenbrodt, E. (1967). Aerodynamik des Flugzeuges, Erster Band. Berlin, Heidelberg, New York: Springer, 14 ff.

diameter of, for example, one meter. Now, something remarkable has been observed: When this flow velocity is exceeded, generally when exceeding the critical Reynolds number for any sphere, the resistance of the smooth sphere suddenly becomes significantly smaller (!).[15]

This leads us to another peculiarity of the motion of objects in the air. Although exceeding a critical Reynolds number initially leads to the formation of turbulence on the surface experiencing flow, which increases the flow resistance, the formation of a local turbulent boundary layer on non-flat (especially convex) surfaces can reduce the resistance. This can be understood in the case of a sphere: In the subcritical Reynolds number range, a smoothly polished sphere has a drag coefficient of approximately $c_{d0} \approx 0.4$, caused by early flow separation. Above the critical Reynolds number, the drag coefficient decreases to $c_{d0} \approx 0.1$, despite the additional local turbulence generated on the previously smooth surface of the sphere. Apparently, this turbulent boundary layer formed prior to flow separation allows the flow to remain attached for a longer distance (see the chapter "What Keeps the Flow Attached?") in the subsequent separation region, resulting in an overall lower flow resistance.

Of course, one can also utilize this effect in the subcritical Reynolds number range by roughening the surface of the sphere instead of polishing it, thereby creating an artificial turbulent boundary layer that leads to better flow attachment in the subsequent separation region. For example, when comparing a sphere made of rough material like Styrofoam to a smoothly polished sphere in the subcritical Reynolds number range, a significantly lower drag

---

[15] Schlichting, H., Truckenbrodt, E. (1967). Aerodynamik des Flugzeuges, Erster Band. Berlin, Heidelberg, New York: Springer, 14 ff.

coefficient of approximately $c_{d0} \approx 0.23$ can be observed. And, of course, this effect is also significant for flying: Not only birds of prey but also model gliders with roughened surfaces (foam gliders) fly remarkably well. It can be assumed that this effect is also responsible for achieving extremely low drag coefficients in sharks, dolphins, and penguins.

The reason why modern high-performance gliders have smooth surfaces despite the observation with the smooth sphere is that their gliding involves flying in the supercritical Reynolds number range. The critical Reynolds number for airfoil profiles of such aircraft is approximately 1,000,000. This means that with $Re = 73,500 \cdot l \cdot v_{\infty}$ and a wing depth of $l = 1m$, a flight velocity of $50km/h$ is reached. This speed is easily surpassed by modern gliders due to their wing loading alone (see the following chapter "Quality of Flight"). Unlike birds of prey, modern high-performance gliders, as well as commercial aircraft, fly in the supercritical Reynolds number range due to their high flight velocities, and therefore, they are equipped with as smooth surfaces as possible. This applies to both the wings and all other parts of the aircraft (fuselage, tailplanes).

Figure 47

In Figure 48, the case of a subcritical flow (left panel) and a supercritical flow (right panel) over a wall are depicted. In the case of subcritical flow, layers of increasing flow velocities extend from the surface with zero flow velocity up to a certain distance from the surface (laminar flow) until reaching the free stream. When the critical Reynolds number is exceeded, either due to a higher free stream velocity v_∞ or a longer length l of flow over the surface, a reversal of flow direction can occur immediately above the surface, as shown in the right panel. This helps to understand why a local vortex (a "bubble") forms near the surface. Flying in the transitional range from subcritical to supercritical flow is feared due to the risk of larger flow separations on the wing, leading to a collapse of aerodynamic lift. To safely fly a glider in either the subcritical or supercritical range, it is necessary to have at least some knowledge of the critical Reynolds number for the specific airfoil used, which remains a constant subject of aeronautics research. If a glider is designed in such a way that it can only fly in the subcritical range (like birds of prey and many model gliders), the only solution is to use a sufficiently rough surface to artificially generate a turbulent boundary layer.

Across the entire wing depth, let us consider the flow stratification in the immediate vicinity of the surface as depicted in Figure 48, left panel. This region is referred to as the boundary layer in the scientific literature. The formation of such a boundary layer requires time. Therefore, at the beginning of an overlying surface, the boundary layer is thin and gradually thickens later. For model gliders, the average thickness is on the order of millimeters, while for sailplanes, it is on the order of centimeters. This leads to the appearance of the boundary layer depicted in Figure 49, immediately adjacent to the surfaces, using the example of a flat plate moving through the air. At the trailing edge of the flat plate, as well as at the trailing edge of each wing, a so-called "Nachlauf" (wake vortices or turbulence) forms, consisting of a thin layer of vortices. The resulting resistance can usually only be estimated, and a reasonable value is given by the drag coefficient $c_{d0} \approx 0.006$. Let us consider such a value as the lower limit for that portion of resistances that can potentially be avoided but have not been eliminated so far. This is referred to as parasitic drag, which arises from the formation of a boundary layer over the surfaces subject to flow.

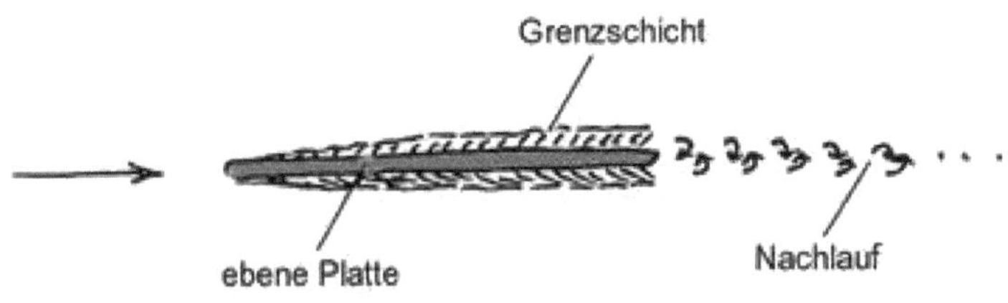

"Grenzschicht:" Boundary Layer; "Ebene Platte:" Flat Plate; "Nachlauf:" Wake Vortices (thin zone of small vortices)

Figure 48

Next, we need to describe the most important unavoidable resistance, known as induced drag. It occurs when a wing generates lift and has finite span. Around the wing, there is a reduced pressure compared to atmospheric pressure, and below the wing, the pressure is less reduced, as explained in the chapter "Aerodynamic Lift". At the wingtips, there must be a pressure equalization, resulting in a flow of air from below to above the wingtips. It is easy to imagine the consequences of this during the forward motion of the wing through the air: Vortices form at the wingtips, as shown in Figure 42. Figure 50 provides a rear view of a glider, illustrating the direction of rotation of these lift-induced vortices. This vortex formation can be clearly observed by releasing a model glider through a fog screen created by a theatrical smoke cartridge and observing behind the glider.

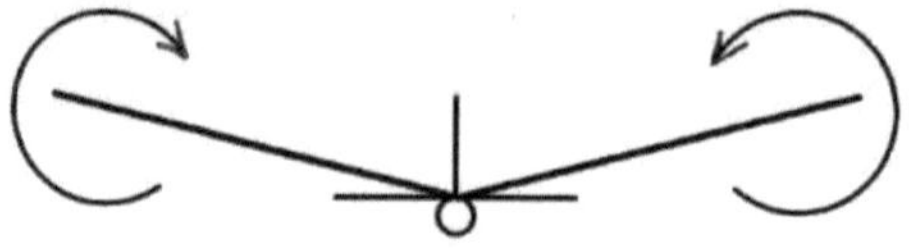

Figure 49

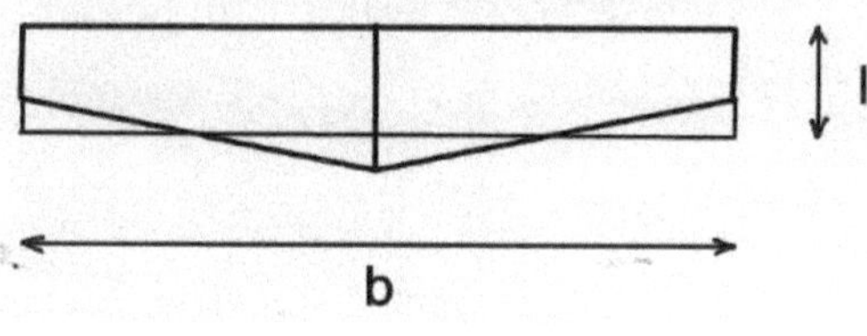

Figure 50

The generation of such lift-induced vortices requires work, hence the resistance. It is possible to estimate the magnitude of this induced drag because it depends on both the magnitude of the aerodynamic lift and the wing's shape, as explained on page 182. The wing's shape is represented by its aspect ratio, denoted as Λ, as shown in Figure 51. The aspect ratio of the wing affects the induced drag because a high aspect ratio (large Λ) corresponds to a short chord length (l) of the reference wing, and a short chord length provides only a limited length of wingspan for the formation of the lift-induced vortices.

The derivation of a good approximation for the magnitude of the induced drag on page 182 assumes an idealized glider with zero parasitic drag, meaning $c_{d0} = 0$. However, the total drag of a freely flying glider includes a contribution from parasitic drag: $c_{dtot} = c_{di} + c_{d0}$. While the contribution of induced drag can be reliably estimated, the contribution of parasitic drag is a relatively unknown quantity for a given glider. Unless you have a wind tunnel where such drag can be

91

measured, you either have to rely on an empirical value for c_{d0} or have specific flight data for the glider in question. In the case of the flight data of the ASW 17 high-performance glider,[16] shown on page 182, it demonstrates how to determine a reasonable value for the magnitude of the parasitic drag coefficient for this particular glider. This value is quite good and can be attributed to the careful design of the aircraft, which focuses on reducing parasitic drag.

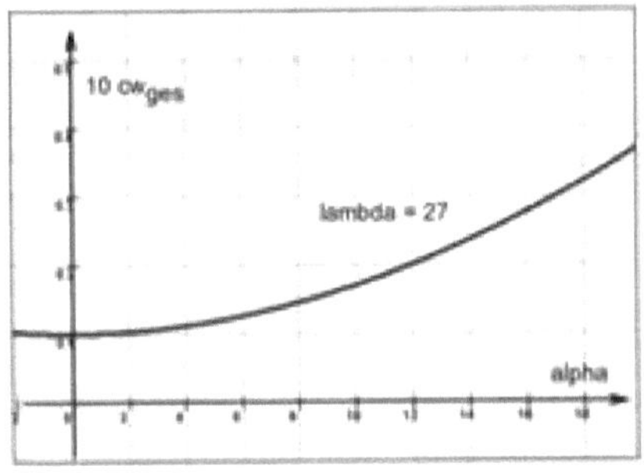

Figure 51

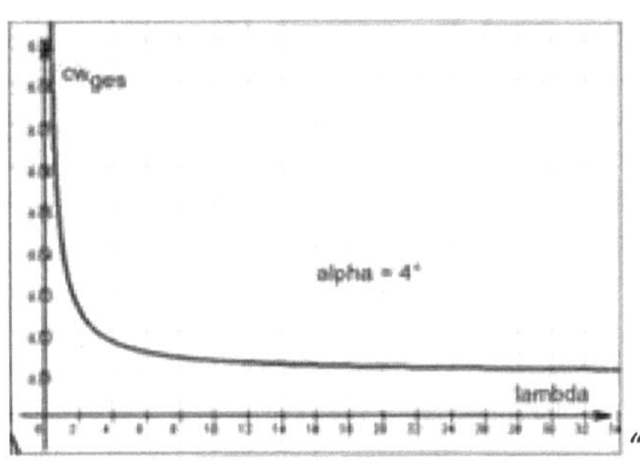

$"c_{wges}": c_{dtot}$

In Figure 52, two diagrams are shown for the ASW 17 high-performance glider, illustrating the dependence of the total drag on the angle of attack alpha (see page 182) with the data $c_{d0} = 0.01$ and $\Lambda = 27$ (left diagram, exaggerated by a factor of 10), and the dependence on the aspect ratio lambda with the data $c_{d0} = 0.01$ and $\alpha = 4°$ (right diagram). It can be observed that the induced drag only increases significantly at higher angles of attack α. Furthermore, the influence of the aspect ratio on the total drag becomes minimal for aspect ratios above $\Lambda = 20$.

An important note is necessary. The considerations on Page 180 involved a general lift coefficient, which is certainly correct when considering a flat plate or moderately thick symmetrical airfoil

---

[16] Buch, H. (1980). *Segelfliegen*. Berlin: transpress VEB, 185.

profiles. However, in the case of a cambered plate (or cambered airfoil), the lift coefficient c_l consists of two components, as described on page 180. Since the induced drag is proportional to the square of the lift coefficient, caution is required. Instead of using $c_{ltot}^2 = (c_l + c_{l0})^2$, the correct formulation is $c_{ltot}^2 = c_l^2 + c_{l0}^2$. In the case of the ASW 17 sailplane with a cambered airfoil profile under normal flight conditions, where $c_{di} \approx \frac{1}{3} c_{d0}$, the error is small. This issue will be further discussed in the chapter "What Are Polar Diagrams Used For?"

Quality of Flight

The frequently encountered statement that measuring in a wind tunnel is indispensable for predicting the gliding characteristics of an aircraft is incorrect, as can be seen immediately. The lift coefficient $c_l \approx \frac{2F_g/\rho A}{v_\infty^2}$ mentioned on page 182 for the ASW 17 sailplane is approximately 0.9. This sailplane already comes quite close to an ideal glider, meaning that flow problems, especially at the wing, leading to additional drag, are largely minimized. Assuming such an approximation to ideal gliding, it can be stated that all unpowered gliding aircraft fly with a lift coefficient c_l close to 1. Consequently, a base velocity $v_\infty \approx \sqrt{\frac{2F_g}{\rho A}}$ for free, unpowered gliding can be predicted for such a glider. This base or reference velocity does not depend on typical aerodynamic data. The flight velocity of an unpowered glider is solely determined by its wing loading F_g/A and the air density. This means that if deviations from this base velocity are observed during free flight of such a glider (and deviations can only be towards higher speeds), there is an issue with minimizing drag. Initially, avoidable parasitic drag may be the cause. If such drag has been eliminated or minimized, there may be an issue with the flow around the wing, such as additional drag and flow separation causing reduced lift, as discussed in the chapter "What Keeps the Flow Attached?" For the ASW 17 sailplane, the calculated base velocity and measured flight velocity largely agree. Therefore, a wind tunnel is not required to determine if an aircraft glides well enough. Simply measuring the flight velocity and comparing it to the easily determinable base velocity is sufficient. If the deviation is small, one can be satisfied with the optimization of gliding. This statement can be verified with several examples.

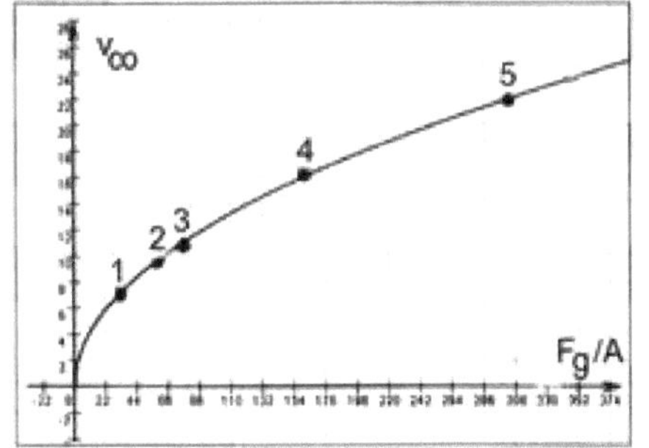

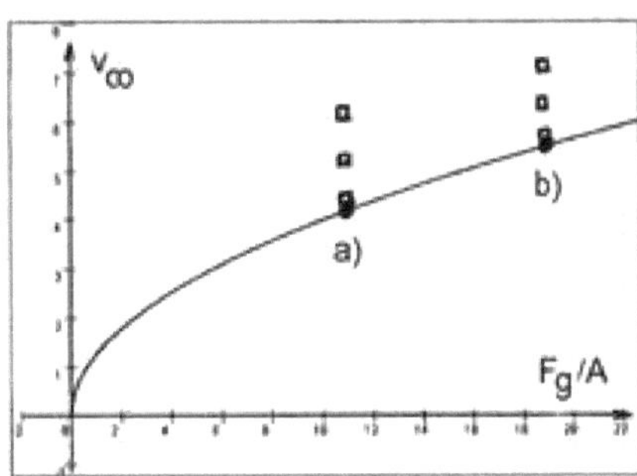

Figure 52

glider data:	wing surface	basic speed v_∞	v_∞ observed	glide ratio ε	rate of descent v_s
surface load	balsa untreated	5.56 m/s	6.45 m/s	10	0.65 m/s
= 19 N/m²,	foil covering	5.56 m/s	7.15 m/s	8	0.9 m/s
camber 6 %,	sandpaper 100	5.56 m/s	7.18 m/s	10	0.66 m/s
stretch 6	sandpaper 40	5.56 m/s	5.85 m/s	11	0.52 m/s

Table 1

In Figure 53, the base velocity $v_\infty \approx \sqrt{\dfrac{2F_g}{\rho A}}$ is plotted against the wing loading, ρ being the standard air density. The left diagram contains data for: 1 Red Kite; 2 Tern; 3 Stork; 4 Albatross; and 5 ASW 17 sailplane. The proximity of these points to the base velocity indicates that both parasitic drag has been well prevented and the flow around

94

the wing is well attached. In contrast, in the right diagram of Figure 53, we have the simple homemade gliders from Figure 24 with cambered plates as wings (Group b) with data from Table 1, where the observed values have an error margin of 10%). It is noticeable that the wing with a coarse sandpaper surface provides the closest approximation to the base velocity, while the smooth wing covered with ironed foil shows the poorest performance. This is because all gliders listed in Table 1 always fly in the subcritical Reynolds number range, as discussed in the preceding chapter, for which a smooth wing surface is unsuitable. These simple observations already provide an initial deeper insight into the conditions for good gliding.

In the right part of Figure 53, another group of investigated gliders from Figure 24 is represented as Group a). These gliders consist of untreated balsa wood wings with a wing loading of $11\ N/m^2$ but varying degrees of wing camber. The glider with the greatest deviation in flight velocity from the base velocity is the one with a flat wing (plane plate), while the one with the smallest deviation has a wing camber of 6%. Therefore, the flat wing experiences the greatest difficulties in generating lift during flow around it. This demonstrates the validity of the considerations presented in the chapter "The Purpose of Airfoils" regarding the purpose of wing camber in a simple yet compelling manner.

In the chapter "Forward Sinking — What is It?" the two parameters glide ratio and sink rate were introduced. We can now attribute a significance to these parameters that goes beyond the knowledge presented in that chapter, as shown on page 183. There, the glide ratio and sink rate are determined as a function of the actual flight velocity v in relation to the base velocity v_∞. Controlled aircraft can fly at variable lift coefficients (c_l values) and, therefore, different speeds v. The equations provided in that section for the glide ratio and sink rate will now be used for further investigations.

For the aforementioned ASW 17 glider with the provided data c_{d0}, v_∞ and Λ from page 182, the diagrams in Figure 54 follow, using an average base velocity of $v_\infty = 23.5\ m/s$: glide ratio and sink rate as a function of flight velocity. Although the initial equations are only approximations, reasonable values are obtained: a maximum glide ratio of approximately 46 and a minimum sink rate of about $0.5\ m/s$. However, the curves in Figure 54 at larger distances from the base velocity should not be taken too seriously, as the underlying equations are approximation equations whose validity is questionable in extreme flight conditions. However, trends are correctly represented: when an aircraft is "pushed down," it flies faster with lower c_l values, resulting in lower glide ratios and higher sink rates. When the control stick is "pulled back," the aircraft flies slower, the angle of attack increases, and it flies with higher c_l values, again resulting in lower glide ratios and higher sink rates. In the extreme case of complete flow separation, the vertical descent described in the chapter "How Does Sinking Work?" occurs, with a "glide ratio" of zero and a sink rate that is approximately equal to the base velocity during gliding. Model aircraft enthusiasts are familiar with this flight condition after activating the so-called thermal brake.

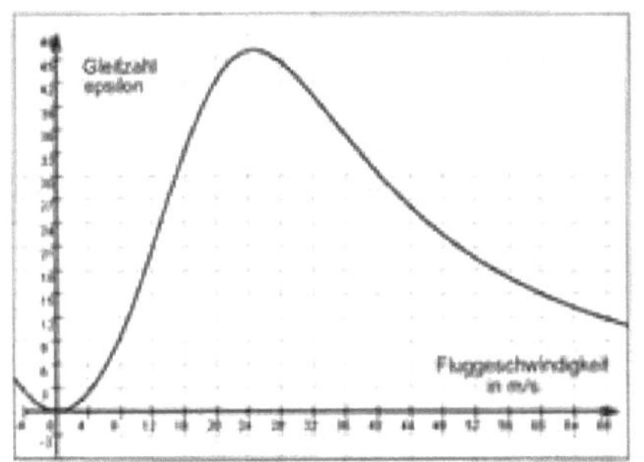

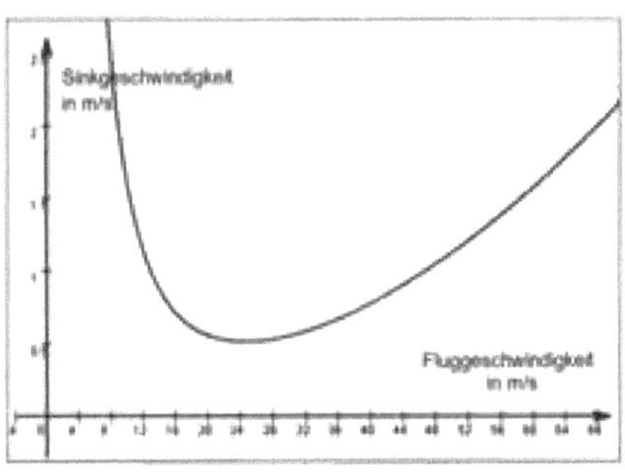

"Gleitzahl:" Glide Ratio; "Fluggeschwindigkeit:" Flight Velocity; "Sinkgeschwindigkeit:" Sink Rate

Figure 53

If the sink rate is plotted as a function of flight velocity, as shown in the right diagram of Figure 54 but reversed as in Figure 55, it creates a graph that appears in a similar form in sailplane data sheets and is referred to as the glide polar. This graph contains two essential pieces of information for the pilot, including the two marked points: the flight velocity corresponding to the minimum sink rate can be read at the maximum of the curve, and the negative slope of the tangent to the curve passing through the origin, which is the tangent at the point next to it on the right, gives the reciprocal of the best glide ratio as well as the corresponding flight velocity (these data are not particularly precise). To reiterate, these flight conditions, minimum sink rate and best glide, can only be achieved with controlled aircraft. Birds of prey and glider pilots utilize this capability to quickly gain altitude within a thermal updraft (such as a thermal bubble) by circling slowly with minimum sink rate, and to fly through a downdraft zone in search of the next updraft zone at the best glide rate.

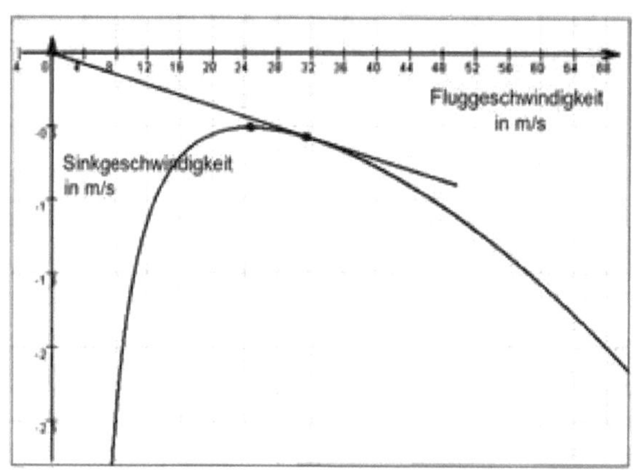

"Sinkgeschwindigkeit:"
Sink Rate

"Fluggeschwindigkeit:"
Flight Velocity

Figure 54

If only an estimation of the expected performance of a glider is needed, the simple equations provided on page 184 are sufficient, as

$v \approx v_\infty$. With these equations, there exists a user-friendly toolkit for assessing the quality of flight. In this case, either reasonable estimated values for c_{d0} need to be used, or the flight velocity can be measured to determine a value for c_{d0}, as shown on page 182. Unless more precise information is required, wind tunnel measurements are not necessary.

Parameters of Practical Gliding

The equations on page 183, which describe practical flying, contain three parameters whose respective influence on gliding can be studied: wing loading $\frac{F_g}{A}$, the coefficient of parasitic drag c_{d0}, and the aspect ratio Λ of the wing. By conducting computational analysis with two of these parameters held constant while varying the third, interesting results can be obtained.

a) Dependency of glide ratio and sink rate on flight velocity with variable wing loading:

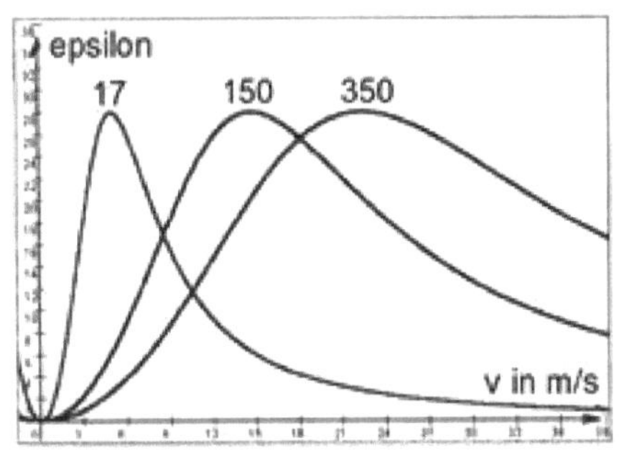

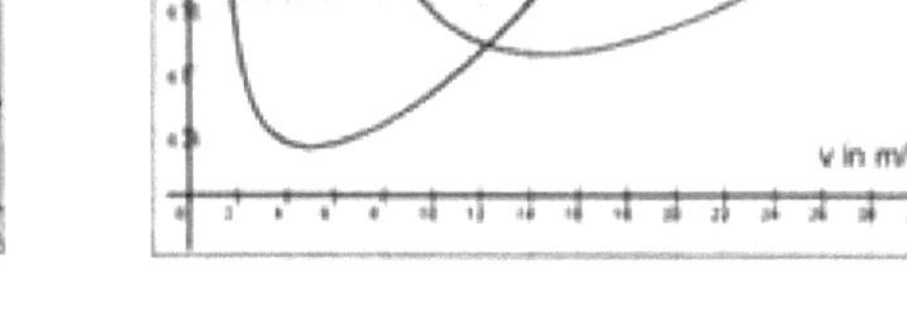

Figure 55   Figure 56

For the diagrams in Figures 56 and 57, fixed values of $c_{d0} = 0.02$ and $\Lambda = 20$ have been chosen. The lowest parameter value for wing loading could correspond to a modern model glider, the medium value to an old glider type, and the highest value to a modern glider. Surprisingly, the observation is that the best glide ratio (epsilon) is independent of wing loading, while the measure of the lowest sink rate increases as expected with wing loading (specifically, with the square root of wing loading). The independence of the best glide ratio from wing loading is also observed in practice.

b) Dependence of glide ratio and sink rate on flight velocity for variable parasitic drag coefficient:

For the diagrams in Figures 58 and 59, the fixed values of $\frac{F_g}{A}$ and Λ are chosen. It is evident that the influence of the drag coefficient is significant on the best glide ratio, but relatively less pronounced on the minimum sink rate. This observation is also made in practice, especially with uncontrolled competitive model gliders: The surface condition of the glider's wings can be somewhat "sloppy" (with repairs) without a significant impact on performance.

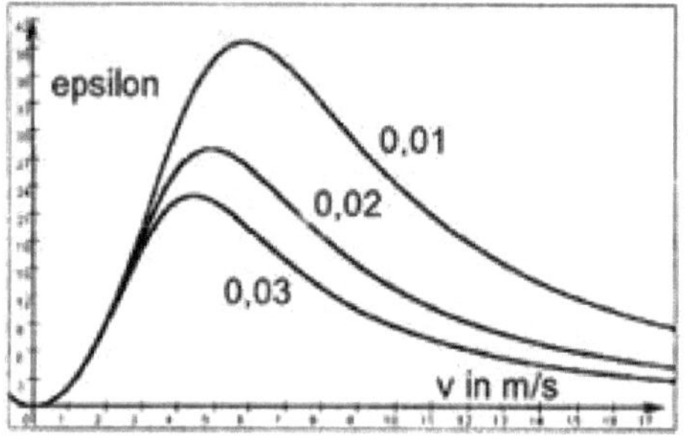

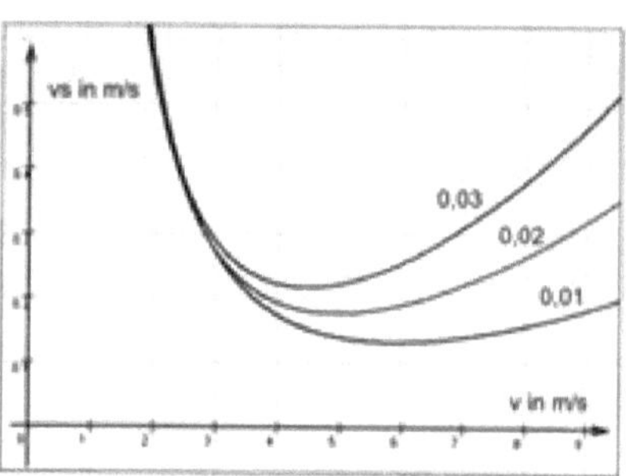

Figure 57   Figure 58

c) Dependency of the glide ratio and sink rate on the flight velocity with variable aspect ratio of the wing:

For the diagrams in Figures 60 and 61, the fixed values of $\frac{F_g}{A} = 17 \frac{N}{m^2}$ and $c_{d0} = 0.02$ are chosen. Significant influences of the aspect ratio of the wing are observed in both the glide ratios and sink rates. It is evident that larger aspect ratios result in "better" values for both parameters. However, there are mechanical limitations, such as bending and torsional stiffness, that impose constraints on increasing the aspect ratio. In modern glider design, the aspect ratio is typically limited to around 30, as shown in Figure 91.

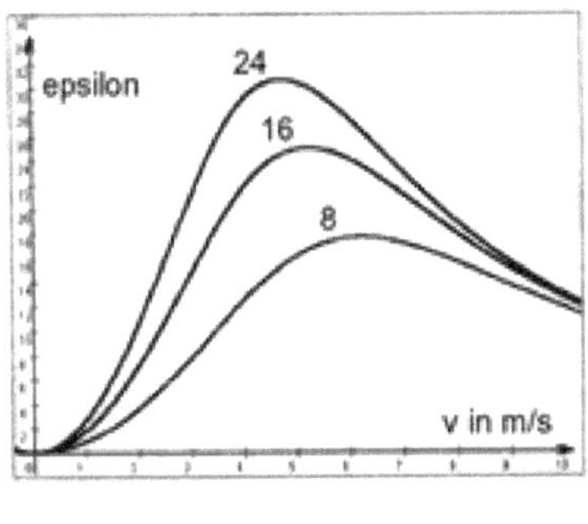

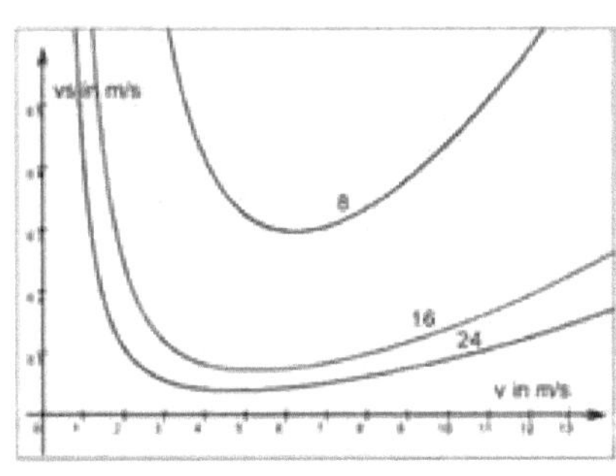

<table>
<tr><td>Figure 59</td><td>Figure 60</td></tr>
</table>

The diagrams shown in Figures 56 to 61 reveal two philosophies for designing "good" gliders: the high-performance glider and the low sinker. For a high-performance glider, low drag and high aspect ratio are crucial, while wing loading plays a less significant role. In other words, a good glider can be heavier without compromising its performance. This design philosophy is commonly found in modern gliders and most remote-controlled competition model gliders.

On the other hand, for a low sinker, low wing loading and, if technically feasible, larger aspect ratios are important, while drag is less critical. This means that the surface of such a glider, especially in the wing area, does not need to be exceptionally smooth. This aligns perfectly with the insights from the chapter "Where Does Drag Come From?". Due to the low wing loading, the low sinker flies at slower speeds, which typically results in subcritical flow over the wings. The turbulence layer induced by surface roughness prevents premature flow separation on the usually more cambered wing surfaces of such gliders. The design philosophy of the "low sinker" is commonly found in free-flight gliders, which rely on thermals and hope for long flight times while leaving their aircraft uncontrolled in the hands of nature.

Are there only two alternatives: a good glider or a poor sinker? Those who require an aircraft for a specific purpose will typically have to choose between these two options. The free-flight enthusiast will construct a lightweight model that flies slowly, with extreme maneuvers being avoided. On the other hand, those seeking to perform aerobatics and master extreme flight maneuvers will design a heavier and faster aircraft capable of executing specific aerial maneuvers.

Modern gliders, as well as large commercial aircraft, are designed as "compromise" configurations aiming to achieve both capabilities: flying slowly with reduced sinking or flying faster with improved gliding performance. The standard method employed to meet these dual requirements in the same aircraft is the use of stationary or deployable camber flaps and often supplemented with deployable leading edge slats.

In Figure 62, it is illustrated how the wing of a commercial aircraft can be modified to meet the requirements of high-speed cruising and efficient gliding on one hand, and low-speed takeoff and landing with minimal sink rate on the other hand. As clearly visible, such flaps or leading edge slats can significantly alter not only the effective wing area but also the camber of the wing.

It may have been noticed that when referring to the lift coefficient, the term "c_l" was generally used, although for the cambered wing, the appropriate term would be "c_{ltot}" as mentioned on page 180. In most cases, this is correct because, under the assumption of good flow around the wing, a cambered wing can be replaced by a flat wing with a correspondingly large lift coefficient without leading to incorrect statements. However, it is important to always remember that the lift coefficient of a cambered wing is composed of two components. This was significant at the end of the chapter "Where Does Drag Come From?" and should also be considered in the following chapter.

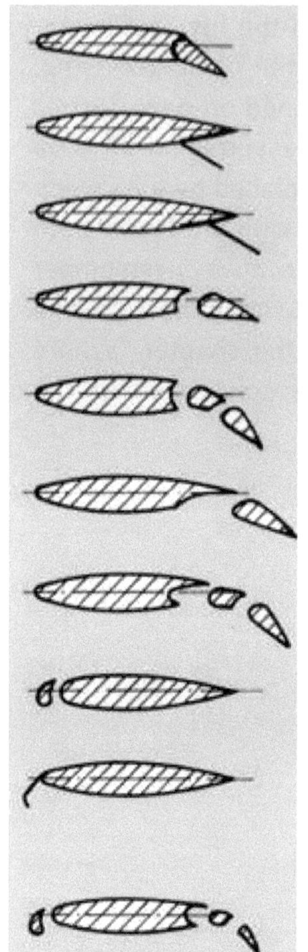

Figure 61

(see R. Kutter[17])

Takeoff and Landing As Well As Cruising Flight in Commercial Aircraft

Up at an altitude of 10 km, the Airbus roars along at about 900 km/h, while down during takeoff or landing, it should only be about 250 km/h fast. How can one achieve such a thing in one's own aircraft? The basic speed during gliding on page 184, does not provide such a range of flight speeds, especially since the wing loading F_g/A is fundamentally unchanged both below and above. In the lift equation on page 180, the two quantities air density p and lift coefficient c_l appear, which have an influence on lift. This lift equation is rearranged according to flight speed and F_l is replaced by F_g: $v_\infty = \sqrt{2F_g/\rho A c_l}$. At an altitude of 10 km, the air density is about 0.3 times that near the earth's surface. Since air densities appear under the square root, the factor generated by the difference in density is $\sqrt{1/0.3} \approx 1.83$. By using flaps and/or slats during takeoff or landing, a lift coefficient of 2.0 or more can be generated. At an altitude of 10 km, the aircraft, due to its flapless slim airfoil and propulsion, can fly with a lift coefficient of about 0.5. This results in a factor of $\sqrt{2/0.5} = 2$, which is caused by the difference in lift coefficients. Both factors combined result in a factor of about 3.66, by which the takeoff and landing speed can be lower than the cruising speed above. This means: Takeoff and landing can occur at 250 km/h, and the runways do not need to be unnecessarily long. However, during takeoff and landing, commercial aircraft fly just above a critical condition where the flow over the wing can separate ("stall"), as discussed in the chapter "What Keeps the Flow Attached?"

---

[17] Kutter, R. (1983). *Flugzeugaerodynamik, technische Lösungen und struktureller Aufbau*. Stuttgart: Motorbuch Verlag, 60.

What Are Polar Diagrams Used For?

Polar diagrams have been used since Otto Lilienthal to depict the relationships between the aerodynamic forces of lift and drag for specific airfoils and angles of attack against the free flow. Over the following decades, various formats of such diagrams have been employed. In modern polar diagrams, the lift coefficient is plotted against the drag coefficient, often with the indication of typical wing angles of attack, in the form of $c_l(c_d)$. Due to $\varepsilon = \frac{c_L}{c_d}$, information about the glide ratio can also be derived from these diagrams. The principle of such diagrams can already be studied in the case of forward sinking discussed in the chapter "Forward Sinking — What is It?"

a) Polar diagram of a forward sinker

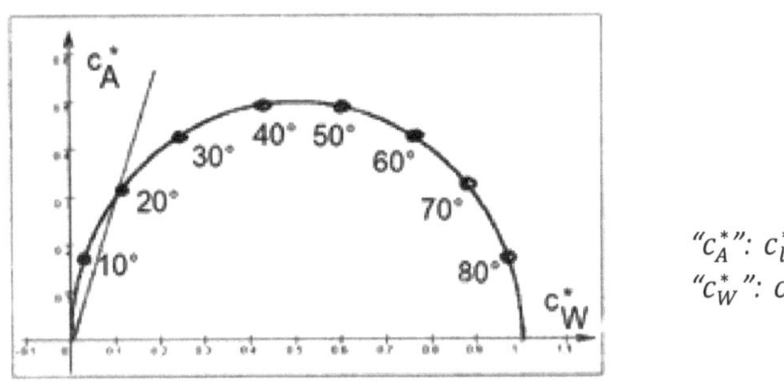

Figure 62

In Figure 63, the polar diagram of a forward sinker is depicted according to the equation given on page 184, with a constant drag coefficient (c_d) of 1. This polar diagram takes the shape of a semicircle. Along the curve, several annotations are provided for the angle of attack (α). The lift coefficient is highest at an angle of attack of 45°, but it does not correspond to the maximum glide ratio

$(\varepsilon = \frac{c_l^*}{c_d^*})$, which is 1 at that point. Higher glide ratios are achieved at smaller angles of attack. A reference line, approximately at an angle of attack of 20°, is included in the diagram. The corresponding glide ratio, determined as the slope of this line, is approximately 3. Theoretically, larger glide ratios can be obtained as one approaches the origin. However, as explained in the chapter "Forward Sinking — What is It?", this movement is not feasible at angles of attack less than 20°.

b) Polar diagram of the flat plate

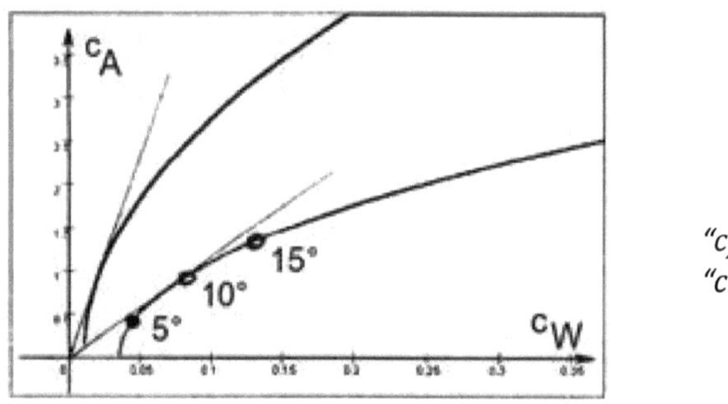

Figure 63

In Figure 64, the polar diagram of the flat plate is depicted according to the equation provided on page 184. The unlabeled curve corresponds to the previously mentioned ASW 17 sailplane, but in reference to an uncambered wing. The glide ratio, represented by the slope of the tangent line at the origin, is 46. The labeled curve corresponds to the simple homemade glider shown in Figure 24, with an aspect ratio (Λ) of 6 and a coefficient of drag (c_{d0}) of 0.035. The theoretical glide ratio of this glider is obtained from the slope of the tangent line, resulting in approximately 12 at an angle of attack (α) of about 9°. However, such values for a flat plate as a wing are purely theoretical. As described in the following chapter, "What Keeps the

Flow Attached?", the flow over a flat plate at such an angle of attack will separate. In practice, achieving glide ratios around 10 are optimal.

c) Polar diagram of the cambered airfoil

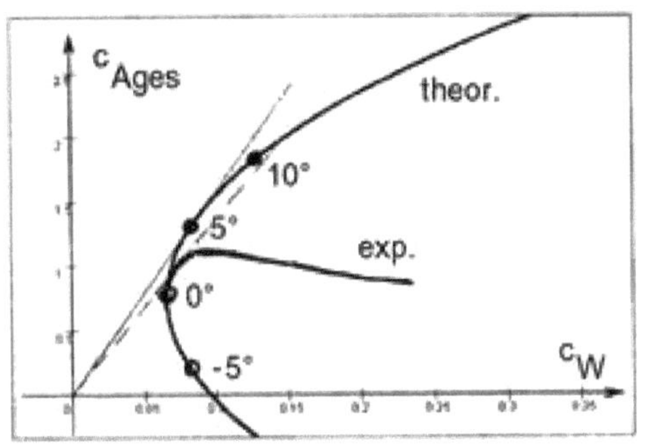

$$\text{"}c_{Ages}\text{": } c_{ltot}$$
$$\text{"}c_W\text{": } c_d$$

Figure 64

In Figure 65, the polar diagram of the cambered airfoil is depicted according to the equation given on page 180, using the approximation $c_{A0} \approx 4\pi(\frac{w}{l})$ and parameters $\Lambda = 6$, $\frac{w}{l} = 6\,\%$, and $c_{d0} = 0.035$. It is immediately apparent that the horizontal parabola from Figure 64, representing the flat plate, has shifted to the right and upwards. This shift is due to the camber of the airfoil.

Just like with the flat plate, the polar diagram of the cambered airfoil above an angle of attack of approximately 4° is purely theoretical. Due to flow separations, higher lift coefficients cannot be achieved. The theoretically possible maximum glide ratio (as the slope of the origin tangent) of about 16 is reduced to approximately 12 as a result. This is still better than the flat plate as a wing. As described in the chapters "The Purpose of Airfoils" and "Quality of Flight" better results can be obtained by both airfoil profiling and surface design of the wing.

What benefits could theoretical polar diagrams have? The literature is abundant with "experimental" polar diagrams for specific airfoil profiles (e.g. from wind tunnel measurements). The term "experimental" is put in quotation marks here because it is not always clear whether theoretical components were used in such diagrams. For the purposes of this book, we limit ourselves to polar diagrams based on the equation for the cambered airfoil provided on Page 180. Two aspects could constitute the usefulness of such theoretical diagrams: (1) The approximate best glide ratio for a given glider can be determined from the slope of the origin tangent to the polar curve, and (2 The dependence of this best glide ratio on parameters such as camber, aspect ratio, and parasitic drag can be studied. It is assumed that the used equation is valid not only for the cambered airfoil but also for cambered wings with moderately thick profiles, as depicted in Figure 29, with sufficient approximation.

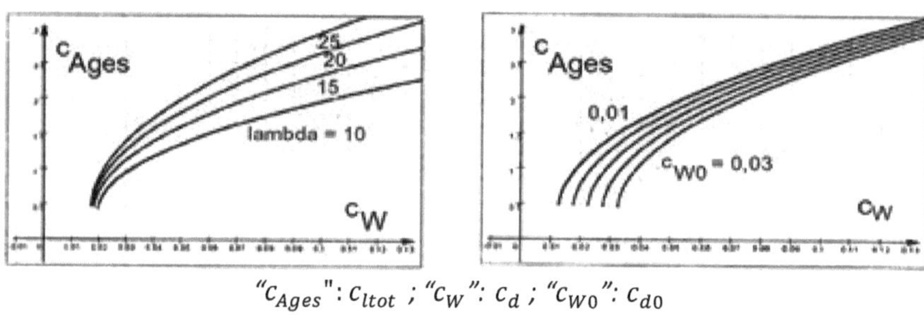

$$\text{"}c_{Ages}\text{"}: c_{ltot} \; ; \; \text{"}c_W\text{"}: c_d \; ; \; \text{"}c_{W0}\text{"}: c_{d0}$$

Figure 65
Figure 66

For the following investigations, the base parameters for a competition glider of the international F3J class are used: aspect ratio $\Lambda = 20$, parasitic drag coefficient $c_{d0} = 0.015$, and wing camber ratio $\frac{w}{l} = 3\,\%$. We hold two of these parameters constant and vary the third one. The dependence on aspect ratio, with constant parasitic drag and consistent camber, is illustrated in Figure 66 (only the upper halves of the transverse parabolas are drawn for clarity). It is clearly noticeable that as the aspect ratio increases, the polar curve shifts higher, indicating a higher maximum glide ratio. This result was to be expected.

When keeping the aspect ratio and camber constant, the magnitude of the parasitic drag determines the position of the curve, as shown in Figure 67. Again, the expected result is observed: The higher the parasitic drag coefficient, the more the curve shifts to the right, resulting in a lower maximum glide ratio.

Finally, the dependence on the camber of the airfoil, while keeping the aspect ratio and parasitic drag constant, is illustrated in Figure 68. The camber varies from 0 to 12 % in increments of 3 %. Here, something unexpected emerges: The transverse parabola (of which only the upper half is drawn) shifts both upwards and to the right with increasing camber. The maximum glide ratio (determined by the slope of the origin tangent) initially increases with increasing camber but then decreases again. The absolute maximum achievable glide ratio (which is a computationally non-trivial determination) for the data of the competition model used here is approximately 5% camber.

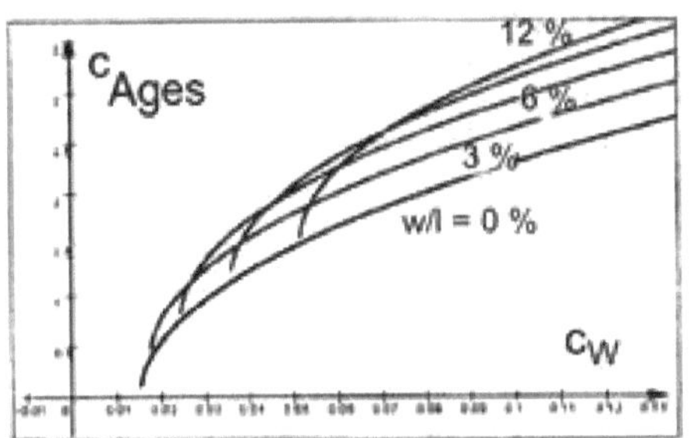

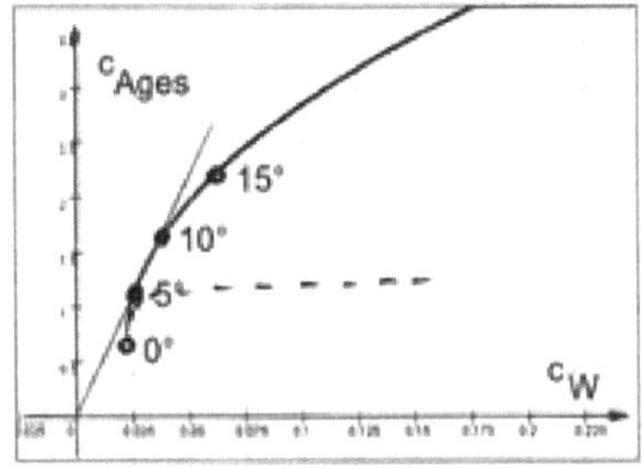

$$\text{“}c_{Ages}\text{”}: c_{ltot} \; ; \; \text{“}c_W\text{”}: c_d$$

Figure 67   Figure 68

We should check if this can also be achieved in practice. Therefore, in Figure 69, the polar diagram for the glider described in Figures 66 to 68, with a camber of 5% (only the upper half of the transverse parabola is shown), is plotted. Additionally, some wing angles of attack are included. Considering that, as described earlier and in the next chapter, flow problems occur above an angle of attack of 5 degrees, it can be assumed that the range of the maximum achievable glide ratio beyond this angle of attack may no longer be reachable. Therefore, there are good reasons to consider airfoils with a camber of 3 to 3.5 % as optimal for high-performance gliders. Both in the construction of high-performance gliders and in the model-building of remote-controlled competition gliders, such wing cambers are predominantly found.

What Keeps the Flow Attached?

By now, there has been so much discussion about flow problems associated with angled and cambered wings that it is high time to take a closer look at what these problems actually entail. Regardless of whether we are dealing with ideal flows characterized by laminar or, above the critical Reynolds number (see the chapter "Where Does Drag Come From?"), turbulent flow in a thin layer above the surface, or whether we are dealing with inherently turbulent flow near rough surfaces, the fundamental question arises:

What causes the necessary "attachment" of the flow over convex surfaces to maintain sufficient lift?

After this question has been clarified:

Can one understand the tendency for flow separation over convex surfaces?

The literature on the first of these two questions remains largely silent! Some who have pondered this question, while considering the observation in Figure 70, believe in some kind of cohesive interactions of the surrounding air that would be responsible for attracting approaching air masses to the flowed-over convex surfaces. These surfaces would then have to provide the necessary impulse current for this purpose, resulting in something like dynamic lift.

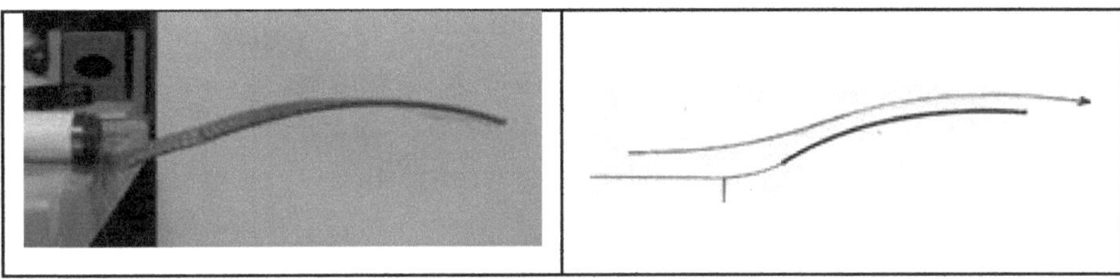

Figure 69

As described in Figure 34, in Figure 70, a jet of air from a fan is directed towards a cambered cardboard plate that is hinged with a tape hinge and has ridges perpendicular to the flow direction. The plate is lifted, experiencing lift. Despite the presence of surface turbulence caused by the ridges, the flow seems to adhere to the curved surface. Now the question is: Does the flow adhere to the curved surface because it is "attracted" by the cambered plate, and therefore, due to the inertia of the redirected air parcels, it has an uplifting effect on the plate?

Such an interpretation of the observation in Figure 70 may sound reasonable, but it assumes that air parcels can be pulled or attracted to one another, implying some form of cohesion between layers of air. However, based on our understanding of the properties of air, this is not the case. If it were, air would not behave as a gas at normal temperatures, and there would be significant cohesive properties among its particles. On the contrary, at room temperature, an air parcel will expand to fill any available volume. This property of air is utilized in the kinetic theory of gases, which, along with the adhesion of air particles to a surface upon collision (as discussed in the chapters "Hydrodynamic Paradox, What is It?" and "Bernoulli Equations"), provides us with the alternative Bernoulli equations. Therefore, an air parcel can be subjected to pressure but not to tension. It needs to be demonstrated that the observation depicted in Figure 70 can be explained by this property of air.

Due to our existence within an enveloping air layer, humans lack a direct sense of air pressure, and this unfamiliarity gives rise to misconceptions about it. In the chapter "Aerodynamic Lift" we have already discussed the astonishing observation that a person can lift an Airbus A380 solely with the power of their lungs. However, a lack of understanding regarding the effects of air pressure becomes evident even in cases where it is believed that there is a vacuum between the panes of insulating glass (because vacuum has the lowest thermal conductivity). If that were the case, there would be two elephants exerting pressure on each square meter of the glass surfaces, and no glass pane of such thinness could withstand that force (the average atmospheric pressure against a vacuum is approximately $10^5 \ N/m^2$ or 10 tons per square meter). Lastly, the phenomenon described in the chapter "Hydrodynamic Paradox, What is It?" remains one of the greatest mysteries surrounding the effects of air pressure.

To understand the effect of a cambered plate on an air flow, let us examine Figure 71. Air parcels flow along both sides of a cambered plate, and an observed transverse force F_Q is present. On the right side of the plate, as depicted in Figure 71, air parcels labeled R flow along the concave side. It is unquestionable that these parcels must follow the camber and contribute to the transverse force due to their inertia. However, the behavior of the air parcels labeled L, which flow along the convex side, is still not fully understood. While it is evident that these parcels also contribute to the observed transverse force due to their inertia (refer to page 186), the mechanism that drives them to move in this manner remains to be clarified. Some scientists refer to a phenomenon known as the "Coandá effect"— named after a Romanian aviation pioneer who, around 1910, inferred from oil and gas traces at the tail of an aircraft that the flow from the propellers adhered to the curves of the aircraft fuselage. However, they usually do not provide a comprehensive explanation for this phenomenon unless one assumes cohesive properties of air (see page 245 for further discussion).

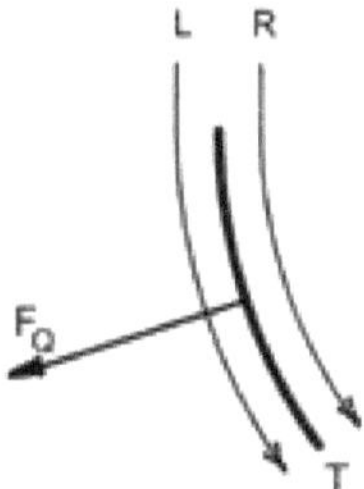

Figure 70

An explanation for the air flow pattern L in Figure 71 can be derived by considering the presence of external air pressure. In the absence (or insufficient presence) of cohesion, the fluid parcels flowing along the convex side of the curved surface cannot follow the curvature due to their inertia. Consequently, a region of reduced air density would form between the straight flow path of L and the separation surface T, creating a "wedge." However, the formation of this region is prevented by the external air pressure acting from all sides. As a result of this air pressure, the fluid parcels flowing past conform to the convex curved surface. The inertia effect still contributes to the transverse force F_Q, and the quantitative value of this contribution is provided on page 186.

Is it all just theoretical? Can the attachment of a flow to a convex curved surface be made visible? In the case of the fluid air, there are difficulties. In the case of the fluid water, it is easier. Water is often chosen as an exemplary fluid in aeronautics and other fields to illustrate certain phenomena, such as vortex formation behind flowing obstacles. However, water, as mentioned in the chapter "Bernoulli Equations", is much less understood in terms of the effects of its particle structure. In particular, noticeable cohesive properties of water particles exist; otherwise, water would not be liquid at room temperature and would not crystallize just a few degrees below. H_2O molecules have a significantly smaller mass than the gas molecules O_2 or N_2 at room temperature, and thus, one would expect them to be in a gaseous state at room temperature. Therefore, observations using water should be approached with caution.

Figure 71

In contrast to air, it is possible to create thin films from water and study their flow behavior. In Figure 72, a well-known observation is depicted: a water film produced from a water jet flows around more than a quarter of a round object, defying gravity and centrifugal force, before detaching and falling in the shape of a parabolic arc. One can doubt whether such an observation can be solely explained by the cohesion of water particles. To explore more extreme conditions, refer to Figure 73. Here, a thin water film is first deflected to the left (concave) by a curved sheet of metal and then sent over an "edge." The result in the left image is expected but can only be achieved with a sufficiently high flow velocity. At a lower flow velocity, the middle image is obtained: the water film follows the bent metal sheet (!), which represents an extremely convex section of the sheet. The perhaps "expected" behavior in the right sub-image occurs only when the edge is "sharpened" with an approximately 1 mm protruding strip of adhesive tape (not visible in the image). An interesting question arises: Can the behavior in the middle image still be explained by cohesion?

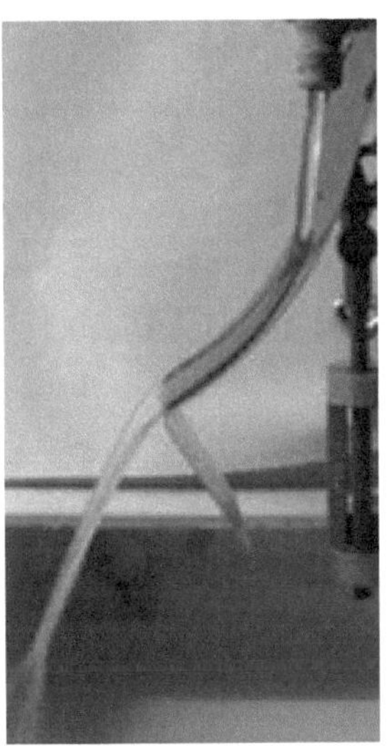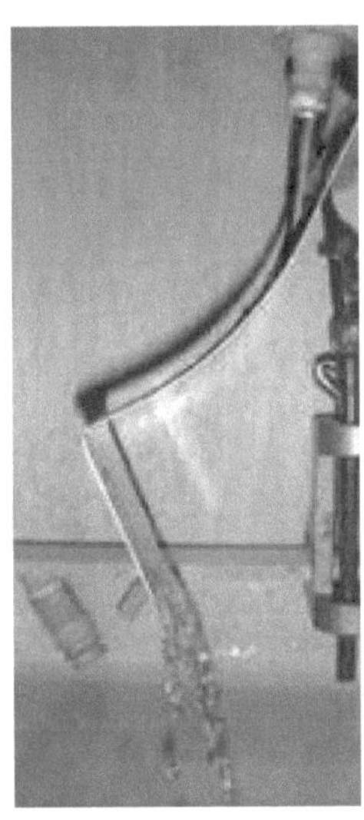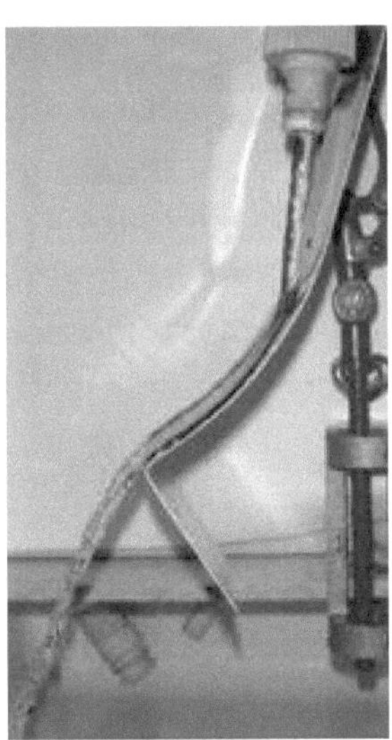

Figure 72

Here, a relatively elementary calculation can be helpful, as described on Page 185. When an object with velocity v and mass m is moved in a circular path with radius r, a centrifugal force is generated, causing the object to accelerate perpendicular to the direction of motion with $\frac{v^2}{r}$. Let us consider this object is a water portion. If this water portion is flowing with a velocity of $v = 1 \ m/s$ in a circular path with radius $r = 10 \ cm = 10^{-1}m$, an acceleration of $\frac{v^2}{r} = 10 \ m/s^2 \approx g$ (acceleration due to gravity) is generated. This means that a centrifugal force is created, equivalent to the weight of the water portion. However, observations of water droplets hanging from a ceiling indicate that the cohesion between water particles is not always sufficient to hold the weight of the droplet.

The conditions depicted in Figure 73 are indeed considerably more extreme. On page 185, the centrifugal force generated by a water portion moving in a very narrow circular path is provided. Since there is no air between the water film and the surface of the metal sheet, and thus no air pressure acting there, a counterforce ΔF is exerted due to the external air pressure, with ΔA representing the wetted area of the deflection region. This results in a critical velocity at which the centrifugal force is equal to the "pressure force." Using practical data such as $r = 5 \cdot 10^{-4}m$, $d = 10^{-3}m$, $p = 10^5 \ N/m^2$, and $\rho = 10^3 \ kg/m^3$, a critical velocity of $v_{critical} \approx 7 \ m/s$ is obtained. Only at this theoretical flow velocity will the water film be able to detach from the surface of the metal sheet in the region of the "edge" due to its inertia. In practice, this critical velocity is lower due to the uneven thickness of the water film and the lack of uniformity in the shape of the "edge." Based on this data, it can be concluded that, even for the water film, the adherence of such a film around the edge is caused by the surrounding air pressure and not by the cohesion between water film particles.

After addressing the first question regarding the mechanism that causes flow adherence over curved surfaces with the prevailing air pressure, some remarks should be made regarding the second question about the causes or tendencies of separation. If one were to understand the separation of a flowing layer of air from a curved surface as a result of its inertia, similar to the separation of a water film, extraordinarily high flow velocities would be required. Let us consider an example: Imagine an air layer with a thickness of $d = 1\ cm = 10^{-2}m$ flowing over a curved surface with a radius of $r = 1\ m$ at a velocity of v. According to the equation $v_{critical} = \sqrt{rp/\rho d}$ provided in Appendix Page 184, with a density $\rho = 1.25\ kg/m^3$, the critical velocity would be approximately $v_{critical} \approx 2830\frac{m}{s} = 10182\ \frac{km}{h}$. Therefore, at the much lower flight velocities of our aircraft or model airplanes, one would not expect a tendency for separations to occur. However, experience shows that separations can indeed occur even at low flight velocities.

As described in the chapter "Where Does Drag Come From?", a fully laminar flow over a (flat or curved) surface is stratified according to flow velocities because, due to the adhesive behavior of air particles near the surface, a boundary layer forms densely above this surface. Initially, it is difficult to imagine how separations could occur in such a stratified laminar flow due to the inertia of air parcels. However, the acceleration of air parcels in the boundary layer leads to an "accumulation" of energy density compared to those air parcels in the free flow far away from the wing – while simultaneously reducing pressure, as discussed in the chapter "Hydrodynamic Paradox, What is It?" (at this point, one can see the need for caution when assuming an equivalence between pressure difference and change in energy density; both are terms that describe a relative state). This increased energy density can be dissipated through the formation of vortices and thus separations, as shown in, for example, Figure 48.

Consequently, initially fully laminar flow stratification is highly susceptible to separations. This is particularly the case with subcritical flow over a smooth surface, as already mentioned in the chapter "Where Does Drag Come From?"

The true flow conditions around wings, however, are different. In the case of supercritical flow, as described in the chapter "Where Does Drag Come From?" there exists a turbulent layer close to the smooth surface, which reduces or ideally even prevents the "accumulation" of energy density. In the case of subcritical flow, this thin turbulent layer can be generated by an uneven surface (sandpaper, Styrofoam, bird feathers, shark skin, etc.). Therefore, the problem of separation formation is reduced to the assessment of flow over curved surfaces with an existing thin turbulent layer – which makes the matter clearer but not easier. It is no coincidence that aeronautics research is particularly intense in this area.

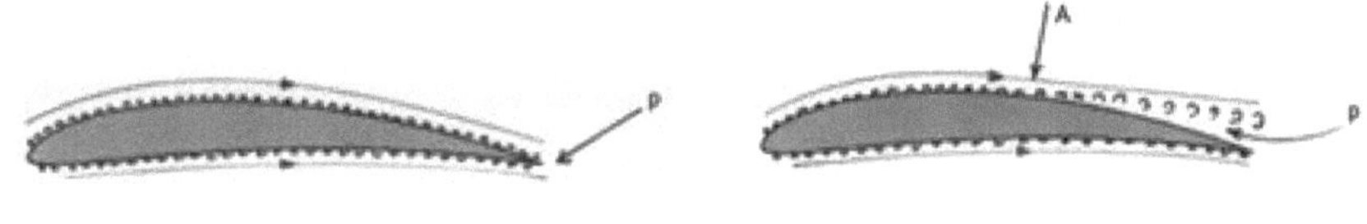

Figure 73

The occurrence of separation in the case of a predominantly laminar flow over a curved surface with a thin turbulent layer can be visualized as follows: In the exaggerated depiction shown in the left image of Figure 74, the flow over an airfoil with a thin turbulent layer is idealized, and the flow remains quasi-laminar throughout. However, there is a weak point where the external air pressure, denoted as p, can act upon this flow pattern, and that weak point is at the trailing edge. As illustrated in Figure 49, a wake is formed at the trailing edge. If the external air pressure succeeds in "penetrating" from behind, as sketched in the right image of Figure 74, the previous low-pressure region at that location becomes equal to the ambient pressure, and the air particles continue to flow straight without being pressed against the downward-facing airfoil. Starting from point A on the upper surface, separation of the flow begins. Such separations reduce lift and increase drag. The location of the "penetration" of the ambient air pressure can be seen in Figure 72.

As the equation $Re = 73{,}500 \cdot l \cdot v_\infty$ in the chapter "Where Does Drag Come From?" illustrates, the Reynolds number can "control" such processes. The flow velocity v_∞ and the length l of the surface being flown over are crucial for the temporal extent of the boundary layer and the risk of "penetration" of external air pressure from the wing's trailing edge. This reveals that faster flying aircraft are less prone to such risks compared to slower ones, assuming comparable wing depths. When the flight velocity is low, the formation of separations must be anticipated. In this context, it is interesting to note a trick used by birds of prey when soaring in thermal currents at low speeds. As soon as a separation, as shown in the right part of Figure 74, threatens to spread, the bird folds up a few of its flexible small covert feathers on the upper surface of its wings, effectively "eliminating" the separation. In aircraft construction, a similar technique has not been replicated; instead, methods such as "suction" are used in the separation-prone area of the wing.

Which wings are prone to separation? Firstly, wings with significant camber, such as those found on commercial aircraft during takeoff and landing, as discussed in the chapter "Parameters of Practical Gliding". Secondly, wings that are heavily pitched against the air flow (e.g., due to elevator input). In both cases, localized separations ("bubbles") can propagate over the entire upper surface of the wing, resulting in a flight condition that pilots particularly fear: the "stall." This condition corresponds to an angle of attack exceeding the critical value, as described in the chapter "Forward Sinking — What is It?", and occurs at glide ratios of approximately 3. If such a situation occurs during takeoff or landing, it causes a sudden loss of lift, potentially leading to a hard touchdown on the runway if the aircraft is still at a low altitude. Alongside this well-known phenomenon of separation occurring at the wing, there exists a much less familiar occurrence that can lead to a decrease in lift, a phenomenon discussed in an article starting on page 226.

Truly Symmetrical?

When observing the shape of birds and conventional aircraft, one becomes convinced that symmetry is a crucial requirement for flight. Instructions for model aircraft construction also emphasize the importance of ensuring that all dimensions, angles, and mass distributions are "correct," and that the construction maintains the best possible symmetry in dimensions, angles, and mass distributions. Such guidance is absolutely correct and essential for beginners to avoid the unfortunate situation where the first flight of a new glider becomes the last due to negligence. Occasionally, there are subtle hints that all aircraft and their models are ultimately built with unavoidable construction inaccuracies that make them asymmetrical. However, the significance of these necessary inaccuracies is rarely contemplated.

Let us assume that a designer manages to achieve the demand for comprehensive symmetry. In rare cases, this may happen, perhaps even by chance. It seems peculiar, however, when the designer realizes that as they approach the perfection of symmetry, the glider's flight characteristics deteriorate. Such a glider flies in a peculiarly "floaty" manner, exhibiting a tendency to oscillate around the pitch and roll axes (see Figure 87). Moreover, in terms of its performance, such as glide ratio and sink rate (see the chapter

"Quality of Flight"), it often performs significantly worse than a glider belonging to a colleague that was not meticulously trimmed for perfect symmetry. The latter glider can be flown with more ease and remains less perturbed by gusts. These observations raise contemplative questions: Could certain deviations from symmetry not only be desirable but even necessary for stable gliding? Or, more radically, is symmetry even important for stable gliding?

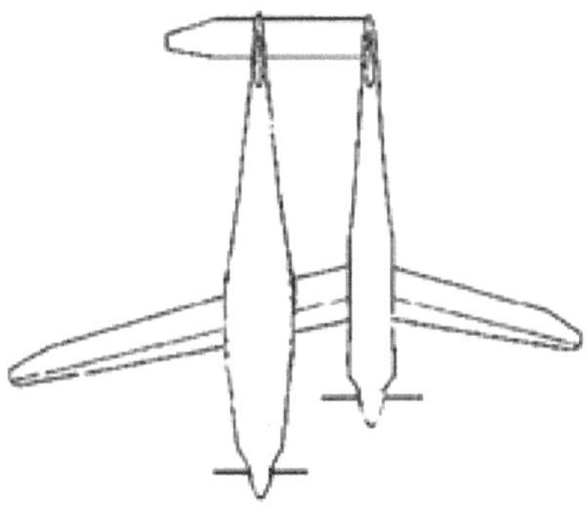

Figure 74

Currently, aircraft or gliders designed with inherent asymmetry remain extremely rare. The most "unconventional" bird the author has heard of is a research glider from NASA, a flying wing with a wing dihedral ranging from 35 to 68 degrees. The only information available about its flight characteristics is that the dihedral significantly reduces drag. Other examples of less radical asymmetrical birds are the World War II reconnaissance aircraft BV 141B (Blohm & Voss) and Burt Rutan's "Boomerang" (see Figure 75). Reports on the flight characteristics of the Boomerang state that it "behaves more stably and gently in the air than machines with 'conventional' design... flies like it is on rails. In all situations, the pilot regains control of the Boomerang immediately. Even with an engine failure, the aircraft continues to fly straight ahead. The airplane consumes less fuel than comparable others." The author has witnessed an incident where one of two remote-controlled model gliders lost about 2/3 of its right wing half due to a collision, yet it remained stable and controllable, successfully returning to the launch point. Such accounts significantly challenge our notion of preserving symmetry as best as possible. Should we then build asymmetrical gliders? Calculating and designing asymmetrical gliders undoubtedly belong to the most demanding endeavors in aircraft construction. However, the prospect of discovering successful asymmetrical glider types through trial and error in model aviation can be enticing. It presents a vast and highly interesting, yet largely unexplored, field of research.

If someone intends to conduct experiments with asymmetrical gliders, the most urgent problem is the mastery of fundamental stabilization. If one happens to discover a "stability island" amidst the ocean of unstable flight conditions, possibly by chance, the high level of stability is astonishing and leads to the core question: Why does such a bird, subject to moderate disturbances, fly with greater static and perhaps even dynamic stability than our conventionally designed gliders optimized for maximum symmetry? A definitive answer to this question is currently impossible, as we are only at the beginning of a development that could bring us many more adventurously designed aircraft in the future. However, at this stage, what we can do is clarify a series of conditions that are also significant for understanding the stabilization of ordinary-looking symmetric gliders. One such condition is why a certain minimum level of asymmetry is not only beneficial but critically necessary for the stabilization of gliders in general. But first, let us clarify what we mean by the term "stability."

"A system is in a statically stable equilibrium when it is situated at a (smooth) minimum of potential energy." This or similar definitions can be found in physics textbooks. Such a broadly applicable definition, which is also applicable in aviation, can be valid for various situations, as depicted in Figures 76 and 77. A ball is situated at the lowest point of a shallow spherical shell or a narrow paraboloid, within the depression on the slope of an ascending potential hill, or in a depression in the summit region. In a preliminary understanding, one would say: The ball is more or less securely positioned there, as long as it is not subjected to strong impacts.

<table>
<tr><td>Figure 75</td><td>Figure 76</td></tr>
</table>

When considering static (and even more so, dynamic) stability, we are dealing with open systems. Such systems seem alien, as the examination of physically closed systems appears more pleasant to us in many respects. This is presumably why stability considerations are often difficult to grasp, and the literature on this topic is challenging to read. Therefore, we will try to simplify it as much as possible. A system is open when there is an energy flow possible from the outside to the inside, or vice versa (which is prevented in a closed system). For a system, there exists an equilibrium state in which the system can be left to itself, as depicted in Figures 76 or 77. If an energy increment ΔE flows into the system, it is referred to as a disturbance, and if this energy increment can flow out again, it is considered the restoration of equilibrium.

Let us first consider the equilibrium situation depicted in Figure 76. Under the influence of a disturbance, the ball will leave its equilibrium position. It is a determining factor whether the minimum of potential energy is flat, as shown in the left part of the image, or narrow and steep, as shown in the right part of the image. In a flat minimum, even slight disturbances, i.e., low energy increments, are sufficient to induce significant amplitudes of oscillations around the equilibrium position. In the case of a narrow and steep minimum, such amplitudes are much smaller. With sufficient friction, the supplied energy increments are quickly dissipated. If energy wells, as sketched in Figure 77, are located in the flank or summit region of a potential mountain, a sufficiently intense disturbance can cause the system to no longer be able to return to its original equilibrium state; the system "tips" into a different equilibrium state. Such occurrences, which are generally considered curiosities, happen more frequently in our gliders than one might expect, as we will see.

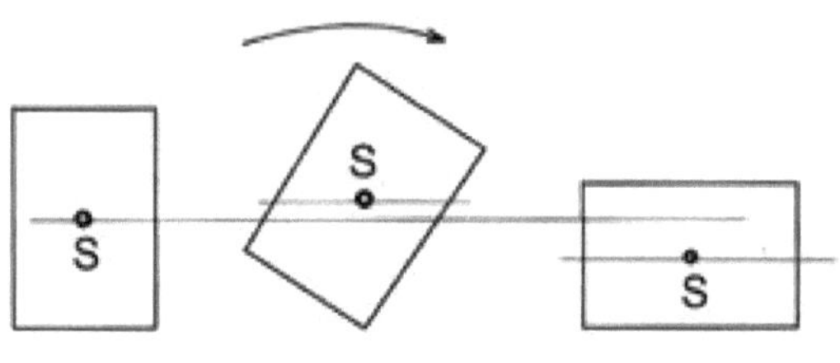

Figure 77

If we are looking for a system that exhibits such behavior in an illustrative way, we can consider a cuboid-shaped game piece, as shown in Figure 78. When placed on its smallest face, it can wobble but eventually return to an upright position if the disturbance is $< \Delta E_{lim}$, where ΔE_{lim} represents the potential energy difference between the resting state and the tipping state of the game piece, as indicated by the height of the center of gravity S in Figure 78. However, if the disturbance exceeds ΔE_{lim}, the piece will irreversibly tip over and assume a new equilibrium position. In this scenario, the game piece was situated on a "stability island," surrounded by a sea of instability with another stability island on the horizon.

We encounter such stability islands more frequently in our seemingly symmetric gliders than we might realize. Let us consider a well-known example. A free-flight glider designed for competitions (with a lifting horizontal tailplane, as discussed in the chapter "Tandem Glider") behaves reasonably well under minor disturbances and returns to its equilibrium position. However, with a more significant disturbance, such as a thermal gust, it suddenly enters a state of nose-down pitching or "undershoot" from which it cannot recover due to the increasing flight velocity and the worsening of this condition. The flight ends with a crash. In this case, the glider was situated on a possibly small stability island. On the other hand, the aforementioned asymmetric flying objects seem to reside on considerably larger stability islands, where even strong disturbances have no lasting impact on their gliding performance.

Is stability "measurable?" The above-mentioned definition of static equilibrium brings to mind mathematics taught in school. Let $E(\varphi)$ be a given function for the potential energy. Where the first derivative is zero (a necessary condition for the presence of a local extremum), the second derivative (or another higher even-order derivative) must be nonzero, positive in the case of a local minimum. Let φ in $E(\varphi)$ be a suitable "coordinate" for the upcoming discussion, and let φ_{min} be the location of the local minimum. Then the reasoning mentioned on page 188 is to be evaluated.

Equilibrium problems are now reduced to two-dimensional cases. In this context, we can use a spatial coordinate ($x, y,$ or z), but it is often more meaningful to use an angular coordinate φ. Let us consider Type I equilibrium, which corresponds to paragliding and can be represented by a swing suspended at point D with a length l, as shown in Figure 79. When disturbed, this swing is displaced from its equilibrium position ($\varphi = 0$) by an angle φ. There is a restoring moment acting around the suspension point D (which corresponds to the center of pressure mentioned in the chapter "How Does Gliding Work?"), caused by the weight F_g acting at the center of gravity S. The connection l (which can be considered nearly massless, similar to a paraglider) is assumed to be massless.

Now let us consider the disturbance that sets the swing in motion. To lift the swing by a distance Δl, work must be done, resulting in an increase in the potential energy $E(\varphi)$ of the system. For small angles of displacement φ, the graph of $E(\varphi)$ is shown in Figure 80. The significance of the grey-coded areas will be discussed in detail later. Applying the reasoning mentioned on page 188, we obtain a stability condition of the form $F_g l > 0$, where l represents a measure of stability. In the case of paragliding, this measure is extremely large.

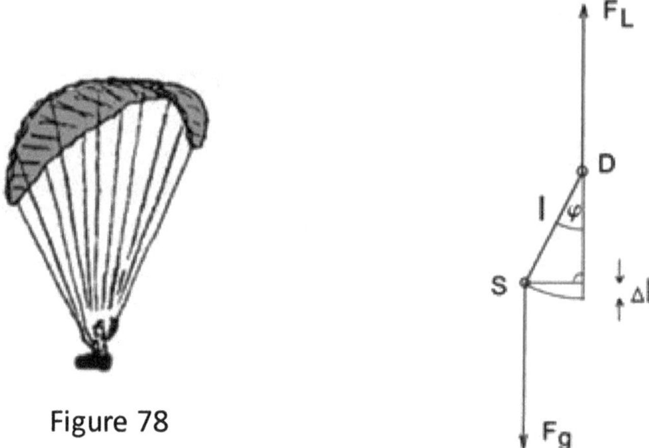

Figure 78

In addition to the Type I equilibrium illustrated in Figure 79, another important Type II equilibrium is relevant in the context of flying. It involves the wind vane effect of a surface exposed to a flow, as depicted in Figure 81. The cross-section of a flat plate (which can be, for example, a horizontal or vertical stabilizer) is shown, capable of exposed to a flow with velocity v. The restoring force F_H, as long as the flow is not separated, has an approximate magnitude given on page 188, resulting in a restoring moment. For an angle of displacement $\varphi > 0$, the point of attack of the aerodynamic force F_H shifts by approximately $a\,sin\varphi$ for small angles φ, which means work must be done, approximately given by $W \approx \frac{1}{2}F_H(0)a\,sin^2\varphi$ (the factor of $\frac{1}{2}$ arises from the force being practically proportional to the displacement for small angles). This leads to an increase in potential energy $E(\varphi)$ for a wind vane. Once again, we apply the reasoning mentioned above, resulting in the same conclusion as in Figure 79, as the terms $1 - cos\varphi$ and $\frac{1}{2}sin^2\varphi$ practically do not differ for small angles φ. Figure 80 is equally applicable to the case depicted in Figure 81.

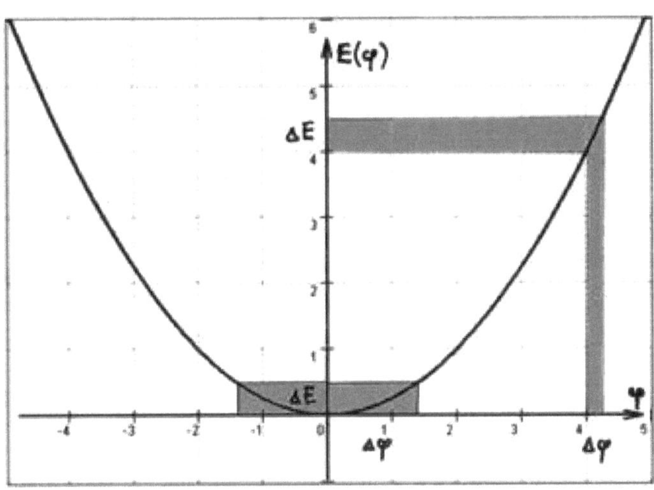

Figure 79

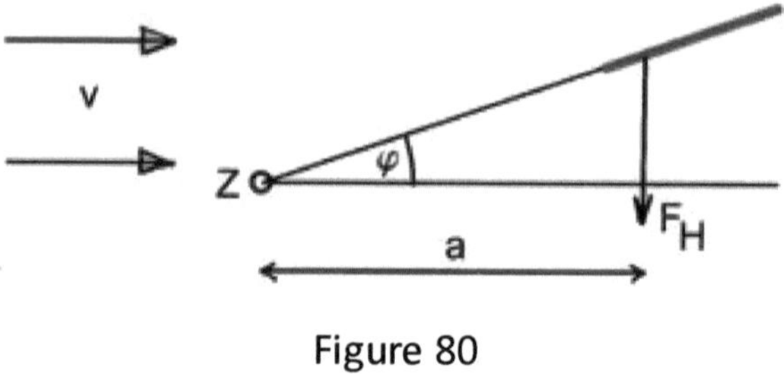

Figure 80

Before delving into the effects of disturbances in flight, a few remarks should be made regarding dynamic stabilization. From the swing in Figure 79, we know that it can oscillate. Oscillation is a dynamic process, and just like in the static case, there is a definition of stability: a statically stable system is also dynamically stable if it returns to the equilibrium position after a disturbance. It can be observed that there are different manifestations of dynamic stabilization: (1) The equilibrium position is reached after many oscillations with slowly decreasing amplitudes, and the oscillation is weakly damped (example: a steel ball suspended on a string in the air); (2) The equilibrium position is reached after a few oscillations with rapidly decreasing amplitudes, and the oscillation is strongly damped (example: a steel ball in water); (3) Oscillation does not occur at all, and the motion proceeds slowly with extreme damping (example: a steel ball in honey). While the onset of oscillation is related to the influx of a portion of energy (disturbance), the different manifestations of damping are determined by the rate of energy dissipation.

In the case of flying, the dissipation of energy after a disturbance occurs through drag. And thus, we find ourselves amidst a conflict in the practice of flying. Good gliding means minimizing drag as much as possible. On the other hand, effective dynamic stabilization requires sufficiently high drag. Aviation, therefore, involves an optimization problem. A super glider with very low drag offers limited opportunities for energy dissipation, causing the glider to react to disturbances with multiple oscillations. These oscillations not only disturb the pilot but also lead to reduced performance. In contrast, a "tangle of wires" (referring to reproductions or models of early human-piloted gliders like Lilienthal glider) due to its high drag provides sufficient energy dissipation and exhibits stable dynamic behavior. However, it quickly loses altitude due to the high drag. The trend in aeronautics, as well as in performance models, is more towards damping the oscillations of controlled super gliders through appropriate rudder deflections. This requires the skills of the pilot unless automated systems (such as a "Phygoid" control) are employed.

The characteristic of a dynamically unstable system is that the oscillation initiated after a disturbance does not cease around the equilibrium position. The oscillation amplitude either remains constant (undamped oscillation) or even increases (resonance catastrophe). Since unavoidable friction processes always lead to a decrease in oscillation amplitudes, an undamped oscillation can only occur when energy is periodically supplied in the "correct" phase. A dynamically unstable system, therefore, requires an external energy reservoir that can be tapped periodically. If we look for such a combination of a system capable of oscillation and an energy reservoir among our gliders, we will find it in the case of longitudinal instability caused by a specific disturbance. In some uncontrolled gliders, one can observe how they enter a weak, then increasingly strong wave-like flight motion after a disturbance, which eventually leads to the dreaded "pumping" motion. The energy reservoir from which it draws is the potential energy of the glider, causing it to lose altitude faster and, in most cases, result in a crash. The fatal aspect of this process is that the improperly adjusted glider itself controls this periodic energy supply optimally. While dynamic stabilization is important and interesting, we should limit our discussion to these few remarks and return to problems of static stability.

As mentioned earlier, a disturbance was described as a short-term supply of an energy portion ΔE, which, without considering friction, leads to a maximum displacement $\Delta\varphi$, as shown in Figure 80. In the case of a constant disturbance, assuming a constant ΔE, this maximum displacement and its impact on the system are greatest when the system was initially in equilibrium at $\varphi = 0$. As Figure 80 illustrates, this maximum displacement decreases as the system deviates further from the equilibrium state, i.e., when it is in a state with $\varphi > 0$. The previously referred to as a weak equilibrium state is strengthened by such either randomly existing or intentionally induced manipulation, as disturbances have less severe effects, resulting in smaller fluctuations $\Delta\varphi$. We will see that such "manipulated" equilibria are common in our gliders, which is why these gliders tend to be quite stable in flight.

One can attempt to illustrate the strengthening of a weak equilibrium through a mathematical analysis, as shown on page 189. In connection with Figure 79 and page 188, we have found that an energy amount of $E(\varphi)$ is required for an angular displacement of φ. For a further displacement beyond φ by an angle $\Delta\varphi$, a correspondingly higher energy of $E(\varphi + \Delta\varphi)$ is needed. Assuming a constant disturbance ΔE, a relationship is established between the disturbance angle $\Delta\varphi$ and a predetermined displacement angle φ. For small angles φ, a graph illustrating this relationship is shown in Figure 82; the numbers 0.01 to 0.05 refer to the constant parameter $\Delta E/F_g l$.

One can observe a strengthening of the equilibrium as the angle φ increases: the amplitudes $\Delta\varphi$ decrease. A note on the execution of the calculations: the approximation $cos\varphi \approx 1$ should not be used since it is precisely applicable to the range of small angles. For the other equilibrium type II based on the wind vane effect, as shown in Figure 81, a result similar to Figure 82 is obtained, as described on page 188, because the relationship present there, given by $1 - cos\varphi \approx \frac{1}{2}sin^2\varphi$ for small angles φ, corresponds to the one mentioned above for Figure 79.

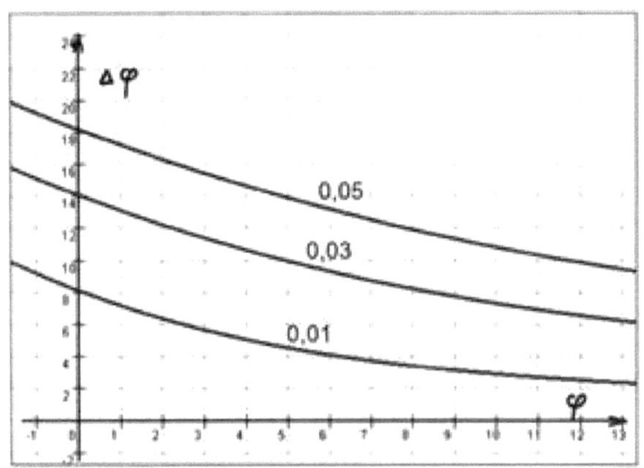

Figure 81

In addition to the weak equilibria described above, a concept of *strong equilibrium* plays a particularly important role in flying. This equilibrium is not easy to grasp, as it is based on the moment situation depicted in Figure 21. If one may say so, the pitching moment generated by the separation of the points D and S where the aerodynamic force and weight act is an example of an extreme "manipulation" of a weak equilibrium. How can this be understood?

As described in the chapter "Circulation: Just a Mathematical Trick?" the equilibrium state depicted in Figure 21 is primarily generated by the circulation flow. This equilibrium state is represented by the angle $\varphi = 0$ in Figure 83. A disturbance of this equilibrium state results in an angle $\varphi \neq 0$. In the following, we assume that immediately after the occurrence of a disturbance, the flight parameters such as velocity and lift have not yet changed (although these parameters do change moments later, which complicates the treatment of the problem considerably). The quantities mentioned below, along with their corresponding equations, are noted on page 190.

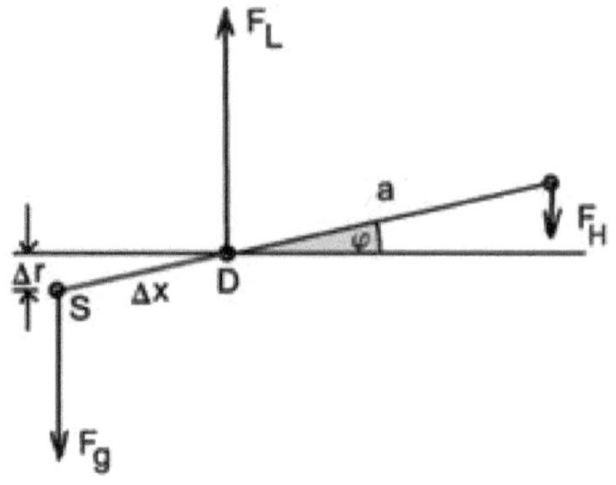

Figure 82

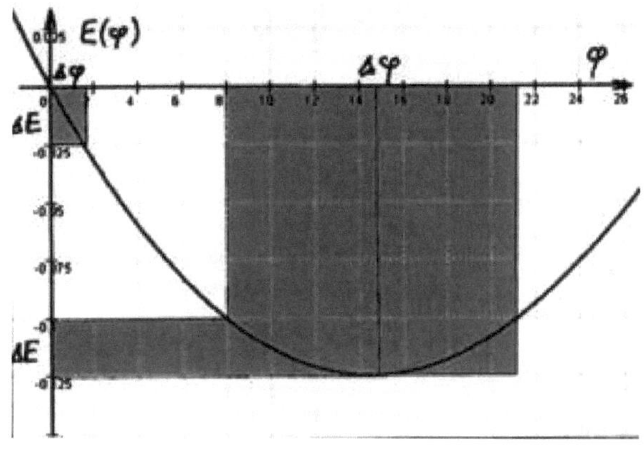

Figure 83

After the disturbance, a restoring moment, caused by a force F_H acting at a lever arm a, will restore the equilibrium state, as shown in Figure 83. This force can be understood as the wind vane effect of the horizontal tailplane. When lowering the (center of) gravity point S by a distance Δr, an energy increment $\epsilon(\varphi)$ is released. At the same time, in order to deflect (the longitudinal axis of the aircraft) by the angle φ as described above, work $W(\varphi)$ needs to be done. Therefore, the increase in potential energy amounts to $E(\varphi) = W(\varphi) - \epsilon(\varphi)$. A non-calibrated graph of this progression for small angles φ is sketched in Figure 84. It demonstrates how a strong equilibrium for $\varphi = 0$ (small fluctuation $\Delta\varphi$ for a disturbance ΔE) weakens as φ increases (large fluctuation $\Delta\varphi$ for the same disturbance ΔE).

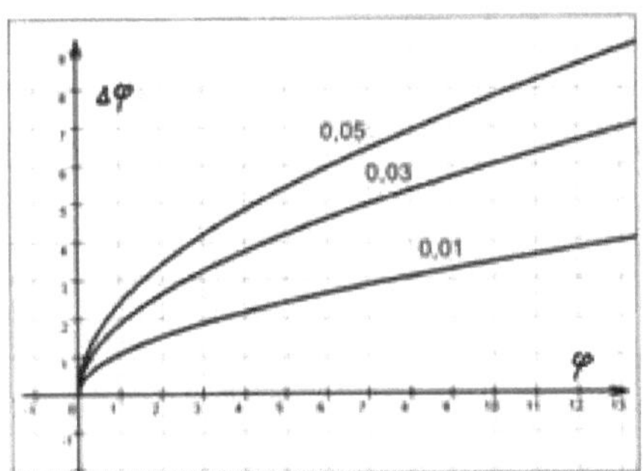

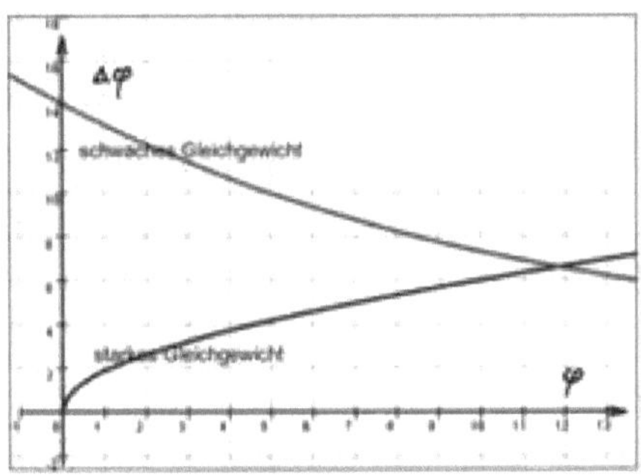

"Schwaches Gleichgewicht:" Weak Equilibrium
"Starkes Gleichgewicht:" Strong Equilibrium

Figure 84   Figure 85

Let us retrace the aforementioned line of reasoning, as outlined on page 190, yielding the result for the local minimum, replacing the unknown moment $F_H(0)a$ with $(F_g\Delta x)/sin\varphi_{min}$. It can be observed that for a small angle φ_{min}, despite the small stability measure Δx, this expression becomes quite large, which is indeed an expression of this strong equilibrium. As before, let us consider the impact of a disturbance in this case. The inconvenient equation is significantly simplified by the approximation $sin\varphi_{min} \approx sin\varphi$. Figure 85 illustrates the relationship $\Delta\varphi(\varphi)$ for this case of a strong equilibrium. The numbers 0.01 to 0.05 again refer to the constant parameter

$\Delta E/(F_g\Delta x)$. In contrast to Figure 82, while the equilibrium weakens with increasing angle φ, it does so from a considerably higher level (to recall: strong equilibrium entails small fluctuations $\Delta\varphi$ for disturbances, whereas weak equilibrium involves larger fluctuations for the same disturbances). This can be demonstrated by a direct comparison, as shown in Figure 86. The curves $\Delta\varphi(\varphi)$ for the same parameter value $\Delta E/(F_g\Delta x) = 0.03$ are plotted there. Noticeable differences in the strength of the equilibria can be observed for small angles φ. Only at an angle φ of approximately 12° do they become equally strong or equally weak.

After grappling with equilibria for quite some time, we need to address the question of how it relates to our gliders. To do so, we must define a basic or equilibrium state for our glider during flight, as well as the main types of disturbances. The normal flight attitude of a glider in space can be described as follows: the longitudinal axis points in the x-direction, the lateral axis in the y-direction, and the vertical axis in the z-direction. The longitudinal axis runs parallel to the symmetry line of the fuselage, the lateral axis parallel to the quarter-chord line of the (reference) wing projected onto the plane (see the chapter "What Are the Consequences of the Wing's Camber?"), and the vertical axis perpendicular to the other two axes. Any angles will be referenced to these axes. Let us agree that the axes intersect at the glider's center of gravity. This means that the axes are glider-related and essentially move with it. However, as we will see shortly, the flight direction does not necessarily align with the direction of the x-axis (!). By referencing the spatial coordinate system to the center of gravity, we avoid considering the torques caused by the applied weight from the outset. Instead, moments caused by the applied aerodynamic forces become decisive. Therefore, the center of rotation is the center of gravity, S. However, occasionally it may also be useful (and easier to calculate) to choose a different center of rotation, such as the center of pressure.

Disturbances in the flight attitude of a glider typically involve rotations around all three spatial axes simultaneously, or in other words, rotations around some axis with changing orientation. It is easy to lose track in such situations! Let us recall the limited degrees of freedom that a glider has in the wind tunnel (see, for example, the chapter "Forward Sinking — What is It?"). A more practical approach is to categorize the disturbances into those that involve rotations around each of the three spatial axes individually, as shown in Figure 87.

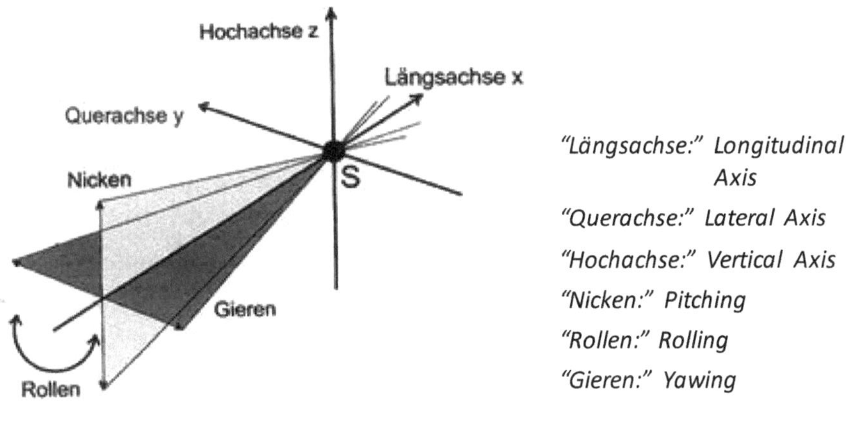

"Längsachse:" Longitudinal Axis

"Querachse:" Lateral Axis

"Hochachse:" Vertical Axis

"Nicken:" Pitching

"Rollen:" Rolling

"Gieren:" Yawing

Figure 86

And these are:

a) Pitching movements of the longitudinal axis ("pitching") through rotation around the lateral axis

b) Yawing movements of the longitudinal axis ("yawing," "turning") through rotation around the vertical axis

c) Rolling movements of the lateral axis ("rolling") through rotation around the longitudinal axis

Note: The terms "yawing" and "rolling" are historically derived from seafaring terminology. The term equivalent to "pitching" called "heaving" is not used in aeronautics.

When considering the moments acting on a freely flying glider, a distinction must be made between uncontrolled and controlled gliders. In the case of an uncontrolled glider, which inherently flies in a stable manner and is subject to atmospheric disturbances, there are no arbitrary control moments available. Only two forces and the resulting restoring moments can be utilized: the weight of the glider acting at the center of gravity and the aerodynamic force acting at the center of pressure. In such a case, the challenge lies in understanding how to suppress continuous pitching, yawing, and rolling motions.

In the case of a controlled glider, additional arbitrary control moments are introduced through movable control surfaces. These control moments may either compete with the restoring moments of the stabilized glider or, in their absence, enable the compensation of disturbances. As a further basis, let us now examine the conditions of an uncontrolled glider, which inherently flies in a stable manner.

The paraglider, as seen in Figure 79, and also the Forward Sinker discussed in the chapter "Forward Sinking — What is It?" (see Figures 15 and 16), are in a statically stable flight attitude when the center of pressure is located above the center of gravity. This is achieved primarily through the V-shape of the wing, as seen in Figure 88 from a front or rear view, with an exaggerated V-shape for clarity. The equilibrium established in this manner is a weak equilibrium, where Δz represents a measure of stability. In the case of a glider, Δz is small, but for a paraglider, it is extremely large due to the fact that the "wing" has a negative V-shape, as shown in Figure 79, instead of a positive V-shape as in Figure 88.

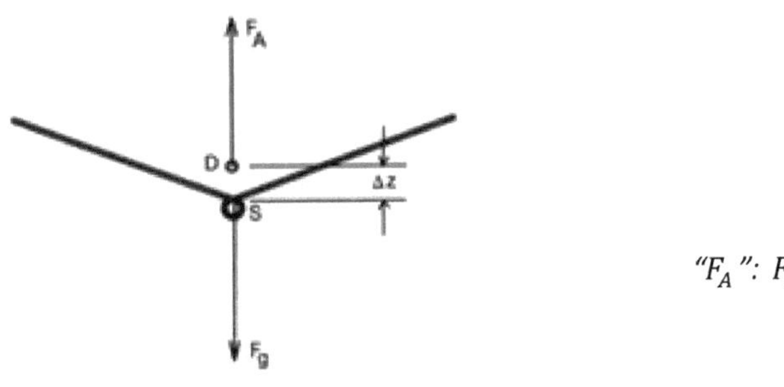

Figure 87

This simple method of stabilization suppresses rolling tendencies, i.e., rotations around the longitudinal axis. The degree of suppression of a rolling disturbance increases with a greater V-shape chosen for the glider's wing. However, a drawback is apparent: an increase in the V-shape reduces the effective surface area (projected onto the plane) required to generate lift. This simple form of stabilization immediately leads to an optimization process with conflicting sub-processes. Therefore, it is advisable to rely on empirical values. For uncontrolled gliders, an (effective) V-shape of approximately 8° per side (as the angle between half of the wing and the horizontal) is recommended, while for controlled gliders, such as those used by recreational pilots, about 3° per side is sufficient. Only in the case of aerobatic gliders will a minimal V-shape be chosen, which requires the pilot to make numerous control corrections (aileron inputs) due to constant disturbances.

Flying wing gliders, as seen in Figures 22 and 23, do not require vertical stabilizers, unlike conventional aircraft. On the other hand, commercial aircraft have relatively large vertical and horizontal stabilizers. The reason for this difference lies in the long fuselages, particularly ahead of the wing or center of gravity. This phenomenon is related to the concept of the quarter-chord line of a surface in the air flow, as discussed in relation to Figure 13. The quarter-chord line represents a torque-neutral position of the surface in the flow. Determining the quarter-chord line is relatively straightforward for rectangular surfaces but becomes more challenging for highly segmented surfaces. The silhouette of a glider viewed from the side is an example of such a complex surface, as shown in Figure 89 (determining the quarter-chord line for certain surface contours to calculate the surface moments may require the use of integral calculus).

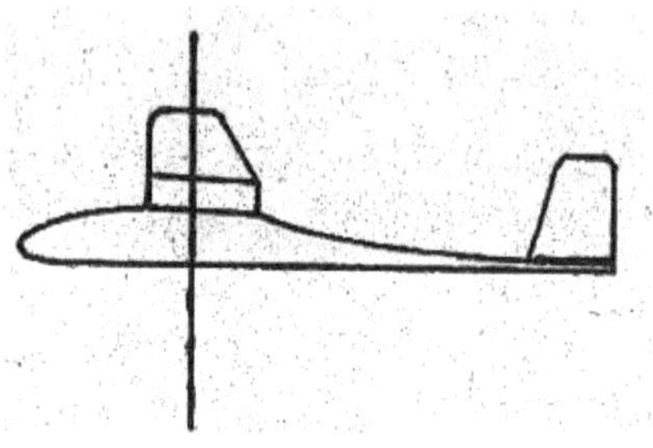

Figure 88

For a wing section to remain stable like a weathervane in the air flow, it must be positioned just ahead of the quarter-chord line (see the chapter "Forward Sinking — What is It?"). If the glider shown in Figure 89 had no or a too small vertical stabilizer, this condition would not be fulfilled. As a result, the glider would constantly tend to align itself more or less perpendicular to the air flow, rotating around the vertical axis. This behavior naturally hinders gliding and generates additional drag. The stabilizing effect of a vertical stabilizer relies on a weak equilibrium, as depicted in Figure 81. Disturbances that cause yawing, i.e., rotation around the vertical axis, are corrected by the action of the vertical stabilizer, allowing the glider to become "directionally stable." Both here and earlier in discussing roll stabilization, efforts are made to strengthen these two weak equilibria. Otherwise, even the slightest disturbances would result in noticeable oscillations around the longitudinal and vertical axes.

The third equilibrium in a glider pertains to pitching, which has been described as a strong equilibrium in connection with Figures 84 to 86. When the center of gravity and center of pressure are separated by a distance Δx in the direction of flight, a stabilizing mechanism is provided by the horizontal tailplane in the event of a disturbance in longitudinal stability, such as a pitching disturbance or rotation around the lateral axis. The strength of this equilibrium is a crucial factor in achieving longitudinal stability in gliding flight. Even in the presence of significant disturbances, only minor changes in the pitch angle of the longitudinal axis should occur. Unlike the two other weak equilibria for rolling and yawing, the pitching equilibrium still incorporates an additional effect, which is the generation of lift. If the pitching equilibrium were as weak as the other two equilibria, disturbances would result in not only oscillations around the lateral axis but also a wave-like flight pattern caused by varying lift forces depending on the angle of attack against the air flow. Similar to the generation of lift, the importance of a sufficiently large stability measure Δx, as shown in Figure 83, should be emphasized in this context.

Based on the assessment of the three equilibria that must exist around the three principal axes of a self-stable aircraft, we can now address the question raised earlier: How can we achieve stabilization of the glider solely through the action of two forces, namely weight and aerodynamic force, without using control surfaces? The answer is now apparent, but it requires us to depart from the notion of symmetry evoked by the external appearance of conventional aircraft. If we remove everything that appears symmetric externally in the glider and look inside, we encounter the symmetry break depicted in Figure 90. The weight acts at the center of gravity, denoted as S. The three axes of the aircraft, as shown in Figure 87, pass through S in the $x, y,$ and z directions. The center of pressure, where the aerodynamic force acts, is now shifted by a distance Δx in the backward direction along the longitudinal axis, by a distance Δy offset from the longitudinal axis in the y-direction, and by a distance Δz above the longitudinal axis in the z-direction.

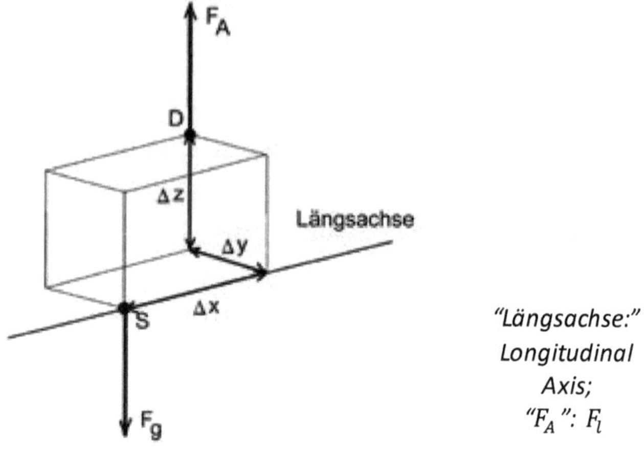

Figure 89

The Δx displacement leads to a strong equilibrium and can be intentionally achieved by correctly determining the position of the center of gravity. The Δz displacement is achieved by choosing the (effective) V-shape of the wing. The Δy displacement contributes to strengthening the weak equilibrium for rolling, and together with the Δz displacement, it strengthens the weak equilibrium for yawing. The Δy displacement is usually not intentionally introduced in the construction of symmetric-looking gliders but arises from inevitable construction inaccuracies. If one were to build strictly symmetrically and eliminate Δy, gliding performance would be compromised because even the slightest disturbances would have significant effects on yawing.

This glimpse into our normally symmetrically designed and perceived gliders shows how asymmetrical they are in terms of their moment distributions. It is the asymmetry depicted in Figure 90 that enables smooth and self-stable gliding. Our gliders do not fly exactly aligned with their longitudinal axis. They exhibit a slight pitching motion, a slight tilt, and a slight sideslip, meaning the direction of the longitudinal axis does not align perfectly with the flight direction. This can also be described as the wings and stabilizers being slightly "loaded" during gliding. This fact is significant not only for self-stable gliders but also for controlled gliders. Even in straight and level flight, uncommanded control surfaces should be slightly loaded. If they were not, the pilot would notice a delayed and initially sluggish response from the control surfaces. Only control surfaces that are preloaded enable direct and immediate response. Regarding the direction assumed by the glider during flight, we should not adhere to the notion that it can be determined by connecting points S and D in Figure 90. The situation depicted in this Figure represents the pre-flight condition. During flight, all the moments superimpose and result in a mixed state, which is better left to the expertise of specialists for evaluation.

At the end of this chapter, we need to address the question of whether the angles that arise when evaluating the disturbances of equilibrium actually reach the magnitudes assumed in Figures 83 and 86. For this purpose, let us first estimate the extent of a disturbance.

Let us assume that we are flying with the ASW 17 high-performance glider into a downdraft zone with a vertical velocity change of $\Delta v_z = 1\ m/s$ (larger vertical velocity changes do occur, but compared to the sink rate of about $0.5\ m/s$, this disturbance is already considerable). The volume of air acting on the wing during the passage through this disturbance is approximately $8\ m^3$ (wing area times thickness).

The energy transferred to the wing due to this disturbance is then on the order of $\Delta E = \frac{1}{2}\rho V \Delta v_z^2 \approx 5.5\ J$. The weight of the occupied glider is about $4900\ N$, and the stability measure Δx for optimal gliding is approximately $0{,}035\ m$ (relative to the average wing depth of $0{,}74\ m$, this is almost 5 %), thus $F_g \Delta x \approx 171.5\ J$ or $\Delta E/(F_g \Delta x) \approx$ 0.032. This puts us in the vicinity of the curve with a parameter value of 0.03 in Figure 85. Assuming a "built-in" angle $\varphi = 1°$, the effect of the disturbance would be approximately $\Delta\varphi = 2°$ by which the longitudinal axis tilts downward due to the disturbance. This is quite small. The effects are significantly stronger for the weak equilibria. If we calculate the same $\Delta E/(F_g \Delta x) \approx 0.032$ for rolling or yawing, we obtain with Figure 82, assuming the same "built-in" angle $\varphi = 1°$, a $\Delta\varphi \approx 14°$. If the aircraft is not flying vertically but forward into the aforementioned downdraft area, this disturbance will result in a roll of approximately 14° (indicating to the pilot that they are encountering a downdraft area; in the case of encountering an updraft area, the opposite rolling motion occurs, indicating the entry into an updraft area where circling can be performed). However, we have not considered the damping effect of the aircraft's inertial moments when considering the effects of a disturbance (magnitudes of angles). They will ensure that the effects are initially weaker. Taking this into account, it becomes apparent that flight mechanics expands into a mechanically and mathematically complex field, and we should be satisfied with approximate considerations of the kind presented above.

Tandem Glider

Among the stabilizing surfaces, the horizontal stabilizer (also known as the elevator or tailplane) plays a crucial role in providing direct control of the aircraft's movement for the pilot during straight and level flight. As described in the previous chapter, loading the horizontal stabilizer creates an adjustment that results in a slight downward force in the neutral flight position (achieved using an adjustable or setting angle, as discussed in the following chapter). To fulfill this purpose alone, the horizontal stabilizer is given a symmetrical cross-section profile (such as a flat plate or a thin symmetrical airfoil, as explained in the chapter "How to Adjust a Glider"; previously, attempts were made with a negatively cambered horizontal stabilizer (tailplane) at a near 0° setting angle, but with limited success). Surprisingly, a relatively small horizontal stabilizer with a relatively short lever arm is sufficient for longitudinal stabilization, as depicted in the top view of the high-performance glider ETA in Figure 91. The surface area of the horizontal stabilizer is only about 7% of the wing area. However, the horizontal stabilizer should not be much smaller than this, as it would conflict with the weathervane effect discussed in the previous chapter, which applies to the horizontal stabilizer as well. This effect can be particularly dangerous due to its influence on lift. However, modern commercial aircraft, with their elongated fuselages extending well ahead of the wings, typically feature large vertical and horizontal stabilizers, with the horizontal stabilizer comprising around 25% of the wing surface area.

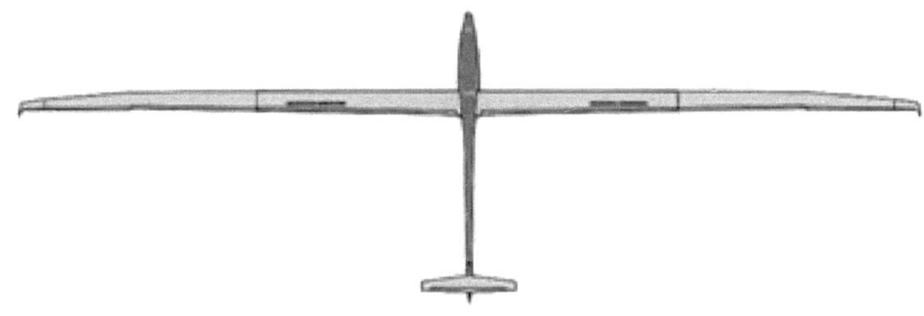

Figure 90

One could be content with the aforementioned significance and design of the horizontal stabilizer, as higher performance has not been achieved through alternative horizontal stabilizer configurations. However, due to practical considerations (including military applications) and a spirit of experimentation, this chapter will cover the topic of tandem gliders, which feature two supporting wings of different or similar sizes. The fundamental arrangements are depicted in Figure 92 using three typical examples. Conventional gliders have a "supporting" horizontal stabilizer, which is airfoil-shaped similar to the main wing. The glider has two wings of approximately equal size. The glider appears to be flying backwards, with the "horizontal stabilizer" at the front (known as canard aircraft – many military aircraft types use this configuration).

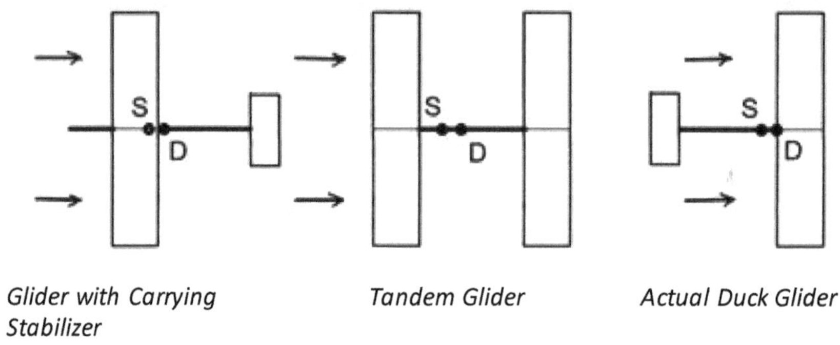

Glider with Carrying Stabilizer | *Tandem Glider* | *Actual Duck Glider*

Figure 91

All three types of gliders with two supporting wings of different sizes are now grouped together as tandem gliders because they share common characteristics in terms of airfoil and wing settings in order to make them flyable. Both the front wing and the rear wing are designed with a camber or airfoil shape that contributes to lift. It is important to note that the effective lift coefficient of the front wing is chosen to be greater than that of the rear wing. In the opposite case, the glider could enter a state of nose-down pitching after a disturbance. This is crucial for uncontrolled tandem gliders and requires intervention from the pilot in the case of controlled gliders. In practice, it is appropriate to use the same camber and airfoil shape for both the front and rear wings, with a negative angle of attack for the rear wing relative to the front wing (approximately 1.5 to 2 degrees). This configuration also achieves the necessary longitudinal stability with a supporting rear wing.

When comparing the top view of an uncontrolled high-performance model glider in the F1A competition class, as shown in Figure 93, with that of the high-performance sailplane ETA in Figure 91, the most significant difference is the significantly larger vertical stabilizer, mounted on a longer lever arm, and the extremely short nose of the fuselage. Such models are optimized for long gliding times and minimal sink rate (see the chapter "Quality of Flight"). Therefore, they are built to be as lightweight as possible (although a lower limit is set by a wing loading of $12 \; N/m^2$) and feature a vertical stabilizer with a similar airfoil shape as the main wing. In principle, this corresponds to a tandem glider as depicted in Figure 92, with two supporting wings of different sizes.

For the configuration of a tandem glider, it is important to note that both the center of pressure D and the center of gravity S are located at different positions compared to a conventional glider. Failing to consider this would prevent such gliders from flying (see Figure 8 and the notes in the chapters "How Does Sinking Work?" and "How Does Gliding Work?"). Let us continue with the competition glider depicted in Figure 93. The changes in the center of pressure and center of gravity positions are illustrated in Figure 94. The center of pressure D is determined by the centers $D1$ of the forward wing and $D2$ of the rear wing, while the center of gravity S is located in front of the center of pressure D (as per the stability measure Δx). According to the chapter "What Are the Consequences of the Wing's Camber?" the center of pressure D of the highly cambered forward and rear wings are located at approximately $35 - 40 \, \%$ of their respective airfoil depths. To determine the position of the center of pressure D, the lift

x_{D1} and x_{D2}, must be carefully matched. The specific alignment can be observed in Figure 94, as detailed on page 191.

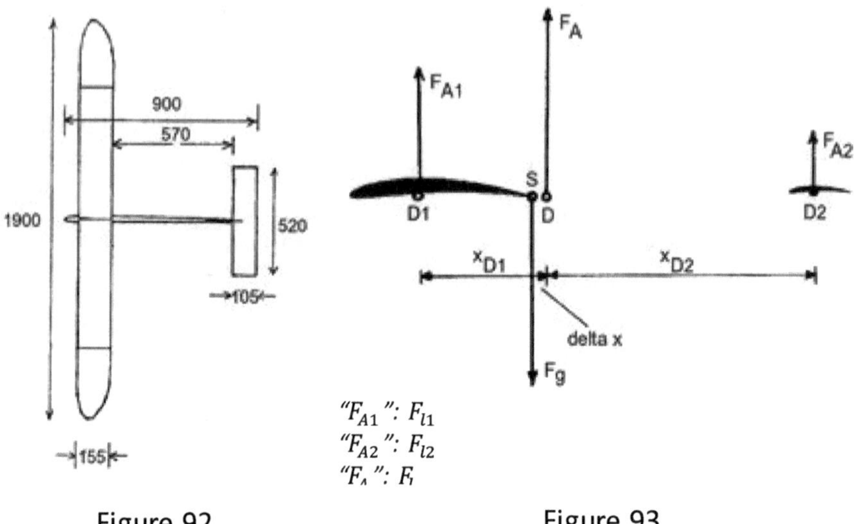

Figure 92   Figure 93

The forward wing generates lift with a lift coefficient c_{l1}, while the rear wing generates lift with a slightly smaller lift coefficient c_{l2} due to its slightly negative angle of attack relative to the forward wing. The forward wing produces a lift force F_{l1}, and the rear wing produces a lift force F_{l2}. There is a moment equilibrium with respect to the center of pressure D, which leads to two equations for determining the center of pressure position, based on specific wing area ratios and lift coefficient ratios. The numerical values provided on page 191 are applicable to the competition glider depicted in Figure 93, with an approximate distance of $L \approx 700\ mm$ between the center of pressure locations of the two wings. The lift coefficient ratio can be obtained from Figure 39, given the known difference in angle of attack between the two wings (e.g., 2 degrees). It yields $x_{D1} \approx 95\ mm$, placing the center of pressure D in close proximity to the trailing edge of the forward wing. The center of gravity S should then be located approximately $\Delta x \approx 8\,\%$ of the depth of the forward wing ahead of the center of pressure D.

The competition glider is required to achieve a flight duration of at least 180 seconds (a "Max") from a height of 50 meters in calm air, without thermal influences. We can verify whether it is capable of achieving this goal using the equations provided on page 183. With a zero-lift drag coefficient $c_{d0} \approx 0.03$ (due to wing and tail surface roughness) and an aspect ratio $\Lambda = 12$, the glide ratio $\varepsilon = 17.7$ is obtained. With a wing loading of $\frac{F_g}{A} = 12\ N/m^2$, the flight velocity is $v_\infty = 4.38\ m/s$. Consequently, the sink rate is $v_s \approx \frac{v_\infty}{\varepsilon} = 0.25\ m/s$. The flight duration from a 50-meter height would be approximately 200 seconds. It seems that the intention to achieve a "Max" flight duration is attainable. However, it should be noted that the equations on page 184 were derived for non-lifting horizontal stabilizers. It is expected that these equations may not be accurate enough for tandem arrangements of two wings.

The determination of a center of pressure according to page 191 and an initial center of gravity location is carried out in a comparable manner for the true tandem glider and the duck glider shown in Figure 92. For the true tandem glider with two wings of equal area, $\frac{x_{D1}}{x_{D2}} = \frac{c_{l2}}{c_{l1}} \approx \frac{1}{1.25} = 0.8$, meaning that the center of pressure D is located approximately $44\,\%$ of L, the length of the fuselage used in Figure 92, when measured from the front. If the wing area ratio for the duck glider is $\frac{A_1}{A_2} \approx 0.1$, as is the case for many military jets, then $\frac{x_{D1}}{x_{D2}} = A_2 c_{l2}/A_1 c_{l1} \approx 8$, indicating that the center of pressure D is located approximately $89\,\%$ of L from the front. We do not have precise information about the center of gravity location. As a precaution, an initial stability margin of $10\,\%$ can be assumed, which means placing the center of gravity $10\,\%$ of the average depth of the larger wing in front of the center of pressure, and observing how the glider behaves. There is not much that can go wrong in this case: if such a stability margin is too small for tandem gliders, the glider will behave more like the Forward Sinker described in the chapter "Forward Sinking — What is It?" For duck gliders, it is known that they behave "peacefully" even after a flow separation on the front wing, and return to the normal flight attitude after a brief nod. With careful shifting of the center of gravity, a stability margin of perhaps 40 to 45 % of the average wing depth can be achieved for true tandem gliders, and about 30 % of the average depth of the larger wing for duck gliders. Accurate calculations of center of pressure and center of gravity positions for tandem gliders are difficult to access. When determining the flight velocities of tandem gliders, significant deviations from the base speed mentioned on page 184 are always found, and these deviations are usually higher. This is not only due to disturbances in the flow around the wings and the influence of the front wing on the flow around the rear wing, but also because the specification of such a base speed, valid for normal gliders, may no longer apply to tandem gliders.

What Else Is of Significance?

**a) Regarding the arrival of air masses at the leading edge of a wing
(German "Stoß")**

Upon closer examination of Figure 40, the first noticeable aspect is the presence of two stagnation points when considering the ideal flow around the airfoil: one at the leading edge and one at the trailing edge. A stagnation point refers to a minuscule portion of air that ideally remains stationary with respect to the wing. In the first third of the wing, air particles need to be accelerated (requiring work to be done), while at the wing's end, they are gradually decelerated over time (resulting in a recovery of some work). In the case of an ideal flow around the wing, these work contributions cancel each other out, resulting in zero drag. However, we know that this is not the case in real flow around the wing. The discussion on what happens at the leading edge will be addressed in more detail. At the trailing edge of the wing, even when the flow is attached everywhere else, there is always a wake formation caused by the boundary layer, as shown in Figure 49.

If we consider the calculated and located stagnation point at the nose of the airfoil in Figure 40 as the point where the incoming air flow divides into an upper and lower portion, it becomes apparent that the paths followed by the separated small air parcels initially close together are quite different, particularly at the beginning. The path below the wing appears "easier" than the one above the wing because the air flow experiences slightly smaller changes in momentum there. In fact, the upward-flowing air parcel in Figure 40 even must flow back a bit to go around the leading edge. This asymmetry in the air flow around the nose of the wing is referred to as "Stoß," as the more significant changes in momentum of the upward-flowing air parcels require work and consequently generate resistance (often referred to as profile drag). "Stoß" is German for "leading edge shock," which refers to the shockwave effect that occurs when air masses at high velocities impinge on the leading edge of a wing or another aerodynamic surface. This can happen at high speeds or in supersonic flight conditions. However, we are talking about significantly lower speeds here. Therefore, the German term "Stoß" is more appropriate. To mitigate this, efforts are made to reduce or even eliminate this shock by appropriately shaping the airfoil. In this regard, a suitable airfoil camber proves to be the means of choice! The understanding of this concept can be gleaned from Figures 96 and 97, as well as Figure 116 on page 206.

In Figure 95, the wing with a symmetrical airfoil profile needs to be inclined at an angle α against the incoming flow to generate lift. However, this creates the aforementioned asymmetry in the air flow around the wing's nose, causing a shock. To effectively mitigate this shock, the nose of the wing needs to be appropriately tilted in the direction opposite to the incoming flow. This can be achieved through wing camber, as shown in Figure 96. With the wing camber, the flow can enter the airfoil with significantly reduced shock. This aligns with the observation made by Otto Lilienthal that a cambered wing interacts with the air flow in a much smoother manner. The relationship between wing camber (γ angle in Figure 96), angle of attack (α), and the direction of the incoming flow just before the wing during lift-producing flight, in a way that largely prevents a shock, is a rather complex matter.

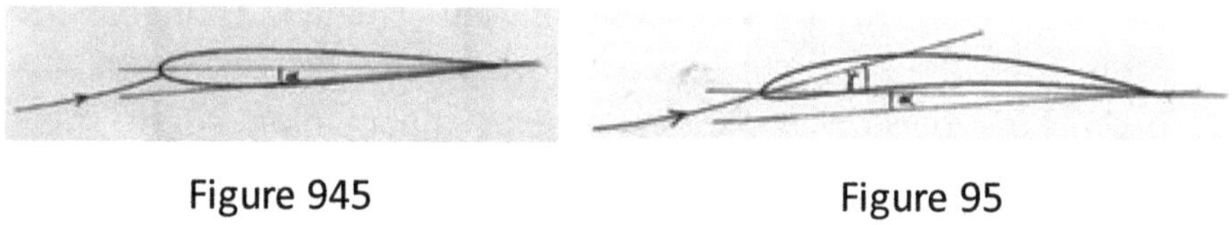

<table>
<tr><td>Figure 945</td><td>Figure 95</td></tr>
</table>

b) Regarding the outflow angle at the trailing edge of the wing

In the chapter "What Are the Consequences of the Wing's Camber?" the issue of angles at the wing trailing edge has already been addressed. It was mentioned casually: The outflow angle at the wing trailing edge allows the determination of circulation and thus the magnitude of aerodynamic lift. This statement is only correct when the wing is not cambered. It has been shown that in the case of a cambered wing, as seen in the Figure 43 on the left, the angle α_0 responsible for the magnitude of lift, known as the zero-lift angle, does not match the actual outflow angle at the trailing edge. This is further illustrated in an exaggerated manner in Figure 97 using the example of a cambered plate: The actual outflow angle γ at the trailing edge is almost twice as large as the zero-lift angle. Therefore, the determination of circulation magnitude needs to be adjusted by a factor of ≈ 2 due to this larger outflow angle. As noted in the chapter "What Are the Consequences of the Wing's Camber?" accurate lift values can be obtained by replacing the cambered plate with a flat plate at the zero-lift angle α_0, effectively determining the circulation magnitude using approximately half of the outflow angle at the trailing edge of the cambered wing.

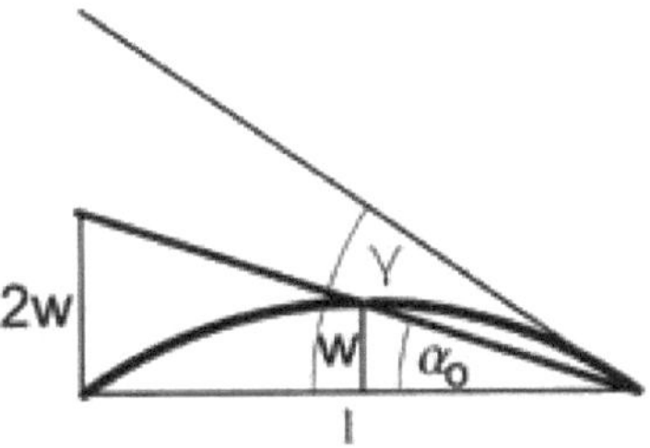

Figure 96

The method pursued in this book, as a result, to determine the magnitude of aerodynamic lift by replacing the cambered wing, assuming good flow conditions, with a flat wing at the corresponding angle of attack, proves to be of importance even when retrospectively assessing the gliding process depicted in Figure 21. If we were to take the actual outflow angle at the wingtip seriously, a flying wing like the one shown in Figures 22 and 23 would not generate lift and therefore would not fly.

Figure 97

This is because the airfoil of a flying wing has the shape outlined in Figure 98 (S-profile, see page 193 ff.), where the outflow angle relative to the direction of free flow would be zero or even negative. In this case, replacing this wing with a flat wing at an appropriate angle of attack is the only simple method to determine lift.

c) Regarding the lift distribution

So far, we have implicitly assumed that our wings generate a uniformly distributed lift, or to phrase it better, we have assumed an averaged and therefore uniform lift distribution over the wing surface. However, in reality, wings with lift exhibit significantly different lift distributions. One reason for this is the longitudinal distribution, i.e., transverse to the angled flat wing, which exists because the center of pressure is located closer to the quarter-chord line of the reference wing (see the chapter "Forward Sinking — What is It?"). In the case of a cambered wing, the center of pressure shifts towards the midline (see Figure 43). Additionally, there is a distribution in the lateral direction, i.e., along the angled flat wing, because the lift at the wingtips becomes zero. Now, two questions arise: (1) How can such lift distributions be described? and (2) What are their consequences?

The simplest pressure distribution in the flow direction, which leads to a "gravity" line at ¼ of the wing depth l above a rectangular flat reference wing surface, is the parabolic one shown in Figure 99, see page 193, where $p(0)$ is an adjustable value. For comparison, the pressure distribution used in aerodynamic literature for an angled flat plate is also shown.[18] Both pressure distributions result in the quarter-chord line as the location of balanced torques, that is

---

[18] Schlichting, H., Truckenbrodt, E. (1967). *Aerodynamik des Flugzeuges, Erster Band*. Berlin, Heidelberg, New York: Springer, 118

$z = \dfrac{x}{l} = \dfrac{1}{4}$. For the purposes of this book, the parabolic model appears to be a more easily understandable approximation, as the root model exhibits an unrealistic infinite value at $\dfrac{x}{l} = 0$ in terms of pressure. The torque caused by the pressure distribution around the leading edge of the wing can be replaced, in the case of an angled flat plate, by the action of an aerodynamic force F_l, which acts in close proximity to the quarter-chord line.

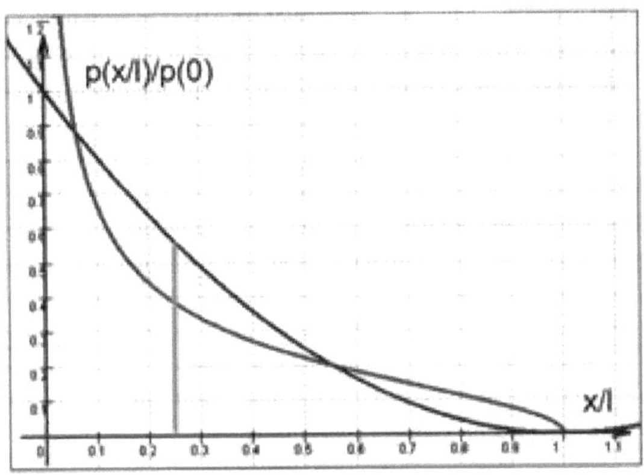

Figure 98

The distribution of lift across the wingspan, i.e., along the wing, is often praised as being particularly favorable when it follows an elliptical distribution. Calculations not further discussed here have shown that the lift distribution over a simple rectangular wing comes surprisingly close to such a distribution, while wing outlines that were initially designed to be elliptical (as seen in the model glider in Figure 93) have proven to be not as favorable. In modern aircraft design, both large and small, trapezoidal wings combined with high aspect ratios have been found to be optimal (see Figure 91).

d) Winglets

In many modern commercial aircraft as well as high-performance gliders, you can find winglets at the tips of the wings. Winglets are upward or angled extensions at the wingtips, resembling the curved tips of bird feathers. The exact aerodynamic effects of winglets in reducing drag are still not fully understood. It is hoped that by creating a broader wingtip, similar to increasing the wing aspect ratio, winglets can contribute to reducing the wingtip vortex area and thus decreasing the induced drag. However, the induced drag (as discussed in the chapter "Where Does Drag Come From?") cannot be completely eliminated because it is a result of generating the necessary lift to counteract the weight and the finite span of the wing. Any reduction in the actual vortex drag caused by winglets may lead to new sources of drag elsewhere on the wing, such as in the inner region near the wingtip.

How to Adjust a Glider

When we step into a commercial aircraft, we have to rely on the fact that the designer knew how to "adjust" that aircraft so that the pilot can fly it afterwards. It is different with a model glider that we may have purchased for a significant amount of money, as its "settings" need to be checked by us before we can entrust it to its element. Adjusting a glider: What does it all mean? Let us start by discussing angles.

It can be quite confusing: In this book, we have discussed the angle of attack of a wing against the free stream, specifically a geometric angle of attack α, which refers to the angle between the chord line of the wing and the oncoming flow. We have also mentioned the "aerodynamic" angle of attack α_0, also known as the zero-lift angle, which is influenced by the wing's airfoil shape. Additionally, the term "setting angle" has been introduced, referring to the setting of the elevator chord line relative to the wing's chord line. This is often referred to in literature as setting angle difference (German "Einstellwinkeldifferenz" or "EWD"). However, since the setting angle itself is already an angle difference, the term "EWD" should actually be called "angle of attack difference." All this talk about angles in this book relates to the chord line of airfoils, a reference direction that can be interpreted differently. Even the definition of the chord line itself can be unclear. And for those who pay close attention, there's another aspect to consider with the setting angle: apart from the geometric setting of the horizontal tailplane relative to the wing, there's an effective setting angle that may be slightly larger, as the horizontal tailplane experiences a weak downward flow behind the lifting wing during gliding (see, for example, Figure 42). Therefore, guidance on glider settings can appear challenging, but it becomes easier if there is an agreement on the specific meanings of certain angle measurements.

Figure 99

Let us start with the chord line of the airfoil. As depicted in Figure 100, the chord line represents the two points furthest apart on a cross-section of the wing (others may interpret the chord line as the line connecting a point on the trailing edge and the deepest point of the highly cambered airfoil). All angle measurements and settings are now referenced to the inclination of this chord line relative to the longitudinal axis of the glider. The easiest angle to describe based on this definition is the setting angle, which represents the difference in direction between the chord lines of the wing and the horizontal tailplane. As shown in Figure 21, for achieving longitudinal stability and generating aerodynamic lift, a slight negative setting of the horizontal tailplane relative to the wing is required. For high-speed gliders with low-camber airfoils, this angle is typically around $-1.5°$, while for slow gliders (with low sink rates) featuring more highly cambered profiles, it is often chosen to be larger, around $-2.5°$. In the case of controlled gliders, a base setting of around $-2°$ may be selected, and the different speed ranges (best glide and minimum sink, as discussed in the chapter "Quality of Flight") can be achieved through trimming of the elevator.

Understanding the angle of attack, which is the angle at which the wing of a glider is inclined relative to the direction of the free stream, is more challenging because this angle is determined during flight. Page 192 provides information that approximately relates the glide ratio to the wing camber and angle of attack. In this context, the angle of attack, denoted as alpha, should be measured in its original form rather than as a percentage.

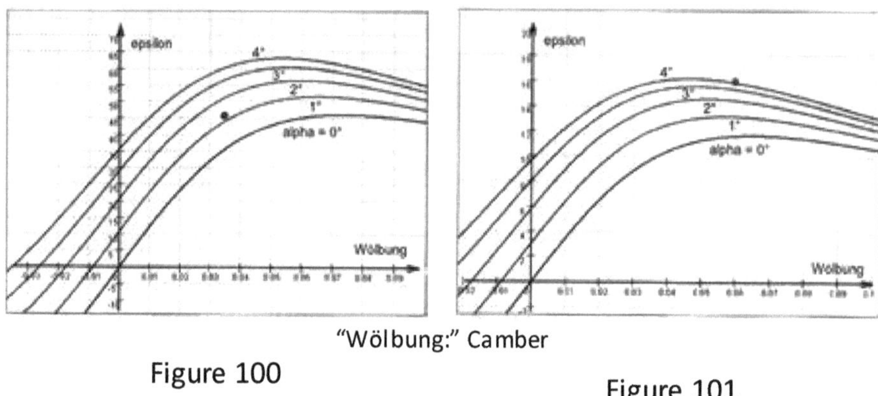

"Wölbung:" Camber

Figure 100

Figure 101

In Figures 102a and 102b, the relationship between the glide ratio (ϵ) and the wing camber ($\frac{w}{l}$) is depicted with the angle of attack (α) as a parameter. For Figure 101, data from the ASW 17 high-performance glider ($c_{d0} = 0.01, \Lambda = 27$) are used, while Figure 102 represents the data of the simple glider shown in Figure 24 ($c_{d0} = 0.035, \Lambda = 6$). The plotted point in Figure 101 corresponds to a glide ratio of $\varepsilon = 46$ for the ASW 17 with a wing camber of 3.5 %. In Figure 102, it represents the (theoretical) glide ratio of $\varepsilon = 16$ for the hobby glider with a wing camber of 6 %, as shown in Figure 65. It can be observed that in the case of Figure 101, an angle of attack of $\alpha \approx 1.2°$ is associated, while in the case of Figure 102, an angle of attack of $\alpha \approx 4°$ is required. Comparing these values with the assumption that the glide angle is approximately equal to the angle of attack ($\varepsilon = \frac{1}{tan\alpha}$, as stated on page 183), the earlier assumption holds quite well. The figures also indicate that the chosen wing cambers do not fall within the range of optimal glide ratios. In the case of the ASW 17, a slightly higher wing camber could potentially result in further improvements in glide ratios, while for the simple hobby glider, a slightly lower wing camber may be beneficial. However, increasing the wing camber of the high-performance glider might lead to flow separation problems (as discussed in the chapter "What Keeps the Flow Attached?"). The diagrams in Figures 102a and 102b also emphasize the significance of wing camber. With a symmetric airfoil profile (i.e., zero wing camber), the achievable glide ratios are considerably smaller compared to those with optimal camber values around 5 % (as depicted in Figure 68).

To properly adjust a glider, two important checks need to be performed before its first flight, which are not easily visible to the naked eye: (1) Checking the setting angle and (2) Checking the center of gravity. During the check of the setting angle, it is sometimes possible to detect major deviations from the setting angle condition by simply observing the glider's fuselage from a side view. It involves ensuring that the alignment of the wing support and the horizontal stabilizer profile is correct. However, it is difficult to determine whether the angle difference is too small, or the inclination differences are too large. Therefore, a more precise check is recommended. One simple method for checking the setting angle is depicted in Figure 103: The fully assembled glider is carefully placed on a pair of stable and straight beams, and the heights h_1 and h_2 are measured. By using the wing and stabilizer depths t_1 and t_2 at the contact point, the setting angle γ can be calculated as $\gamma = arcsin(h_1/t_1) - arcsin(h_2/t_2)$. The setting angle should be within the range of 1.5° (for fast gliders) to 2.5° (for slow sinkers).

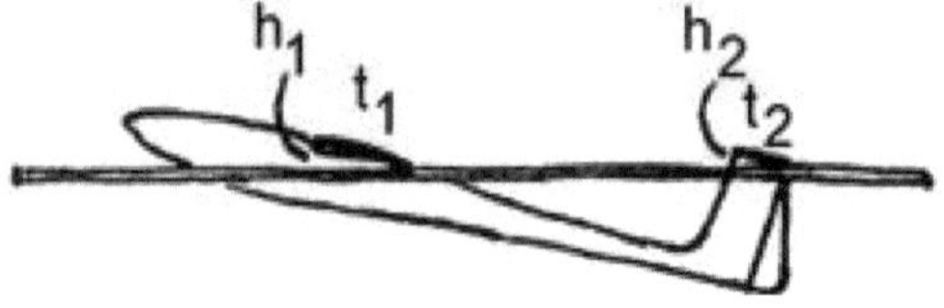

Figure 102

For checking the center of gravity, it is important to understand where the center of gravity should be located. As explained in the chapter "What Are the Consequences of the Wing's Camber?"the position of the center of gravity is determined by the position of the center of pressure along with the required stability measure. The position of the center of pressure, in turn, depends on the shape, camber, and angle of the wing, as well as whether two wings contribute to the lift, as described in the chapter "Tandem Glider".

Once the predetermined position of the center of gravity has been marked on the underside of the wing roots on both sides of the fuselage, the assembled glider is placed on two vertical rods (or even fingers) in such a way that the tips align with the markings. Depending on the inclination of the glider, it may be necessary to adjust the balance using small weights. The adjusted position of the center of gravity may not be the optimal location; its purpose is simply to ensure that the maiden flight of the glider does not end in disaster. Finally, it is checked whether the glider remains balanced and does not tilt to one side when placed horizontally on the ground.

The flight behavior of every model glider should be initially tested through a hand launch from the ground, as shown in Figure 104. It is important, and particularly challenging for beginners (hence, it is recommended to practice with sturdy, simple foam gliders), to perform a hand launch where the inclination of the glider's longitudinal axis, flight direction, and initial velocity closely resemble that of free flight. Proper launching is purely a matter of feel and practice. A wild upward throw (similar to a paper airplane) usually results in the demise of a newly built glider. By performing a controlled hand launch, it can be determined whether the glider tends to climb rapidly, undershoot, or maintain a steady straight flight, as depicted in Figure 104.

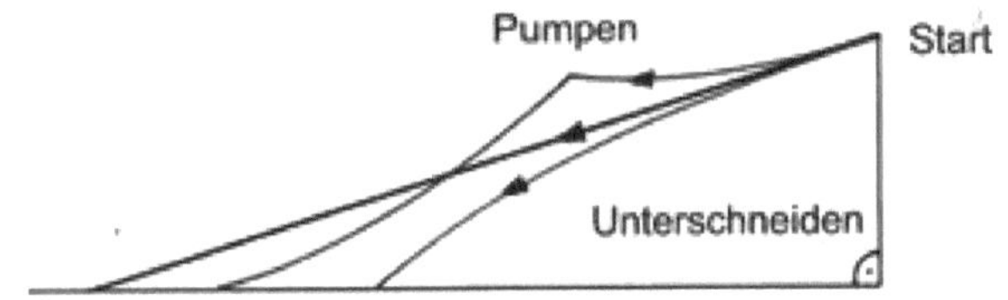

"Pumpen:" Pump; "Start:" Start; "Unterschneiden:" Undershoot

Figure 103

Pumping and undershooting are closely related to inadequate longitudinal stability. After a disturbance, undershooting is less likely to occur in a normal glider with a non-lifting horizontal tailplane, but more common in a free-flying competition glider with a lifting tailplane. Undershooting occurs when the lift coefficient of the horizontal tailplane is too high or when it is insufficiently negative compared to the wing. Undershooting is unavoidable when the center of pressure of the entire glider shifts rearward with increasing flight velocity, but it can be prevented by shifting the center of pressure forward instead. Pumping occurs when the setting angle is too large, and the stability margin is too small. This tendency for pumping arises when the glider is intended to achieve maximum flight times by entering a state of minimum sink. A free-flying glider suppresses pumping by maintaining a pre-set level turn after releasing from the towline or after shutting off a propulsion motor (which also assists in circling within a potential thermal updraft).

As mentioned earlier, a distinction must be made between uncontrolled, free-flying gliders and those that can be controlled. A free-flying glider must be adjusted to stabilize itself against any type of disturbance. In the case of a controlled glider, this requirement is not as strict because a critical flight condition can be corrected by the pilot. However, the more inherently stable a controlled glider is, the more comfortable the pilot's experience will be.

The fine-tuning of a controlled glider will be carried out by an experienced pilot through flight testing. Controlled gliders often have airfoils with around 3.5 % camber and a setting angle of approximately 2 degrees relative to the horizontal tailplane with a symmetrically shaped profile. This results in a recommended center of gravity position at around 30 % of the (reference) wing depth. The challenge of achieving optimal glider performance lies in the need to harmonize two adjustment parameters: the incidence angle and the center of gravity position. One can approach the optimum glide performance when, after a brief disturbance (such as a push), the glider only requires a few oscillations around its lateral axis with decreasing amplitudes to return to a stable glide, and when the center of gravity is positioned as far back as possible without compromising the generation of sufficient lift. This configuration allows for the smallest acceptable stability margin, resulting in reduced drag and improved overall performance.

What Is Missing in This Book

Even with the focus of this book solely on gliding, i.e., flying without propulsion, there are still practical gliding issues that are not addressed here. For example: How can flow problems such as local flow separation on a convex surface be prevented? Or: How does one fly a curve, and what glider properties promote or hinder curved flight? Or: What does "wing twist" mean and when is it necessary? But also, topics such as winch launching, slope soaring, flight in thermals, and everything related to the variable properties of air are either missing or only briefly mentioned. Even without propulsion, it is possible to reach high speeds in controlled dives, provided that the flight device has sufficient stability, exceeding the limits of validity of, for example, the simple Bernoulli equation. What does that mean? When does flutter occur, and what flow phenomena cause flutter (such as wingtip flutter or rudder flutter)? The relationship between wing elasticity under load and its influence on flight behavior is still not thoroughly researched. And related to that is the question: What tricks do birds have? What is still largely lacking are investigations into the significance and consequences of deliberate asymmetries in glider design. Anyone who still believes that flying can be easily explained will continue to face challenges in the future...

A Closing Statement

"How to Fly" is the title of this book. Right from the beginning, critical questions arise: Dear reader, after studying the preceding chapters, do you now feel that you understand how flying works? Or, more accurately, how flying could work? Has it been possible to carve a path of understanding through the tangle of numerous "explanations" about flying? It has certainly been a laborious task, at times quite challenging! This is because an "explanation on a book page" is not feasible.

So, what is flying? Here are a few key statements: "Flying means compensating for weight"—"Flying means generating aerodynamic lift"—"Flying requires a gravitational field and air"—"Flying is only possible if the air consists of particles with specific properties"—"Flying assumes a certain shape of the aircraft"—"Flying is only possible when the center of gravity and center of pressure have specific positions"—"Flying means achieving a movement in the air with minimal drag"—"Flying involves considering certain stabilizations"—"Understanding flying without physics and mathematics is not possible"...

Perhaps there would be a conclusive answer to the question of how flying works if we understood how birds move in the air. However, this question has only been partially answered since humans started observing birds, and even today, it remains incomplete. It can be said that we have only understood the movements of rigid aircraft to the extent to which they have been designed. However, it is possible that understanding our rigid aircraft, as described in this book, brings us closer to understanding bird flight. There is no apparent indication that, despite all the tricks that birds have mastered, fundamentally different conditions exist regarding the generation of lift and the reduction of resistance. After all, birds move through the same air as our aircraft and must deal with the same problems. This is the current state of knowledge in principle.

On a completely different level, we find ourselves in attempting to convey the current state of knowledge. Einstein is attributed with the remark: "If someone cannot explain something, they haven't understood it." Let us briefly look back at the two current and scientifically grounded explanations of the cause of flying that were described at the beginning. Have the respective protagonists been able to fully explain the true cause? It seems not, or only in partial aspects, because otherwise, in our scientifically well-informed society, it would hardly be possible to offer two radically different explanations for the same phenomenon credibly over time. Dear reader, please examine whether the explanations presented in this book on flying are not only credible but will also withstand future advances in understanding. Perhaps there is some truth to what a young person meant about the constantly changing views, not only regarding flight:

In truth, reality is quite different!

Appendix

From the Science Section of "Die Zeit" (2001)

"Here, conventional wisdom is wrong"
Why can an airplane fly? Until today, two American researchers
criticize that it is explained incorrectly

by Ulrich Schnabel

No object between heaven and earth remains permanently hidden from the X-ray vision of modern natural science. Well, that is not always the case! Sometimes, seemingly simple things turn out to be profound mysteries. Let us take, for example, the question: Why can an airplane fly? A ridiculous problem, admittedly; nothing for a science page, one might think. Hasn't this topic been settled since the year 1903 when the Wright brothers first took off? Isn't there a simple explanation in every textbook today?

This is exactly the problem - at least according to David Anderson. "The usual explanation for flight is a kind of myth - it's simply wrong!" protests the physicist from Fermi National Laboratory in Chicago. "But it has taken on a life of its own to the extent that you can even find it on NASA websites and in physics books." That is why Anderson has now taken up the fight against ignorance and, together with aeronautical engineer Scott Eberhardt, published the book Understanding Flight (McGraw Hill). Eberhardt has also observed repeatedly among his students that they do not develop a true understanding of flight physics. "They can explain it mathematically.

But that is not the same as understanding."

Typically, the lift of an airplane is explained using the so-called Bernoulli's principle, named after the Swiss mathematician Daniel Bernoulli, who studied flowing fluids in the 18th century. Bernoulli, who never dreamt of flying machines, discovered a fundamental relationship between the velocity of a flowing fluid and the pressure it exerts. In short, Bernoulli's principle states that the faster the flow (for example, in a pipe), the lower the pressure (on the walls of the pipe). According to many textbooks, this principle can also explain aircraft lift: The air over the curved upper surface of a wing must travel a longer distance than under its flatter lower surface, resulting in faster air flow over the top, which creates lower pressure above the wing, and this pressure difference lifts the airplane.

But for heaven's sake, as Anderson asks, why should the two air streams arrive simultaneously at the end of the wing? That is blatant nonsense. No one forces the air molecules to arrive at the same time. Moreover, according to this logic, aerobatics inverted flight should not be possible at all because according to the textbook logic, the pressure ratio should reverse with the inverted airfoil, and the aircraft should crash. Anderson and Eberhardt, therefore, favor a different explanation. To do so, they initially invoke the so-called Coandá effect, which describes the tendency of air (or other low-viscosity fluids) to adhere to a surface and thus follow its camber when flowing past. Consequently, the air is sucked downward over the top of the wing, creating a lower pressure above the wing. However, the crucial factor for lift is not the wing's profile but its angle of attack: A tilted wing pushes the air downward by exerting force on it. This promptly produces a reaction force (according to Newton's famous law actio = reactio), which lifts the wing upward. Voilà.

Other experts readily admit that Anderson and Eberhardt are right in their criticism of the conventional textbook interpretation. However, they point out that lift can also be explained using the Bernoulli principle. It just needs to be interpreted differently: When the air strikes the front of the wing, it gets compressed like in a bottleneck, thus forced to flow faster. The result remains the same: A pressure difference creates lift. So, the mystery of flying is now theoretically solved twice. All is well that ends well, right? If only it were that simple. "An entirely exact explanation is unfortunately not that easy," says Rudolf Voit-Nitschmann, head of the Institute of Aircraft Design at the University of Stuttgart. For practical aircraft design, both Newton's laws and the Bernoulli formula are too simplistic. Ultimately, the actual lift of a wing can only be determined in a wind tunnel. While there are now elaborate computer programs for calculating complex flow conditions, they still do not provide exact results. And then, Professor Voit-Nitschmann says something quite astonishing coming from a professional aircraft designer after almost 100 years of aeronautics: "Flying is probably one of those phenomena that we observe in nature and simply have to accept."

Who says physics has no more secrets?

Mia Asks

Or: Why "Why" Questions End Up in Nowhere

Mia, who is actually named Emilia, is a bright child of five years old, or rather, soon to be six years old, as she likes to correct. After a Sunday breakfast with her parents, it happened: She is allowed to go to the living room to play while her dad clears the table and takes the breakfast dishes to the kitchen. Suddenly, there is a loud crash and clatter. Mia quickly runs into the kitchen.

"What happened?" she asks.

"A plate fell from my hand," Dad calls out.

"Both of you, out!" scolds Mom. "I have to sweep up the shards."

Mia and her dad flee to the living room. Excitedly, Mia asks, "Dad, why did the plate break?"

"It slipped out of my hand and fell," he replies.

"And why did it fall?"

"Because it's heavy and has weight."

"Why does our plate have weight?"

"Because it is attracted by the Earth."

"And why is it attracted by the Earth?"

Dad senses it: the "why" questioning is starting again. With the following answer, he thinks he can bring the matter to an end.

"When the Earth attracts heavy objects, you can experience it when you jump. Every time you jump up, you fall right back down. That happens because you are being pulled down by the Earth beneath you."

A crease forms on Mia's forehead. Apparently, she realizes that Dad didn't really answer her question. Therefore, she asks again, "But why am I attracted by the Earth when I jump?"

Dad, who actually knows a thing or two about physics, briefly contemplates how to proceed.

"Listen, Mia. I'm going to tell you a technical term that can answer your question. It's called gravity. Some also call it heavyness. But the word gravity describes the matter more generally because the same type of attraction that happens when you jump also exists between the Earth and the Moon or the Earth and the Sun."

Mia ponders for a while. "Could I also jump on the Moon?"

"Yes, but not on the Sun. Why not there?" Dad tries to retaliate with a "why" question of his own. But her response comes quickly.

"That's impossible because it's too hot there!" Mia exclaims. Dad thinks he succeeded, but she has no intention of giving up and continues asking.

"Dad, why does this grav—grav—this gravity exist?"

Dad is starting to feel warm. Oh dear, how do I explain this to my child, he thinks.

"I'll tell you something about it. The most famous scientist who ever lived, a certain Albert Einstein, thought about this question. But he has already passed away, so you can't ask him this question anymore."

"And what did this Albert Einstein find out about gravity?"

Dad is getting warmer and warmer. The child has more questions! I have to find some kind of answer, he thinks.

"Listen, Mia. You know that when it's dark and there are no clouds above you, you can see many points of light in the black sky. And you also know that these points of light are stars similar to our Sun but much farther away. All the stars are located in a vast, vast space called the universe or cosmos. Einstein discovered that this space is curved."

"Dad, what does curved mean?" Mia interrupts.

"Curved is something similar to bent."

"Like my long ruler that I can bend?"

"Yes. But you have to imagine it differently in space. Einstein discovered that a light beam, like the one from your flashlight that you think always goes straight ahead, can be bent similar to your flexible ruler. Do you know what that means? I showed you the North Star (Polaris) recently. When you see it, you think: it is exactly where I see it, in the north. But it may not be true because it might be somewhere else, as the light from it has been bent due to the curvature of space. Einstein discovered that gravity is related to this curvature of space."

Dad pauses, observing Mia's thought process in her head, but also because he himself doesn't really know how this will continue. Soon Mia will come alive again.

"Dad, why is space curved?"

Now Dad really starts to sweat: What should he answer to that?

"Einstein found out that the curvature of space is caused by the stars present in this space. These stars have a property called mass. If you hold a small stone and a large stone in your hands, you will notice that they have different masses. Compared to a stone, the entire Earth has a huge mass. But the masses of the stars are much, much larger. And these enormous masses curve the space."

Mia sinks into longer contemplation once again. The plate fell because it was attracted by the Earth. This attraction is called gravity. This gravity has something to do with the curvature of space. The curvature of space is caused by the masses of the stars...

"Dad, why do stars have mass?"

"Well, you know, a long, long time ago, there was a huge explosion somewhere, an explosion called the Big Bang. That's when all the masses in space were created."

"Was the explosion terrible?"

"Very terrible, much worse than we can imagine."

"But why did such a terrible explosion happen?"

I have absolutely no idea, Mia's dad thinks and responds, "Because there are laws of nature."

"And why are there laws of nature?"

Now Dad is at the end of his wisdom, and he can only come up with one answer, "Because the dear God made them."

After a while, Mia's face brightens up, and with a smile, she declares, "So, it's the dear God's fault that our plate broke!"

***

How do you like this little story? Perhaps you can test yourself: How do you approach the "why" questions? Do you know that scientists never asks the question "why" (because they cannot answer it), but always asks the question "how"? Hence the title of this book: How to fly.

Quantities and Units

As is customary in the natural sciences in general and physics in particular, a quantity is defined by its numerical value and unit. The numerical value depends on the unit being used. After a historically and regionally grown confusion of terms and units, internationally standardized designations have been agreed upon (known as SI units, from French "système international"). With few exceptions, the initial letters of the English designations are used, capital letters as well as lowercase letters and even Greek letters are used for the quantities and base units. This can be vividly illustrated with the quantity "pressure," which plays a significant role in flying. Pressure is encountered in the context of contact pressure, exerted by a heavy object on its contact area; or water pressure, felt when diving; or air pressure, used to inflate a tire, for example. Depending on the system in which pressure is involved, various units were previously used, such as "Torr" (from Torricelli), "mm water column or mercury column," "at" (from atmosphere), "psi" (from pounds per square inch), and various other units. After standardization, in scientific and technical publications worldwide, the only accepted designation for pressure is "p" (from English "pressure"), and its unit is only "Pa" (from Pascal) or "N/m^2" (Newtons per square meter). Thus, the average atmospheric pressure at sea level is approximately 1,013 hPa (hectopascals) or 101,300 N/m^2. The use of quantities and units in this book follows the international SI system. With two exceptions in German aeronautics: The drag coefficient is designated as "c_W," whereas the international convention uses "c_d" (d for English "drag"); and the lift coefficient is designated as "c_A," whereas the international convention uses "c_l" (l for English "lift").

The Hydrostatic Basic Equation

First, we determine the volume of a portion of water located in a glass cylinder. With the base area A (from English "area") in m^2, the constant cross-sectional area A of the cylinder, and the height Δh in meters (m), the volume ΔV is given by:

$$\Delta V = A \, \Delta h \qquad \text{unit } 1 \text{ m}^3.$$

The notation "Δ" (Greek delta for difference) with h (from English "height") and V (from English "volume") is used to indicate that an increase or decrease in the height h of the water filling the glass cylinder by Δh leads to an increase or decrease in the volume V by ΔV.

The density ρ of a homogeneous object is defined as the ratio of its mass m to its volume V:

$$\rho = m/V = \Delta m/\Delta V \qquad \text{unit } 1 \text{ kg/m}^3.$$

Therefore, the mass Δm of this portion of water is given by:

$$\Delta m = \rho \, \Delta V.$$

This portion of water has a weight. At the Earth's surface, the conversion factor from the mass of an object to its weight is g = 9.81 m/s² (acceleration due to gravity). Therefore, the weight F_g (F for force; g for gravity) of this portion of water is given by:

$$\Delta F_g = g \, \Delta m, \qquad \text{unit } 1 \text{ kg m/s}^2 = 1 \text{ N}.$$

With the definition of pressure as force per unit area, the hydrostatic pressure is given by:

$$\Delta p = F_g/A, \qquad \text{unit } 1 \text{ Pa} = 1 \text{ N/m}^2.$$

Combining the above equations, we obtain the hydrostatic fundamental equation:

$$\Delta p = g \, \rho \, \Delta h$$

Alternatively, in differential form:

$$dp = g \, \rho \, dh.$$

The mathematical notation of the fundamental equation using differentials "d" instead of "Δ" has the practical significance that this equation also holds for infinitesimal and hence flowing changes. Such flowing changes are commonplace in fluid mechanics and therefore in aviation as well. Differentials are well suited for describing flowing changes.

Dynamic Pressure, Drag and Vertical Sink Rate

From Figure 10, we extract that within the time period t, the accelerated volume of air is given by

$$V = As,$$

where A represents the (maximum) cross-sectional area, and s represents a length. The acceleration work is given by:

$$E = \frac{1}{2}mv^2,$$

where m is the mass of the accelerated volume of air, and $v = \frac{s}{t}$ is the velocity of the flow. The mass of the accelerated volume of air is:

$$m = \rho V,$$

where ρ is the density of the air. The dynamic pressure (German "Staudruck") is then:

$$p = \frac{E}{V} = \frac{1}{2}\rho v^2 = \frac{F}{A}$$

with $\frac{E}{V}$ being an "energy density." The force acting on the area A is consequently:

$$F = \frac{1}{2}\rho A v^2$$

The actually swirled volume of air is:

$$V = Asc_d$$

with c_d is the drag coefficient. Consequently, the drag force is:

$$F_d = \frac{1}{2}\rho Av^2 c_d = F_g$$

in the case of uniform sinking. Thus, the drag coefficient is:

$$c_d = \frac{2F_g}{\rho Av_\perp^2} \quad \text{and} \quad v_\perp = \sqrt{\frac{2F_g}{\rho Ac_d}},$$

as the vertical descent velocity. The quotient F_g/A, with units of pressure, is also referred to as the surface loading (German "Flächenbelastung").

Glide Ratio and Sink Rate I

The term glide ratio is understood as follows in accordance with Figure 18:

$$\varepsilon = \frac{s}{h} = \frac{1}{tan\alpha}$$

The sink velocity is given by:

$$v_s = \frac{h}{t}$$

The flight velocity is given by:

$$v_\infty = \frac{\sqrt{s^2 + h^2}}{t}$$

The relationship between flight and sink velocities is:

$$\frac{v_\infty}{v_s} = \frac{\sqrt{s^2 + h^2}/t}{h/t} = \sqrt{\left(\frac{s}{h}\right)^2 + 1} = \sqrt{\varepsilon^2 + 1} \approx \varepsilon,$$

when $\varepsilon > 3$. Therefore, for the sink velocity, approximately:

$$v_s \approx \frac{v_\infty}{\varepsilon}.$$

Forward Sinking and Drag

The drag-producing surface area is given by

$$A \sin\alpha$$

The aerodynamic force is as follows, in accordance with Figure 18 and appendix Page 176:

$$F_L = F_g = \frac{1}{2}\rho A \sin\alpha\, v_\infty^2 c_d$$

Hence, the flight velocity is:

$$v_\infty = \sqrt{\frac{2F_g}{\rho A \sin\alpha\, c_d}} = \frac{v_\perp}{\sqrt{\sin\alpha}}$$

Using Figure 18, the sink velocity is:

$$v_s = v_\infty \sin\alpha = v_\perp\sqrt{\sin\alpha}, \ \ i.e. \ \ y = -v_\perp\sqrt{\sin\alpha}$$

With Fig. 20:

$$tan\alpha = \frac{y}{x} = -\frac{v_\perp\sqrt{\sin\alpha}}{x}, \ \ i.e. \ \ x = -v_\perp\sqrt{\sin\alpha}/tan\alpha \ .$$

Thickness of the Modified Air Layer at the Wing

The weight and wing area of the ASW 17 glider are given as:

$$F_g \approx 5000 \ N \qquad A = 15 \ m^2$$

The sink velocity of the glider is approximately:

$$v_s = \frac{\Delta h}{t} = 0.5 \ m/s$$

The amount of work released per second during descent (difference in potential energy) is:

$$\Delta E_{pot} = F_g \Delta h \approx 2500 \ J$$

The average pressure difference at the wing is:

$$\Delta p = \frac{F_g}{A} \approx 330 \ N/m^2 = \frac{\Delta E_{pot}}{V}$$

From this, we can determine the volume of air with altered pressure created per second:

$$V = \frac{\Delta E_{pot}}{\Delta p} \approx 7.5 \ m^3$$

The area swept by the glider per second is approximately:

$$A_1 \approx 460 \ m^2$$

This leads to the thickness of the air layer with altered pressure:

$$d = \frac{V}{A_1} \approx 1.6 \ cm.$$

A Basic Bernoulli Equation

The momentum of the particle before it impacts the wall is given as:

$\mu \vec{v}_A$, where μ is the mass, and $\vec{v}_A$ is the velocity of the particle.

The wall is moving with a (relative) velocity of $\vec{v}$

The transverse momentum at the moment of collision between the particle and the wall is:

$$\mu \vec{v}$$

Therefore, the momentum of the emitted particle is:

$$\mu \vec{v}_B = \mu \vec{v}_r + \mu \vec{v}$$

Applying the Pythagorean theorem, we get:

$$v_r^2 = v_B^2 - v^2 = v_A^2 - v^2$$

As the altered pressure follows:

$$\frac{1}{2}\rho v_r^2 = \frac{1}{2}\rho v_0^2 - \frac{1}{2}\rho v^2, \quad v_A = v_0$$

and thus, a "Bernoulli" equation follows:

$$p(v) = p(0) - \frac{1}{2}\rho v^2$$

where $p(0) = \frac{1}{2}\rho v_0^2$ represents the surrounding air pressure.

The average particle velocity is:

$$v_0 = \sqrt{\frac{2p(0)}{\rho}} \approx 400 \ \frac{m}{s},$$

from $p(0) = 10^5 \ \frac{N}{m^2}, \ \rho = 1.25 \ \frac{kg}{m^3}.$

Derivation of a Bernoulli Equation

The hydrostatic fundamental equation is given as:

$$dp = \rho g dr,$$

where r is a running coordinate in the field direction. A more suitable formulation of this equation is:

$$g = \frac{1}{\rho}\frac{dp}{dr}.$$

The d'Alembert correction term $\frac{dv}{dt}$ leads to the hydrodynamic basic equation:

$$g - \frac{dv}{dt} = \frac{1}{\rho}\frac{dp}{dr},$$

where v is the local flow velocity. For stationary flows, we have:

$$\frac{dv}{dt} = \frac{dr}{dt}\cdot\frac{dv}{dr} = v\frac{dv}{dr}.$$

In this case, the hydrodynamic basic equation can be expressed as:

$$g - v\frac{dv}{dr} = \frac{1}{\rho}\frac{dp}{dr}.$$

For horizontal motion (flying), we have g = 0. In this case, the hydrodynamic basic equation becomes:

$$dp = -\rho v dv.$$

Taking a step back to:

$$\frac{1}{\rho}\frac{dp}{dr} + v\frac{dv}{dr} = 0.$$

The integration of $dp = -\rho v dv$ within the limits from 0 to v yields:

$$\frac{p(v)}{p(0)} = 1 - \left(\frac{v}{v_0}\right)^2, \quad p(0) = \frac{1}{2}\rho v_0^2.$$

This is a form of Bernoulli's equation and is referred to as Gl. (7).

Alternative Bernoulli Equations

The Boyle-Mariotte's law states:

$\frac{p}{p_0} = \frac{\rho}{\rho_0}$, when temperature T remains constant.

This leads to the modified hydrodynamic basic equation:

$$\frac{dp}{p} = -\frac{\rho_0}{\rho} v dv.$$

Integrating within the limits from 0 to v yields:

$$ln \frac{p(v)}{p(0)} = -\frac{1}{2} \frac{\rho_0}{p_0} v^2.$$

With $p_0 = p(0) = \frac{1}{2} \rho_0 v_0^2$ we arrive at the "Bernoulli" equation:

$$\frac{p(v)}{p(0)} = exp\left(-\left(\frac{v}{v_0}\right)^2\right),$$

referred to as Gl. (8a).

The general gas equation is

$pV = const.\cdot T$, where T is the temperature in Kelvin (K)

Here, the gas equation is used in the following form:

$$\frac{pV}{p_0 V_0} = \frac{T}{T_0},$$

Where p_0, V_0, T_0 are the state parameters of the stationary gas.

For small temperature changes, the density of the gas follows:

$$\frac{V}{V_0} \approx \frac{\rho_0}{\rho} \text{ , i.e. } \rho \approx \rho_0 \frac{p}{p_0} \frac{T_0}{T}.$$

The adjusted hydrodynamic fundamental equation is then:

$$\frac{dp}{p} \approx -\frac{\rho_0}{p_0}\frac{T_0}{T(v)} v\,dv.$$

The particle energy after emission is:

$$\epsilon_r = \frac{1}{2}\mu v_r^2 = \frac{1}{2}\mu(\vec{v}_B - \vec{v})^2 = \frac{1}{2}\mu(v_B^2 - 2\vec{v}_B\vec{v} + v^2)$$

The contribution of scalar products, α being the angle enclosed by $\vec{v}_B$ and $\vec{v}$, is:

$$\sum_n \vec{v}_B\vec{v} = \int_0^\pi \vec{v}_B\vec{v}\,d\alpha = \int_0^\pi v_A v\,\cos\alpha\,d\alpha = 0,\ |\vec{v}_B| = v_A.$$

Because $\epsilon_A = \epsilon_0 = \frac{1}{2}\mu v_0^2$ and $\epsilon_r = \frac{1}{2}\mu(v_B^2 + v^2) = \frac{1}{2}\mu(v_0^2 + v^2)$,

we have: $\dfrac{T_0}{T(v)} = \dfrac{\epsilon_A}{\epsilon_r} = \dfrac{v_0^2}{v_0^2 + v^2}$

This leads to the further adjusted hydrodynamic basic equation:

$$\frac{dp}{p} \approx -\frac{\rho_0}{p_0}\frac{v_0^2}{v_0^2 + v^2} v\,dv$$

Finally, with $p_0 = p(0) = \frac{1}{2}\rho_0 v_0^2$, we get:

$$\frac{dp}{p} \approx -\frac{2v\,dv}{v_0^2 + v^2}.$$

Integrating within the limits from 0 to v yields:

$$\ln\frac{p(v)}{p(0)} \approx \ln\frac{v_0^2}{v_0^2 + v^2}$$

or the "Bernoulli" equation:

$$\frac{p(v)}{p(0)} \approx \frac{1}{1 + (v/v_0)^2},$$

referred to as Gl. (8b).

Lift Equation

The line integral L is defined as the expression:

$$L = \int_a^b d\vec{v}\, d\vec{s},$$

if the line is a streamline between the points a and b. Circulation Γ is defined when the line is closed:

$$\Gamma = \oint d\vec{v}\, d\vec{s}$$

In the case of the circular path shown in Figure 38 with a diameter of l

$$\Gamma = 2\pi \frac{l}{2} v_\perp = \pi l v_\infty sin\alpha = l\Delta v$$

This transition cannot be explained here (Stokes' theorem).

Using the hydrodynamic basic equation $\Delta p = \rho v_\infty \Delta v = \frac{F_l}{A}$, we obtain the lift equation:

$$F_l = \frac{1}{2}\rho A v_\infty^2 c_l$$

where $c_l = 2\pi sin\alpha$ is the lift coefficient.

Lift of the (Inclined) Cambered Plate

For the lift of the un-inclined cambered plate, we have:

$$F_{l0} = \frac{1}{2}\rho A v_\infty^2 c_{l0}$$

with the lift coefficient:

$$c_{l0} = 2\pi sin\alpha_0.$$

The zero-lift angle is approximately:

$$\alpha_0 \approx arctan(2w/l).$$

Therefore, the lift of the inclined cambered plate is:

$$F_{ltot} = F_l + F_{l0} = \frac{1}{2}\rho A v_\infty^2 c_{ltot}$$

with the lift coefficient:

$$c_{ltot} = c_l + c_{l0} = 2\pi(sin\alpha + sin\alpha_0) \approx 2\pi sin(\alpha + \alpha_0).$$

Pressure Point Migration on the Cambered Wing

From Figure 45, we can derive the equilibrium condition:

$$F_l\left(x_D - \frac{l}{4}\right) \approx F_{l0}\left(\frac{l}{2} - x_D\right).$$

Rearranging for $\frac{x_D}{l}$ gives:

$$\frac{x_D}{l} \approx \frac{1}{4}\left(1 + \frac{F_{l0}}{F_{l0} + F_l}\right),$$

With the coefficients:

$$\frac{x_D}{l} \approx \frac{1}{4}\left(1 + \frac{c_{l0}}{c_{l0} + c_l}\right) = \frac{1}{4}\left(1 + \frac{c_{l0}}{c_{ltot}}\right).$$

The moment coefficient around the neutral point is:

$$c_{ltot}\left(x_D - \frac{l}{4}\right) = \frac{l}{4}c_{l0} = c_{m0,25}.$$

Using $\quad c_{l0} = 2\pi sin\alpha_0 \approx 2\pi tan\alpha_0 \approx 4\pi\frac{w}{l}, \quad c_l = 2\pi sin\alpha \quad$ and $c_{ltot} = c_l + c_{l0}$, we get the pressure point migration:

$$\frac{x_D}{l} \approx \frac{1}{4}\left(1 + \frac{c_{l0}}{c_{l0} + c_l}\right) \approx \frac{1}{4}\left(1 + \frac{1}{1 + sin\alpha/(\frac{2w}{l})}\right).$$

The Induced Drag

From the proportionalities $c_{di} \propto f(c_l)$ and $c_{di} \propto \frac{1}{\Lambda}$, we can conclude that $c_{di} \propto \frac{f(c_l)}{\Lambda}$.

The aspect ratio of the wing is defined as:

$$\Lambda = \frac{b}{l} = \frac{b^2}{A},$$

where b is the wingspan, A is the wing's area.

Using Figure 18, we have:

$$\varepsilon = \frac{1}{\tan\alpha} = \frac{F_l}{F_{di}} = \frac{c_l}{c_{di}} \approx \frac{1}{\sin\alpha},$$

if α small. Since $c_l = 2\pi\sin\alpha$, we find that:

$$c_{di} \propto f(c_l) = \frac{c_l^2}{2\pi}$$

and therefore $c_{di} \approx \frac{c_l^2}{2\pi\Lambda}$.

For two wingtip vortices, the induced drag is approximately given by:

$$c_{di} \approx \frac{c_l^2}{\pi\Lambda}.$$

Determination of c_{d0} (Zero Drag Coefficient)

Using the flight data for the ASW 17 high-performance glider:

- Flight speed $v_\infty \approx 90\ \frac{km}{h} = 25\ \frac{m}{s}$ (good gliding speed)

- Wing loading $\frac{F_g}{A} \approx 350\ \frac{N}{m^2}$;

- Wing aspect ratio $\Lambda = 27$;

- Glide ratio $\varepsilon \approx 46$.

With $F_l \approx F_g$, we can calculate c_l as follows:

$$c_l \approx \frac{(2F_g/\rho A)}{v_\infty^2}.$$

Thus, c_{d0} is calculated as:

$$c_{d0} = c_{dtot} - c_{di} = \frac{c_l}{\varepsilon} - \frac{c_l^2}{\pi\Lambda}.$$

Using the flight data of the ASW 17 and air density ρ, we find:

$$c_{d0} \approx 0.01.$$

Glide Ratio and Sink Rate II

The glide ratio is defined as follows:

$$\varepsilon = \frac{1}{tan\alpha} = \frac{F_l}{F_d} = \frac{c_l}{c_d} = \frac{c_l}{c_{d0}+c_{di}} = \frac{c_l}{c_{d0}+c_l^2/\pi\Lambda}$$

Using the lift coefficient c_l with:

$$c_l \approx \frac{(2F_g/\rho A)}{v^2}, \quad \text{and} \quad v_\infty \approx \sqrt{\frac{2F_g}{\rho A}} \quad \text{as well as} \quad c_l \approx (v_\infty/v)^2$$

we can derive the glide ratio as:

$$\varepsilon \approx \frac{(v_\infty/v)^2}{c_{d0}+(1/\pi\Lambda)(v_\infty/v)^4} = \frac{v_\infty^2 v^2}{c_{d0}v^4+v_\infty^4/\pi\Lambda}$$

And the sink rate is given by:

$$v_S \approx \frac{v_\infty}{\varepsilon} \approx \frac{c_{d0}v^4+v_\infty^4/\pi\Lambda}{v_\infty v^2}.$$

Approximate Quality of Flight Metrics

Glide Ratio (ε) is approximately given by: $\varepsilon \approx \dfrac{1}{c_{do}+1/\pi\Lambda}$

Flight Speed (v_∞) is approximately given by: $v_\infty \approx \sqrt{\dfrac{2F_g}{\rho A}}$

Sink Rate (v_S) is approximately given by: $v_S \approx \dfrac{v_\infty}{\varepsilon}$

Regarding the Polar Diagrams

<u>For the forward sinker</u>

Using Figure 18, we have $F_d = F_L \sin\alpha$ and $F_l = F_L \cos\alpha$.

For level flight, $F_g = F_L = \frac{1}{2}\rho A \sin\alpha \, v_\infty^2 c_d$.

Therefore, for forward sinking, we have:

$$F_A = \frac{1}{2}\rho A v_\infty^2 \sin\alpha \cos\alpha \, c_d \text{ as well as } F_d = \frac{1}{2}\rho A v_\infty^2 \sin^2\alpha \, c_d$$

This translates to the coefficients $c_l^* = \sin\alpha \cos\alpha \, c_d$ and $c_d^* = \sin^2\alpha \, c_d$ for lift and drag, respectively.

Using $= \sqrt{1 - \sin^2\alpha}$, we can express c_l^* as:

$$c_l^* = \sin\alpha \sqrt{1 - \sin^2\alpha} \, c_d$$

$$= \sqrt{\sin^2\alpha - \sin^4\alpha} \, c_d = \sqrt{\frac{c_d^*}{c_d} - \left(\frac{c_d^*}{c_d}\right)^2} \cdot c_d = \sqrt{c_d^* c_d - c_d^{*2}}.$$

<u>For the flat plate</u>

The relation is given by:

$$c_l(c_d) = \sqrt{\pi\Lambda(c_d - c_{do})}.$$

<u>For the cambered plate</u>

Using the coefficient of induced drag, $c_{di} = c_d^2/\pi\Lambda + c_{d0}^2/\pi\Lambda$, the relation becomes:

$$c_l(c_d) = c_l + c_{l0} = \sqrt{\pi\Lambda(c_d - c_{d0}) - c_{l0}^2} + c_{l0}.$$

Regarding the Presence of a Thin Water Film

The centrifugal force is given by:

$$F_r = mv^2/r$$

with acceleration:

$$v^2/r.$$

For a water portion with mass $m = \rho\Delta V$, the centrifugal force becomes:

$$F_r = \rho\Delta V v^2/r.$$

The "counter" force exerted by air pressure p is given by:

$$\Delta F = \int p dA = p\Delta A.$$

The limiting velocity of flow (v_{lim}) can be calculated as:

$$v_{lim} = \sqrt{rp\Delta A/\rho\Delta V} = \sqrt{rp/\rho d}.$$

Here, d represents the thickness of the water film.

Interlude on the Significance of Momentum Changes in Flowing Fluids

If Figure 104 (page 112) is drawn with 90 degrees, we have an approximation of the conditions of flow around a wing with a cambered surface. There, the deflection of airflow above and below the wing generates a sideways force, which some believe is ultimately the aerodynamic lift. To test this view, a more detailed calculation should be carried out. To compensate for the weight of the ASW 17 high-performance glider, mentioned several times before, with $F_g \approx 5,000\ N$, a correspondingly large sideways force $F_q = \frac{mv_\infty^2}{r}$ needs to be generated. Here, m represents the mass of the air parcel to be deflected, and r is the radius of a circular path resulting from the camber of the airfoil of this aircraft. This radius is approximately $r \approx 3\ m$, and the flight speed is $v_\infty \approx 23\ m/s$. Therefore, an air parcel with a mass of $m \approx 26\ kg$, equivalent to $20.8\ m^3$, is affected. Since this is a snapshot, it means that with a wing area of $15\ m^2$, an air layer of about $1.4\ m$ thickness is captured by the wing for deflection, in the theoretical case considering only this air layer, significantly more if the entire transitional region to undisturbed flow is affected. Since this seems quite possible, this calculation alone is not sufficient. The consequences of this idea must also be considered, which is illustrated in Figure 104.

In Figure 104, the focus is on an air layer captured by the cambered wing, where the wing (in this case, the curved surface) is positioned in such a way that the undisturbed flow, apart from the influence of the airfoil shape, can enter without any deflection. It is only then (!) that the deflection of airflow can have the desired effect. From Figure 104, it can be observed that the centrifugal force F_r is composed of two forces: the actual sideways force F_q, which corresponds to lift, and the drag force F_d, which is caused by the deflection. The glide ratio associated with this concept is given by $= \frac{F_q}{F_d} = \frac{1}{\tan\left(\frac{\alpha}{2}\right)}$, as indicated in Appendix Page 173 and Figure 18, where $\frac{\alpha}{2}$ is the zero-lift angle, which is approximately 4 degrees for the airfoil of the ASW 17 glider. This results in a glide ratio of $\varepsilon \approx 14$. However, the ASW 17 glider exhibits a glide ratio of $\varepsilon = 46$, which is significantly higher!

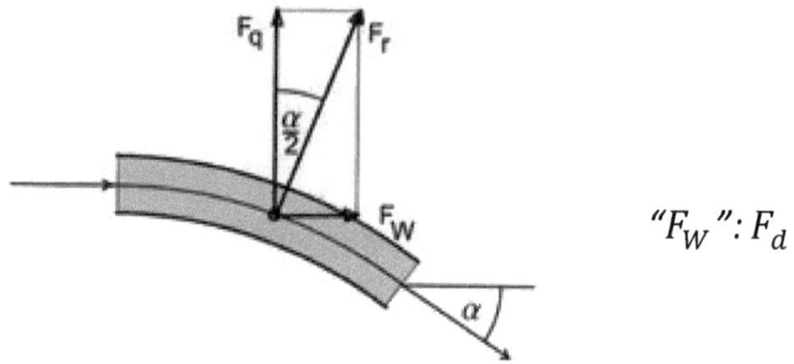

Figure 104

Those who believe in this concept of generating aerodynamic lift will not only encounter the difficulty of achieving small glide ratios. In this explanatory model, the magnitude of the glide ratio is determined solely by the wing's camber, and not by important factors such as the coefficient of drag and the aspect ratio, as described in the chapters "Quality of Flight" and "Parameters of Practical Gliding". However, the need to compensate for the weight of the aircraft has even more significant consequences: the less camber the wing has, the larger the amount of air that needs to be deflected! Therefore, the following conclusion can be drawn: although the concept of deflecting airflow through the wing to compensate for weight does not initially seem impossible for typically cambered wings, a quantitative estimation of the consequences does not yield appropriate results, and in the case of low-cambered wings, it even leads to a contradiction. Consequently, as described in the chapter "Aerodynamic Lift", **any form of impulse flow consideration for aerodynamic lift is**

inadequate. Only the inclusion of pressure phenomena allows for a sufficiently accurate explanation of the magnitude and cause(s) of this lift.

The Weak Equilibrium

One can follow the argument chain familiar from upper-level analysis in mathematics:

$$E(\varphi_{min}) \leftrightarrow \frac{d}{d\varphi}E(\varphi_{min}) = 0 \leftrightarrow \frac{d^2}{d\varphi^2}E(\varphi_{min}) > 0.$$

a) Consider equilibrium Type I, as seen in Figure 80. The restoring moment is given by:

$$M = F_g l \, sin\varphi.$$

Disturbance caused by work = increase in potential energy:

$$W = F_g \Delta l = F_g l(1 - cos\varphi) = E(\varphi).$$

In the local minimum:

$$\frac{d}{d\varphi}E(\varphi) = F_g l \, sin\varphi = 0 \text{ , meaning } \varphi_{min} = 0 \text{, and:}$$

$$\frac{d^2}{d\varphi^2}E(\varphi)|_{\varphi_{min}} = F_g l \, cos\varphi_{min} = F_g l > 0.$$

b) Now, consider equilibrium Type II, as shown in Figure 82. The restoring force is approximately:

$$F_H \approx \pi\rho A v^2 sin\varphi,$$

resulting in the restoring moment:

$$M(\varphi) \approx F_H(\varphi)a = F_H(0)a sin\varphi \text{ with } F_H(0) = \pi\rho A v^2.$$

Work due to disturbance = Increase in potential energy:

$$W \approx \frac{1}{2} F_H(0) a \sin^2 \varphi = E(\varphi)$$

In the local minimum:

$$\frac{d}{d\varphi} E(\varphi) = F_H(0) a \sin\varphi \cos\varphi = 0, \quad \text{meaning } \varphi_{min} = 0 \text{ and:}$$

$$\frac{d^2}{d\varphi^2} E(\varphi)\big|_{\varphi_{min}} = F_H(0) a (\cos^2 \varphi_{min} - \sin^2 \varphi_{min}) =$$

$$F_H(0) a > 0.$$

To Strengthen the Weak Equilibrium

The energy at an angular displacement φ is given by:

$$E(\varphi) = F_g l (1 - \cos\varphi).$$

The energy at an angular displacement $\varphi + \Delta\varphi$ is:

$$E(\varphi + \Delta\varphi) = F_g l (1 - \cos(\varphi + \Delta\varphi)).$$

The change in energy (ΔE) is thus:

$$\Delta E = E(\varphi + \Delta\varphi) - E(\varphi) = F_g l (\cos\varphi - \cos(\varphi + \Delta\varphi)).$$

For a constant disturbance ΔE, we have:

$$\frac{\Delta E}{F_g l} = \cos\varphi - \cos(\varphi + \Delta\varphi),$$

which is also a constant.

This leads to a relationship $\Delta\varphi(\varphi)$:

$$\Delta\varphi = \arccos\left(\cos\varphi - \frac{\Delta E}{F_g l}\right) - \varphi.$$

For equilibrium Type II, we have:

$$\frac{\Delta E}{F_H(0)a} = \frac{1}{2}\left(sin^2(\varphi + \Delta\varphi) - sin^2\varphi\right).$$

The Strong Equilibrium

The restoring force is approximately given by:

$$F_H \approx \pi\rho Av^2 sin\varphi.$$

Energy released when lowering the center of gravity:

$$\epsilon(\varphi) = F_g\Delta r = F_g\Delta x sin\varphi.$$

Work required for displacement:

$$W(\varphi) = \frac{1}{2}F_H(0)asin^2\varphi.$$

Increase in potential energy:

$$E(\varphi) = W(\varphi) - \epsilon(\varphi) = \frac{1}{2}F_H(0)asin^2\varphi - F_g\Delta x sin\varphi.$$

The execution of the arguments yields:

$$\frac{d}{d\varphi}E(\varphi) = F_H(0)asin\varphi cos\varphi - F_g\Delta x cos\varphi = 0,$$

with the local minimum at:

$$sin\varphi_{min} = \frac{F_g\Delta x}{F_H(0)a}.$$

Furthermore:

$$\frac{d^2}{d\varphi^2}E(\varphi)\big|_{\varphi_{min}} = F_H(0)a(1 - 2sin^2\varphi_{min}) + F_g\Delta x sin\varphi_{min} > 0,$$

or

$$\frac{d^2}{d\varphi^2}E(\varphi)\big|_{\varphi_{min}} = F_g\Delta x\left(\frac{1}{sin\varphi_{min}} - sin\varphi_{min}\right) =$$

$$F_g \Delta x \left(\frac{\cos^2 \varphi_{min}}{\sin \varphi_{min}} \right) > 0.$$

Effect of a disturbance:

With $\Delta E = E(\varphi + \Delta\varphi) - E(\varphi)$ and $F_H(0)a = \dfrac{F_g \Delta x}{\sin\varphi_{min}}$, we obtain the inconvenient equation:

$$\frac{\Delta E}{F_g \Delta x} = \frac{1}{2} \frac{\sin^2(\varphi+\Delta\varphi) - 2\sin(\varphi+\Delta\varphi)\sin\varphi_{min} - \sin^2\varphi + 2\sin\varphi\sin\varphi_{min}}{\sin\varphi_{min}}$$

which can be approximated as:

$$\frac{\Delta E}{F_g \Delta x} \approx \frac{1}{2} \frac{(\sin(\varphi+\Delta\varphi) - \sin\varphi)^2}{\sin\varphi},$$

resulting in a relation:

$$\Delta\varphi \approx \arcsin\left(\sqrt{2\sin\varphi \frac{\Delta E}{F_g \Delta x} + \sin\varphi} \right) - \varphi.$$

Pressure Point Location in Tandem Glider

The lift of the leading wing is given by:

$$F_{l1} = \frac{1}{2}\rho A_1 v_\infty^2 c_{l1}.$$

And the lift of the trailing wing is given by:

$$F_{l2} = \frac{1}{2}\rho A_2 v_\infty^2 c_{l2}.$$

To achieve a moment equilibrium, we have:

$$F_{l1} x_{D1} = F_{l2} x_{D2}.$$

To determine the pressure point location, we use:

$$A_1 x_{D1} c_{l1} = A_2 x_{D2} c_{l2}.$$

For example, with a wing area ratio $A_1/A_2 = 5.1$ (as seen in Glider Figure 94) and a lift coefficient ratio $c_{l1}/c_{l2} \approx 1.25$, the resulting equations to determine the location of the pressure point D are:

$$\frac{x_{D2}}{x_{D1}} = \frac{A_1 c_{l1}}{A_2 c_{l2}} \approx 6.37$$

$$x_{D1} + x_{D2} = L.$$

Flat Plate: Pressure Distributions in the Flow Direction

Given the coordinate $\frac{x}{l} = z$, where l is the depth of the plate, the resulting parabolic pressure distribution is:

$$p(z) = p(0)(1 - z)^2.$$

The pressure distribution commonly used in aviation is:

$$p(z) = p(0)\sqrt{\frac{1}{z} - 1}.$$

The torque about the leading edge of the wing is:

$$M = F_l \frac{\int_0^1 z\, p(z)\, dz}{\int_0^1 p(z)\, dz} = F_l \cdot \frac{l}{4}.$$

Glide Ratio, Camber, and Angle of Attack

The glide ratio can be expressed as:

$$\varepsilon = \frac{c_{ltot}}{c_d} = \frac{c_l + c_{l0}}{c_{do} + c_{di}} = \frac{2\pi(\sin\alpha + \sin\alpha_0)}{c_{do} + \frac{c_l^2 + c_{l0}^2}{\pi \Lambda}}$$

$$= \frac{2\pi\left(sin\alpha + sin(arctan\frac{2w}{l})\right)}{c_{d0} + \frac{4\pi}{\Lambda}\left(sin^2\alpha + sin^2(arctan\frac{2w}{l})\right)}$$

For small angles, $sin\omega \approx tan\omega$, so:

$$sin(arctan\frac{2w}{l}) \approx \frac{2w}{l}.$$

Therefore, for the glide ratio, we have:

$$\varepsilon \approx \frac{2\pi\left(sin\alpha + 2\frac{w}{l}\right)}{c_{d0} + \frac{4\pi}{\Lambda}\left(sin^2\alpha + 4\left(\frac{w}{l}\right)^2\right)}.$$

Wing Profile (Airfoil) Design

In several chapters of this book, it has become clear that the wing's airfoil shape (i.e., the design of the wing cross-section) is not crucial for generating aerodynamic lift, but it is crucial for the quality of the wing's airflow. An ideal airflow has been assumed to derive equations like those mentioned on page 184, which have allowed us to make predictions about the performance of an aircraft design when airflow deficiencies are minimal. We have identified various sources of such deficiencies and observed that deficiencies are particularly large when using a flat plate as a wing, while they can be kept particularly small with clever wing profiling. In this regard, two characteristics of such airfoils have proven to be significant: (1) the shape of an elongated drop (instead of a constant thickness like a flat plate), and (2) a slight curvature of the mean or skeletal line (instead of a straight line).

Since the beginning of aviation, the search for optimally shaped airfoils has been a passion for private researchers as well as a major research focus for aeronautical engineers. Some have placed their hopes on the so-called "miracle profile" until it was realized that such a universal profile does not exist — one profile that leads to optimal airflow conditions for both slow-flying birds of prey, fast gliders, and commercial aircraft. Nowadays, airfoils are optimized for their specific purposes. Thus, profiles for uncontrolled, slow-flying gliders look different from those designed for controlled, fast-flying aircraft. Even within these specializations, remarkable discoveries are constantly being made, which is why the search for suitable airfoils remains an ongoing topic of interest for both private and professional researchers.

However, one thing should be clear from the outset: Any alleged "miracle profile" becomes the standard profile when building a glider, unless one invests in technical efforts that go far beyond the capabilities of an average builder. As a consolation, it should be noted that during actual flight, the miraculous shaping of the wing becomes less important, and the pilot's flying skills take precedence. In other words, even a super-optimized glider is of little use in the hands of an inexperienced pilot. In short, a healthy dose of realism is needed when considering which airfoil is suitable for one's glider. And healthy realism means that often, simply drawn profiles are sufficient. It is worth noting how often one has been surprised when looking out of the cabin of a commercial aircraft, observing the "imperfections" of the wings, despite the goal of minimizing drag and thereby saving fuel.

Airfoils can be sketched by hand, drawn more elegantly with a French curve, and ultimately computed and drawn with great accuracy in any size using modern function plotters. A wide variety of airfoils can be found in literature. For most of them, it is not clear what their specific advantages are, such as how certain gliding performances are precisely influenced by these profiles. Therefore, a more practical question is which function equations can be used to draw such profiles and stretch or compress them in any desired scale. The literature does not offer much in this regard, as existing profile contours are either derived from well-executed hand sketches or composed of rather complex functions whose mathematical nature is often difficult to ascertain. This book explains how to create usable airfoils using simple functions that can resemble well-known and proven profiles if desired. The subsequent calculations will demonstrate that anyone can create their own airfoils to test on their gliders, although it is not an easy task, unfortunately.

Mathematically speaking, we can start from a single relation that allows us to generate a complete teardrop-shaped profile contour: it is the shear-transformed square root function along the vertical axis (shearing refers to a specific area-preserving mapping in mathematics, as used in Figure 19, for example). Typically, sheared square root functions have complex relation equations. However, among the square root functions suitable for describing a slender teardrop profile, there is a type with a rather simple equation: $|y| = \sqrt{ax} + bx$, where a and b are freely selectable parameters. The absolute value notation indicates that it describes both the upper and lower profile contours. The appearance of this equation for $a = 4$ and $b = -\frac{1}{5}$ is illustrated in Figures 106 and 107.

The upper half of the sheared square root function depicted in Figure 106 has the equation $y = \sqrt{4x} - \frac{1}{5}x$. The section designated for representing the profile contour is indicated by the dark shading. For the lower part of the teardrop profile sketched in Figure 107, the equation responsible is $y = -\sqrt{x} + \frac{1}{5}x$. An expert immediately recognizes that this is a symmetric profile with a thickness of approximately 10 %. The location of maximum thickness is at around 25 % of the profile depth, precisely where the quarter-chord line of the reference wing, as described in the chapter "Forward Sinking, What is It?", is located.

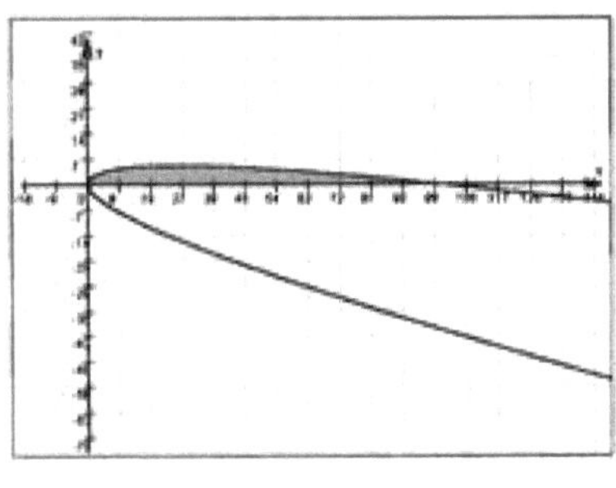

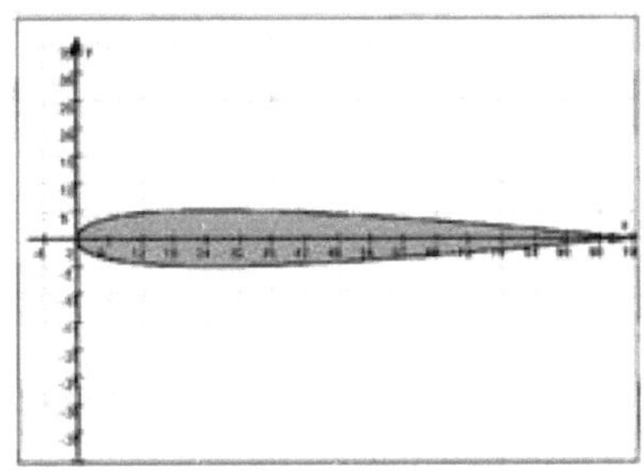

| Figure 105 | Figure 106 |

In Box 1, it is described how to derive a simple contour function for the symmetric teardrop profile from the base function. Profile shapes are usually referenced to a standard depth, such as the standard depth of 100 mm. If the positive root x_0 of the sheared square root function lies at that point, we obtain an initial contour base function. The standard specifications of a profile include the thickness, the location of maximum thickness, and the nose radius, each relative to the profile depth (later also the camber). The location of maximum thickness is determined from the position of the extremum, as explained in Box 1. The thickness D at that point is twice the function value at the position x_e for symmetric profiles. This results in a simple contour function for the symmetric teardrop profile, where D is replaced with the percentage value relative to the profile depth x_0. For example, if D is intended to be 8 % of the profile depth, then $D = 0.08x_0$ should be used.

<u>Box 1: The Symmetric Airfoil Drop</u>

Basic function:

$$|y| = \sqrt{ax} + bx, \text{ with parameters } a,b.$$

Using the normalized depth of the airfoil, x_0, we have:

$$\sqrt{ax_0} + bx_0 = 0 \text{ or } b = -\sqrt{\frac{a}{x_0}}$$

Contour Base Function:

$$|y| = \sqrt{a}\left(\sqrt{x} - \frac{x}{\sqrt{x_0}}\right)$$

At the maximum:

$$y'(x_e) = \sqrt{a}\left(\frac{1}{2\sqrt{x_e}} - \frac{1}{\sqrt{x_0}}\right) = 0, \text{ i.e. } x_e = \frac{x_0}{4} \text{ and}$$

$$y(x_e) = \frac{D}{2} = \left(\sqrt{\frac{ax_0}{4}} - \sqrt{\frac{a}{x_0}} \cdot \frac{x_0}{4}\right) = \frac{1}{4}\sqrt{ax_0}, \text{ i.e. } a = \frac{4D^2}{x_0}.$$

Contour Function:

$$|y| = 2D\left(\sqrt{\frac{x}{x_0}} - \frac{x}{x_0}\right)$$

Contour Function with a General Power Function:

$$|y| = \frac{D \cdot p^{\frac{1}{p-1}}}{2 \cdot \left(\frac{1}{p}-1\right)}\left(\left(\frac{x}{x_0}\right)^p - \frac{x}{x_0}\right)$$

For the nose radius, some more effort is required, as described in Box 2. Initially, we obtain a curvature radius that appears complex, and its value needs to be evaluated as x approaches 0, which is not entirely trivial due to terms with x in the denominator. However, as these terms become increasingly dominant as x decreases, a simple expression for the nose radius emerges in the limit. Thus, for the symmetric profile according to Box 1, the following data determines it: the chosen thickness D at $\frac{1}{4}x_0$ and the nose radius $|\rho| = \frac{2D^2}{x_0}$, where x_0 is the profile depth. In the case of the profile in Figure 102, these values are: $x_D = 25\,\%$; $D = 10\,\%$; $\rho = 2\,\%$ of the profile depth. Figure 108 shows how well the determined nose radius corresponds (it cannot be a perfect match because the contours are those of two slightly inclined square root functions; it fits perfectly only for the horizontally lying square root function).

<u>Box 2: Nose Radius</u>

The curvature radius ρ at a point x of a function y is given by:

$$\rho = \frac{\left(1+y'^2\right)^{3/2}}{y''}$$

In the limit as $x \to 0$, we have $\rho = -\dfrac{2D^2}{x_0}$

Derivatives of $y = 2D\left(\sqrt{\dfrac{x}{x_0}} - \dfrac{x}{x_0}\right)$:

$$y' = 2D\left(\frac{1}{2\sqrt{x_0\,x}} - \frac{1}{x_0}\right) \quad \text{and} \quad y'' = -\frac{D}{2x\sqrt{x_0\,x}}$$

Now, the curvature radius is:

$$\rho = \frac{\left(1+4D^2\left(\frac{1}{2\sqrt{x_0 x}} - \frac{1}{x_0}\right)^2\right)^{3/2}}{\left(-\frac{D}{2x\sqrt{x_0 x}}\right)}$$

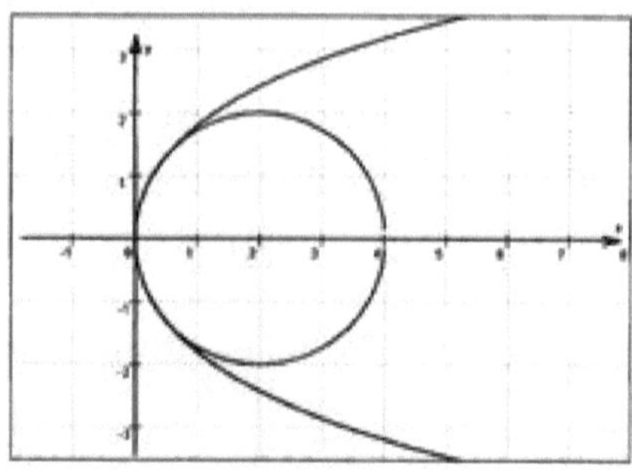

Figure 107

In Figure 109, several symmetric profiles are sketched along with their corresponding data. The profile designations will be explained later.

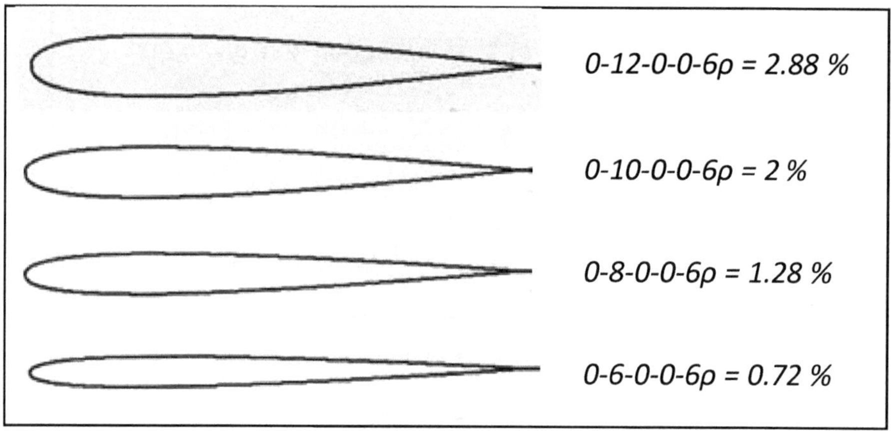

Figure 108

From these symmetric profiles, simple asymmetric profiles of a certain type can be created by using different parabolic segments for the upper and lower contours. If a specific thickness D, such as 10 %, is given, for a given value D_2 for the lower contour, the corresponding

199

value $D_1 = D - D_2$ must be used for the upper contour. Figure 109 illustrates examples for a thickness D of 10 %. It is noticeable that as the difference between the upper and lower contours increases, the nose radius becomes smaller, meaning the profile becomes "sharper," which may be desirable for the quality of the airflow. The profiles also become increasingly cambered as a result. The profile designations will be explained later.

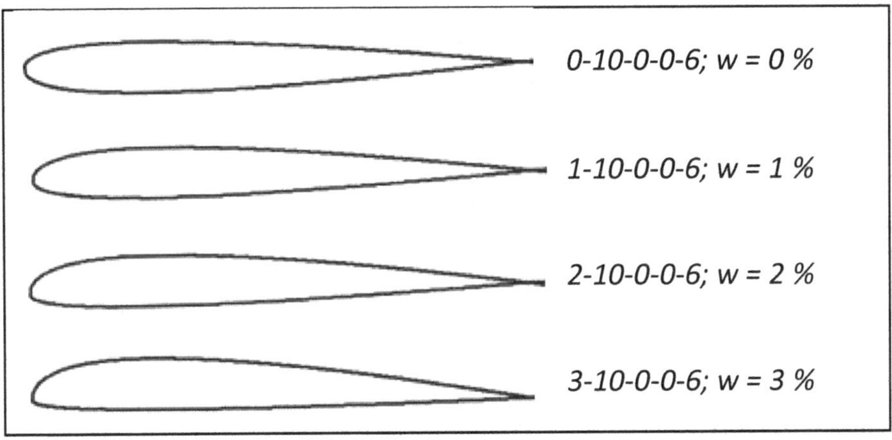

Figure 109

The sheared square root function chosen for the profile contour in Box 1 results in the maximum thickness occurring at 25% of the wing depth and a relatively large nose radius, as seen in the profile examples in Figure 110. However, if instead of the square root function, a general power function is used, such as $y = (ax)^p + bx$, the position of the maximum thickness as well as the nose radius will change. By incorporating the profile data, thickness D, and depth x_0 in the same manner as in Box 1, the contour function given as the last one in Box 1 can be obtained after a slightly more cumbersome calculation. For $p = \frac{1}{2}$, the contour function provided above is derived. For $p < \frac{1}{2}$, the location of the maximum thickness moves further forward, and the nose section becomes "flatter," making it generally unsuitable for airfoils. Interesting values occur for $p > \frac{1}{2}$ (although $p = 1$ should be avoided for understandable reasons); as p increases, the location of the maximum thickness moves backward, the nose radius becomes smaller, and the nose section becomes progressively "sharper." Table I (page 217) illustrates examples of the resulting symmetric profile shapes.

You will get cambered airfoils "pushing" a curved center line, a *skeletal line*, under the contour of the symmetrical profile instead of the straight center line, see Fig. 111. With this type of curved center line, you can also proceed as simply as possible. The shape of the piece of an arc of a circle seems to be obvious. When looking at Figure 108, you can see that the circular line in the area that is of interest the airfoils nestles up quite well with a parabolic line. Parabolas are easier to deal with mathematically than circles; in addition, shifts in the positions of the curvature maxima are also possible with parabolas. Box 3 shows the development of the skeletal line from the parabola line to the general power function.

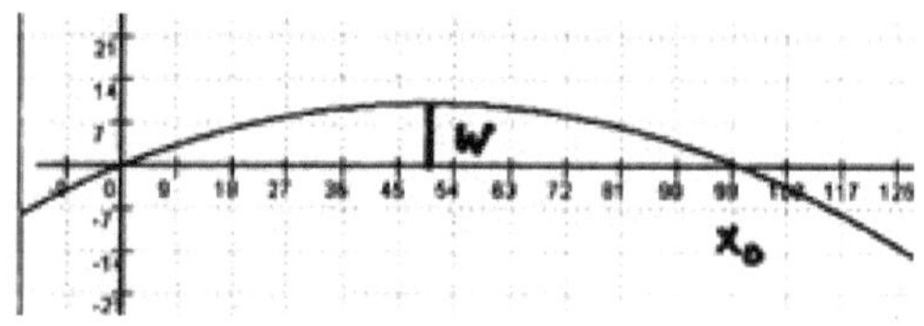

Figure 110

The equation of the skeletal line should use the curvature measure w, expressed as a percentage of the wing depth (similar to D, for example, if $w = 4\,\%$, then $w = 0.04x_0$ should be used, where x_0 is the profile depth). In Figure 112, two cambered profiles are sketched using the equation of the skeletal line derived from a parabolic curve, as described in Box 3. The profile designations will be explained later.

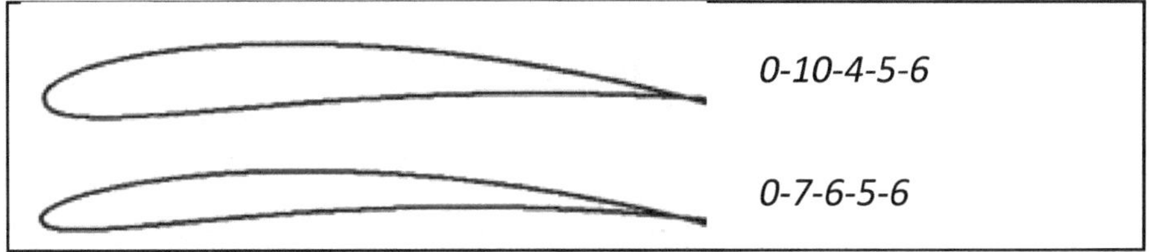

Figure 111

The skeletal line shown in Figure 111 has its maximum curvature at 50 % of the profile depth. If a different location for the maximum curvature is desired, the question arises as to which simple functions can be used for that purpose. Similar to the profile contour described in Box 1, the family of skeletal lines can also be described based on power functions using a single equation, as shown in Box 3. For $p = 2$, the equation of the skeletal line derived from a parabolic curve is obtained ($p = 1$ should be avoided again). Skeletal lines with $p < 1$ are theoretically possible but exhibit irregular behavior near the nose, i.e., at $x = 0$. Figure 113 illustrates examples of skeletal lines with $p = 2,3,4,5$, where the maximum curvature shifts towards the rear as p increases.

Box 3: The Curved Skeletal Line

Parabolic Equation:

$$y = ax(x - b), \text{ with } parameters\ a,b.$$

Skeletal Line Equation:

$$y = w\,\frac{1}{x_0}\left(x - \frac{x^2}{x_0}\right)$$

General Power Function:

$$y = bx - ax^p$$

Root at $x = x_0$, therefore $a = bx_0^{1-p}$

With $y' = b - pax^{p-1}$, we find the maximum at $x_e = \dfrac{x_0}{p^{\frac{1}{p-1}}}$

With $y(x_e) = w = bx_0 \left(\dfrac{1}{p^{\frac{1}{p-1}}} - \dfrac{1}{p^{\frac{p}{p-1}}} \right)$, we get $b = w\, \dfrac{p^{\frac{p}{p-1}}}{(p-1)x_0}$

Skeletal Line Family:

$$y = w\, \frac{p^{\frac{p}{p-1}}}{(p-1)x_0} \left(x - \frac{x^p}{x_0^{p-1}} \right) \quad \text{camber maximum back (*)}$$

Or:

$$y = w\, \frac{p^{\frac{p}{p-1}}}{(p-1)x_0} \left(x_0 - x - \frac{(x_0-x)^p}{x_0^{p-1}} \right) \quad \text{camber maximum forward (**)}$$

The skeletal line shown in Figure 111 has its maximum curvature at 50 % of the profile depth. If a different location for the maximum curvature is desired, the question arises as to which simple functions can be used for that purpose. Similar to the profile contour described in Box 1, the family of skeletal lines can also be described based on power functions using a single equation, as shown in Box 3. For $p = 2$, the equation of the skeletal line derived from a parabolic curve is obtained ($p = 1$ should be avoided again). Skeletal lines with $p < 1$ are theoretically possible but exhibit irregular behavior near the nose, i.e., at $x = 0$. Figure 113 illustrates examples of skeletal lines with $p = 2,3,4,5$, where the maximum curvature shifts towards the rear as p increases.

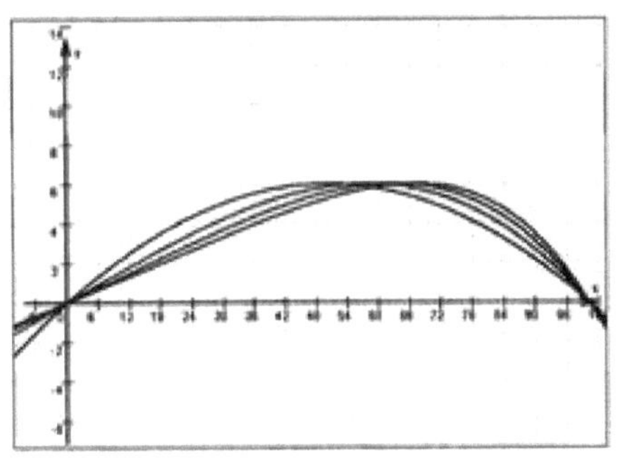

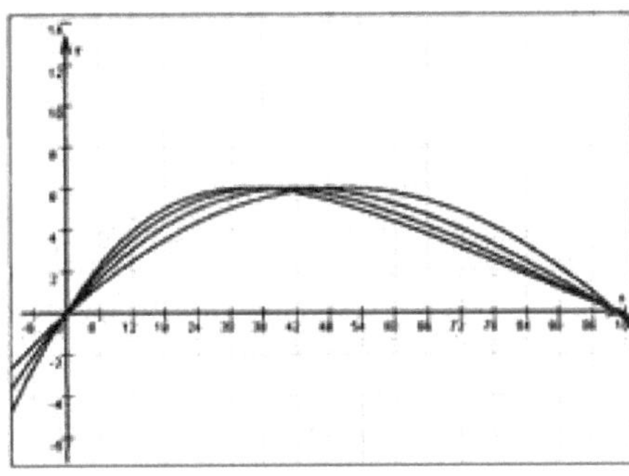

Figure 112

Figure 113

If one wishes to advance the maxima instead, the curves can be mirrored along the y-axis, then shifted to the right by x_0, resulting in the last equation for skeletal lines mentioned in Box 3. For $p = 2$, this equation again yields the skeletal line derived from a parabolic curve (once again, $p = 1$ should be avoided). Figure 114 depicts skeletal lines for $p = 2,3,4,5$ with forward-shifted maxima. The effect of the location of the maximum curvature on profiles, according to the equations in Box 3, is illustrated in Table IV with some examples.

<u>Box 4: The S-shaped Profile</u>

Basic equation of the skeletal line:

$$y = w\,sin\left(\frac{\pi x}{x_0}\right)$$

Extended range:

$$y = w\,sin\left(\frac{k\pi x}{x_0}\right),\ 1,0 \leq k \leq 1,9$$

Second positive root at x_0:

$$y = w\left(sin\left(\frac{k\pi x}{x_0}\right) - \frac{x}{x_0}\,sin(k\pi)\right)$$

Slope of the skeletal line at $x = 0$:

$$y'(0) = w\frac{p^{\frac{p}{p-1}}}{(p-1)x_0} \ \text{ or } \ y'(0) = w\frac{p^{\frac{p}{p-1}}}{x_0}$$

For gliders that do not have a separate horizontal stabilizer, known as flying wings, longitudinal stability is achieved by curving the trailing edge of the wings, similar to the flat plate shown in Figure 21. This requires an S-shaped skeletal line (also known as S-camber). Among the suitable candidates for this purpose, the sine function proves to be the simplest, as described in Box 4. If a larger portion of the sine curve is desired within the range of 0 to x_0, the next equation provides that capability. Furthermore, if it is desired for the second positive root to occur at x_0, which means that the chord line of the profile aligns with the x-axis, the last equation in Box 4 is used for that purpose.

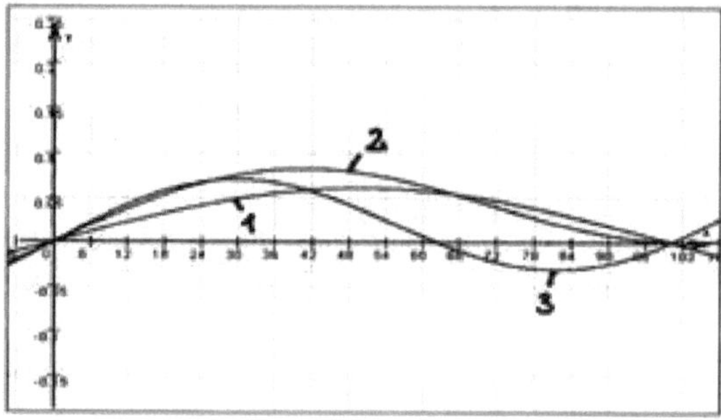

Figure 114

In Figure 115, examples of skeletal lines based on the equations provided in Box 4 are shown. The illustration is exaggerated to demonstrate the different shapes. The numbers 1, 2, and 3 represent different values of the parameter k, where 1 corresponds to $k = 1, 2$

corresponds to $k = 1.4$, and 3 corresponds to $k = 1.8$. The value of w is set to 6 %. In Table VIII, there are several examples of profiles with such cambered shapes.

By using the equations described in Boxes 1, 2, and 4 interchangeably, one can imitate certain well-known profiles if desired. However, these equations cannot describe other well-known profiles, especially those suitable for laminar flow at high Reynolds numbers. This is mainly because the contour functions in Box 1 do not allow for significant thickness distribution without affecting the profile nose. To achieve that, one would need to use two contour functions for the upper and lower contour lines, with the transitions also adjusted accordingly. However, this would deviate from the intention of using as few equations as possible, as pursued in this book.

In the following Figure 116, "imitated" profiles are depicted. The profile designations will be explained later.

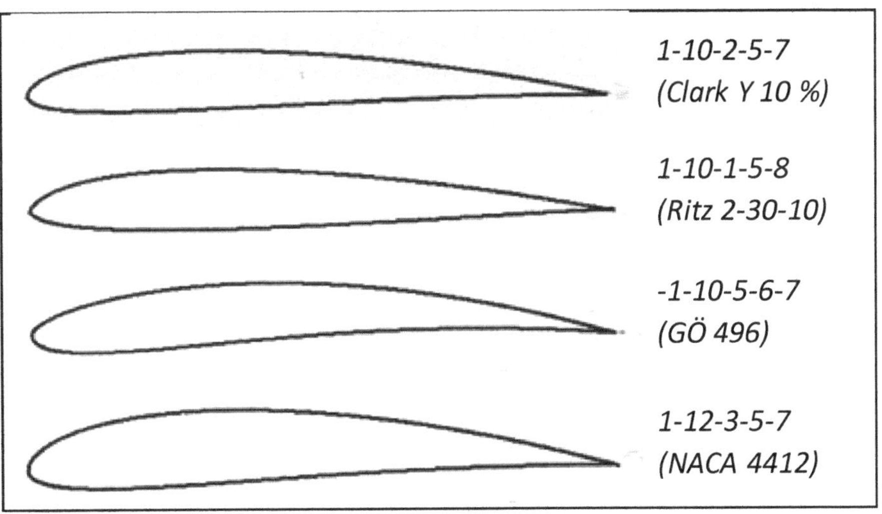

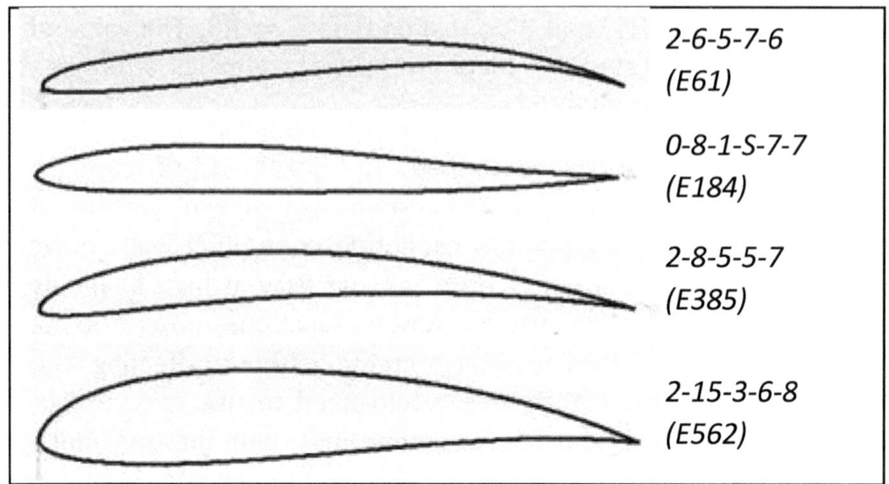

Figure 115

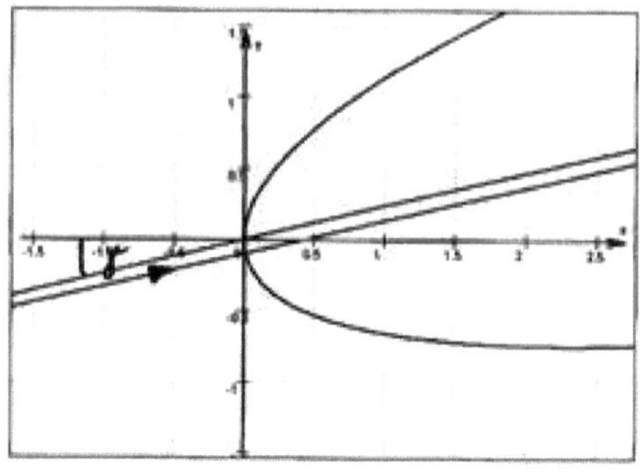

Figure 116

The nose area of profiles can be either rounded or more pointed, depending on whether the profile is designed for a supercritical or subcritical flow. In both cases, achieving the so-called "shock-free flow entry," as described in the chapter "What Else Is of Significance?", involves adjusting the wing position during free gliding so that the flow impinges on the profile nose at the exact angle γ at which the skeletal line is inclined against the profile chord. This is illustrated in Figure 117. The upper line represents the continuation of the skeletal line into the free stream ahead of the wing, while the lower line represents the line that symmetrically intersects the inclined profile nose. Air particles located there have the free choice to continue their path either above or below the wing. Any other inclination of the wing against the flow results in an asymmetric impingement of the respective air particles, thereby limiting their freedom of choice. This leads to a buildup of pressure just ahead of the wing nose, known as a "shock," which increases the resistance or drag.

The favorable flow direction for the profile can be determined from the slope of the skeletal line at $x = 0$. Using the equations for the skeletal line in Box 3, the slope given in Box 4 at $x = 0$ can be obtained. For example, for $p = 2$ and $x_0 = 100$, we have $y'(0) = 0.04\,w$, where w is the wing camber expressed as a percentage. For $w = 5\,\%$, this corresponds to an ideal flow angle of $\gamma = \arctan(0.2) \approx 11.31°$. If the airfoil is inclined at an angle $\alpha = 2°$ against the free stream, the resulting flow angle would be $\gamma - \alpha \approx 9.31°$. However, whether this favorable flow direction for undisturbed flow is present during gliding is a different story. There are many other factors at play (including the deformation of the flow field due to lift generation, as shown in Figure 40). This is why rounded profile noses are typically used, unless one wants to create a turbulent boundary layer by sharpening the nose, which can provide better flow attachment to the upper surface of the wing in subcritical flow conditions.

The application of the equations provided in boxes 1, 3, and 4 allows for a variety of profile variations. For better orientation, the labeling rule depicted in Figure 118 can be used:

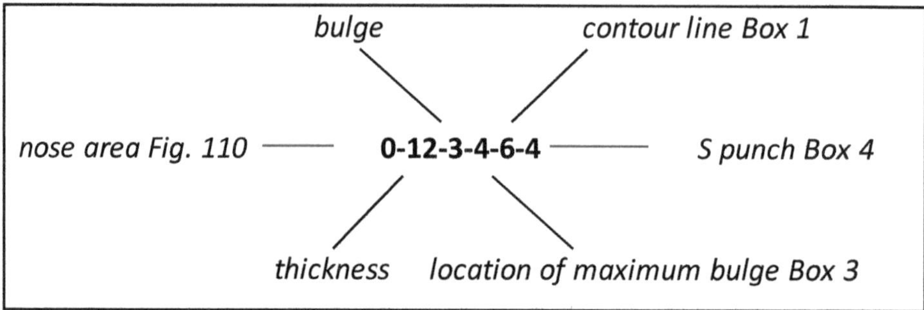

Figure 117

First digit: If it is 0, it indicates a symmetrical contour. If it is 1, it means that 1 % has been subtracted from the lower thickness D_2 and added to the upper thickness D_1, resulting in a 1 % camber with the camber maximum at 25 %. The same applies to digits 2, 3, etc. If it is -1, it means that 1 % has been added to the lower thickness, and so on.

Digit(s) in the second position: It represents the profile thickness as a percentage of the profile depth.

Third digit: It represents the camber measure of the skeletal line as a percentage of the profile depth.

Fourth digit: When using the equations in Box 3 for the skeletal line, it indicates the location of the camber maximum; 1 corresponds to $p = 6$, 2 corresponds to $p = 5$, 3 to $p = 4$, 4 to $p = 3$, 5 to $p = 2$; 1-5 corresponds to the last equation, 6 to $p = 3$, 7 to $p = 4$, and 8 to $p = 5$; and 5-8 corresponds to the penultimate equation. For an S-shaped profile according to Box 4, an "S" is indicated here.

Fifth digit: When using the last equation in Box 1, it indicates the type of contour line; 3 corresponds to $p = 3/12$, 4 corresponds to $p = 4/12$, 6 to $p = 6/12$, 7 to $p = 7/12$, 8 to $p = 8/12$, 9 to

$p = 9/12$, a, b, c, d, e, f, g correspond to $p = 5/6$, 11/12, 101/100, 3/2, 2, 3, 4.

<u>Sixth digit</u>: This digit only appears when an S-shaped profile according to Box 4 is present; it represents the decimal value of the parameter k; 1 indicates $k = 1.1$; 2 indicates $k = 1.2$; and so on up to 9, which indicates $k = 1.9$.

Tables I - XI depict profile "families" that can be plotted using a function plotter by choosing the parameters specified in Boxes 5 and 6.

Based on the previous chapters of this book, we can provide information regarding the use of profiles. Assuming a critical Reynolds number of 1,000,000 for moderately cambered airfoils, the chapter "Where Does Drag Come From?"gives a minimum required flight speed of approximately 13.6 m/s or 49 km/h for gliders with a (average) wing depth of 1 m (sailplane). However, if the (average) wing depth is 0.2 m (model aircraft), a minimum flight speed of 68 m/s or 245 km/h is already required (model of a racing aircraft). In gliders, high flight speeds are accompanied by high wing loadings. For example, the sailplane ASW 17, which glides well at around 90 km/h, needs a wing loading of approximately 350 N/m² to reach these speeds without propulsion. The flight speeds and wing loadings can be lower if a lower critical Reynolds number is known. For instance, the flight speed can be halved, and the glider can be lighter if the critical Reynolds number is 500,000. Gliders with wings flying in the supercritical Reynolds number range should have particularly smooth surfaces in the wing area to minimize the drag coefficient c_{d0}.

Kasten 5

Daten für die Zeichnung von Profilen:

Kontur:

$$y = \frac{D}{2\left(\frac{1}{P}-1\right)\left(\frac{1}{P}\right)^{\frac{1}{P-1}}}\left(\left(\frac{x}{x_0}\right)^{P} - \frac{x}{x_0}\right)$$

siehe Kasten 1

Exponent P	1/4	1/3	1/2	7/12	2/3	3/4	5/6	11/12	1,01	3/2	2	3	4
Nenner $2\left(\frac{1}{P}-1\right)\left(\frac{1}{P}\right)^{\frac{1}{P-1}}$	0,948	0,776	0,5	0,392	0,296	0,211	0,134	0,064	-0,007	-0,296	-0,5	-0,776	-0,948
Dickenmaximum bei $\left(\frac{1}{P}\right)^{\frac{1}{P-1}}$	15,7%	19,1%	25%	27,4%	29,7%	31,6%	33,5%	35,2%	37%	44,4%	50%	57,7%	63%
Kennziffer	3	4	6	7	8	9	a	b	c	d	e	f	g

Hinweis: $x_0 = 100$ verwendet

211

Kasten 6

<u>Daten für die Zeichnung von Profilen:</u>

Skelettlinie:
$$y = w\,\frac{P\cdot(P)^{\frac{1}{P-1}}}{(P-1)x_0}\left(x - \frac{x^P}{x_0^{P-1}}\right)$$ siehe Kasten 3 Gleichung (*)

$$y = w\,\frac{P\cdot(P)^{\frac{1}{P-1}}}{(P-1)x_0}\left(x_0 - x - \frac{(x_0-x)^P}{x_0^{P-1}}\right)$$ siehe Kasten 3 Gleichung (**)

Exponent P	6	5	4	3	2	3	4	5
Vorfaktor $\dfrac{P\cdot(P)^{\frac{1}{P-1}}}{(P-1)x_0}$	0,017	0,0187	0,0212	0,026	0,04	0,026	0,0212	0,0187
Wölbungsmaximum bei $\dfrac{x_0}{(P)^{\frac{1}{P-1}}}$	31,1%	33%	37%	42,3%	50%	57,7%	63%	67%
Anwendung von Gleichung	(**)	(**)	(**)	(**)	(*)/(**)	(*)	(*)	(*)
Kennziffer	1	2	3	4	5	6	7	8

Hinweis: $x_0 = 100$ verwendet

Skelettlinie S-Schlag: $$y = w\left(sin\left(k\pi\,\frac{x}{x_0}\right) - sin(k\pi)\cdot\frac{x}{x_0}\right)$$ siehe Kasten 4

Model gliders with (average) wing depths of around 0.15 m and wing loadings of around 20 N/m² fly at a base speed of approximately 5.7 m/s, corresponding to a Reynolds number range of around 63,000. This is significantly below the critical range, which makes it futile to strive for a smooth surface on the wings of these gliders. On the contrary, a certain roughness of the entire wing surface or specific turbulators can be used to create artificial turbulence and improve flow attachment even in the subcritical range.

Profiles can be broadly classified into thinner and thicker profiles, as well as less cambered and more cambered profiles. Thicker profiles allow for the construction of more stable wings that can withstand bending and torsional stresses. Thicker profiles are also necessary when the wing needs to serve as storage space, such as for fuel reserves, in addition to generating lift. Therefore, profiles with a thickness significantly greater than 10 % of the wing depth are suitable for stable glider wings with high aspect ratios, flying in the supercritical Reynolds number range (high-performance gliders). Thinner and less cambered profiles are suitable for fast gliders or aircraft with propulsion. For commercial aircraft flying at Mach 0.8 with lift coefficients of approximately $c_l \approx 0.5$, well into the supercritical Reynolds number range, so-called laminar profiles with around 9-10 % thickness, small leading edge radius, significant thickness taper, and low camber have gained recognition.

More cambered profiles are typical for high-lift gliders, which means lift coefficients of around 1 and above. This applies, among other things, to the wing design of commercial aircraft during takeoff and landing, where the aircraft weight needs to be compensated for at low flight velocities. This is achieved using leading edge slats and flaps, which are extended during takeoff and landing and retracted during cruise. In a simplified manner, only the camber of the airfoil is adjusted using a control surface at the wing's trailing edge. For lightweight model gliders that fly slowly in the subcritical Reynolds number range, rough wing surfaces, as well as more cambered and thinner airfoils, are well-suited to achieve low sink rates.

If sharper-pointed profiles are used in the nose area, the relationship between the direction of the approaching air and the direction of the skeletal line in the nose area should be considered, as mentioned above, unless one intends to incorporate a turbulator through the sharpening, which promotes better flow attachment to the airfoil under subcritical flow conditions.

Below are tables of airfoils that have been calculated using the equations and parameters provided in Boxes 5 and 6.

Table I

Profiles with the contour described in Box 1, with a constant thickness of 8 %. It demonstrates how various positions of the maximum thickness in symmetrical profiles affect the profile. The changes in the nose area are noteworthy.

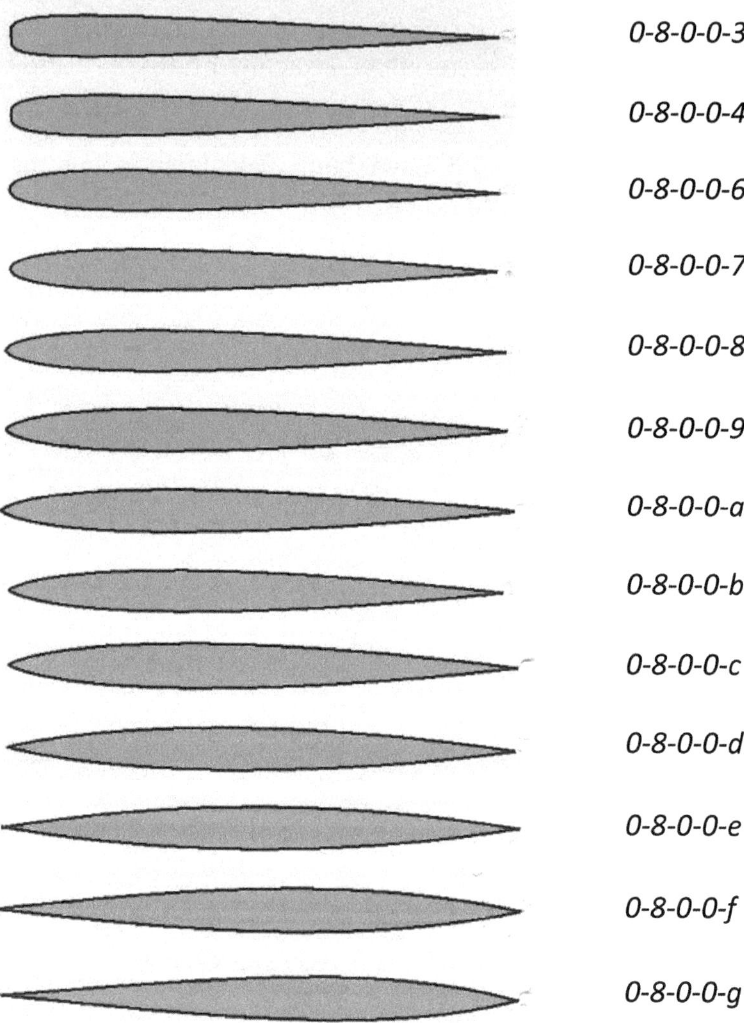

Table II

Profiles with the contour line from Box 1, constant overall thickness of 8 %. Table I shows two example profiles that demonstrate how different upper and lower thicknesses, without a curved skeletal line, result in a certain degree of camber. However, this camber is fixed, and its maximum always coincides with the position of the maximum thickness. The profiles 4-8-0-0-d and 6-8-0-0-d may be suitable for boomerangs. Sharp leading edges of profiles are useful where the flow direction at the profile nose is known. Otherwise, sharp leading edges can function as desired turbulators in subcritical flow conditions.

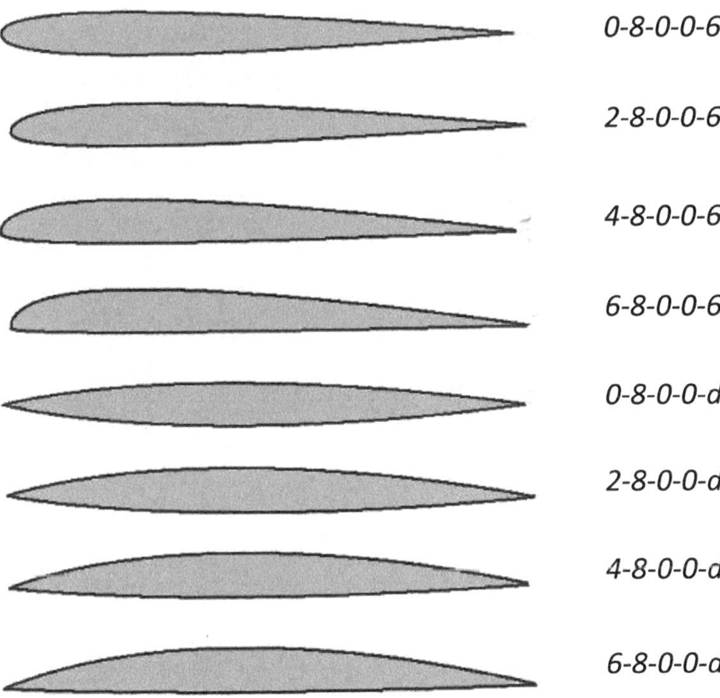

Table III

Cambered profiles according to Box 5, constant thickness of 8 %. Starting from the base profile 0-8-0-0-7 in Table I, three profiles are drawn with increasing camber and increasing camber position. The profile 0-8-2-4-7 has an almost straight lower surface.

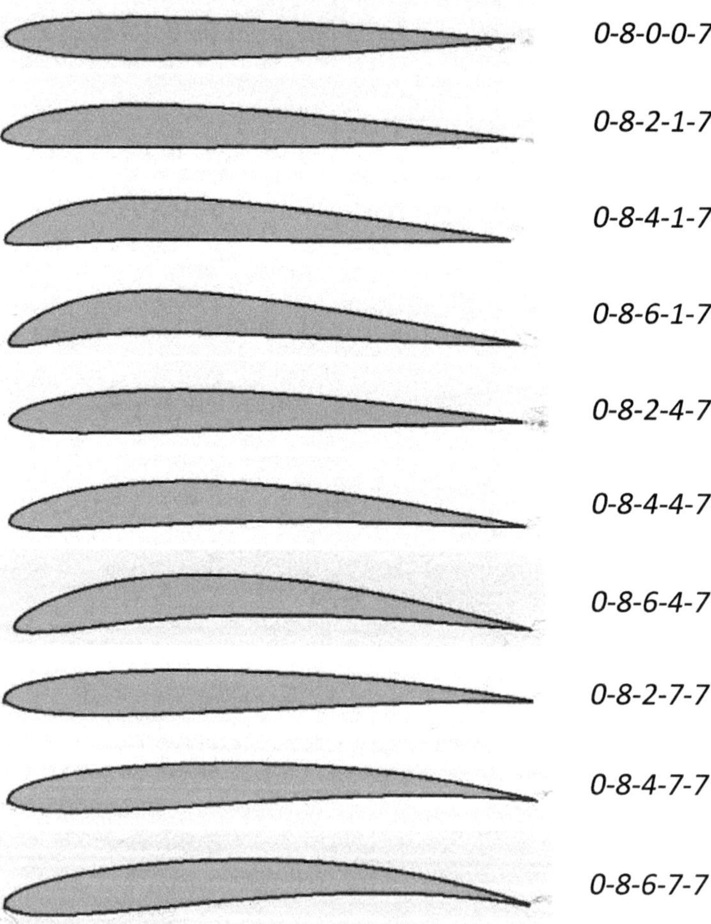

Table IV

Profiles according to Box 5, constant thickness of 8 % and camber of 5 %. It is shown how the various positions of the camber maximum affect the profile while keeping the remaining data constant. As the camber maximum shifts backward, the highest point of the profile and the pressure distribution on the upper surface also shift backward (towards a longer laminar flow attachment).

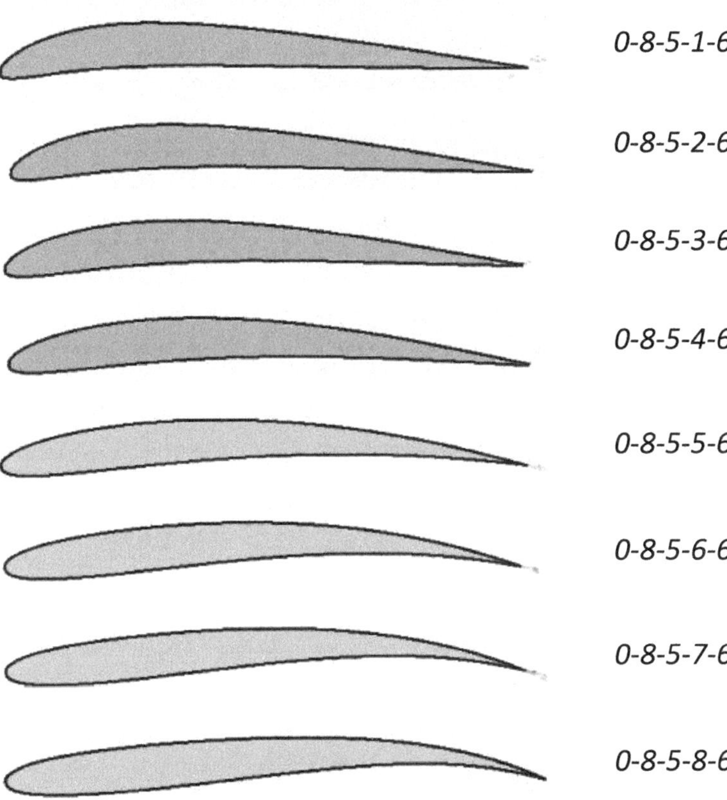

Table V

Profiles according to Box 5, constant thickness of 4 %, increasing camber, decreasing thickness. These thin profiles, inspired by cambered plates, are suitable for gliders. The weak camber is suitable for fast gliders, the strong camber for slow gliders, and the moderate camber is a compromise between the two. The starting profile is the profile 0-4-0-0-e.

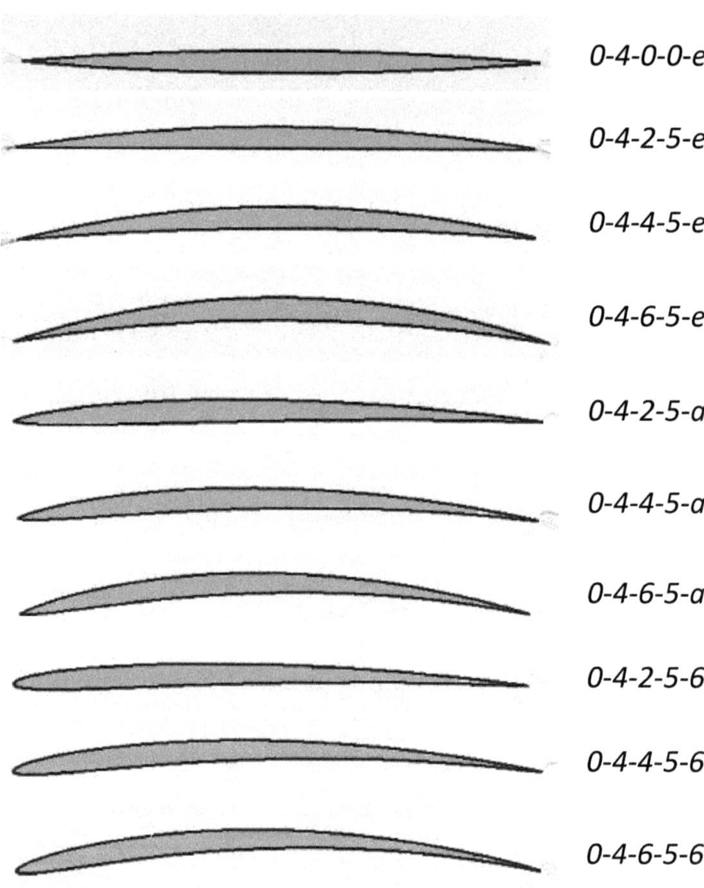

Table VI

Profiles according to Box 5, constant effective camber of 5 %, increasing thickness. A camber of 5 % is considered optimal for achieving the highest glide ratios. However, the development of the profile noses becomes problematic with larger thicknesses; for improvements, refer to Table VII. Strongly rounded profile noses like those in profiles 2-12-3-5-6, 2-14-3-5-6, and 2-16-3-5-6 require a supercritical flow.

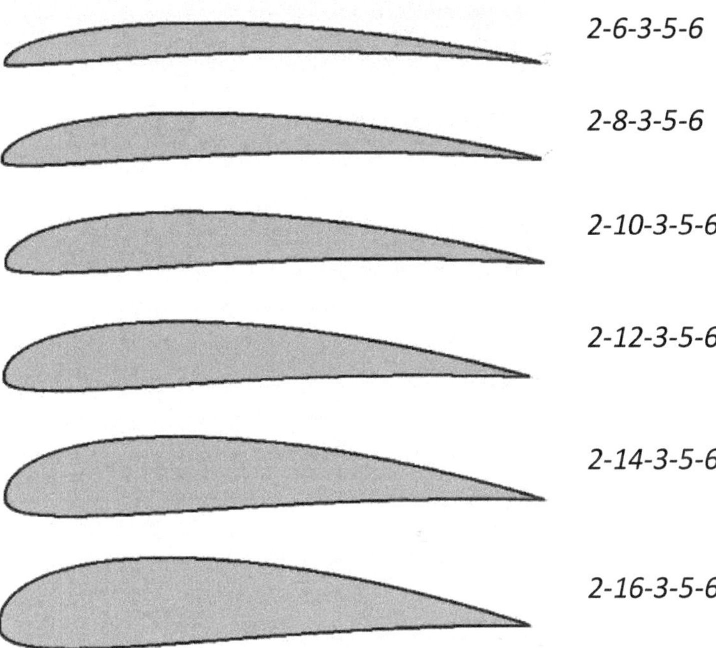

Table VII

Profiles according to Box 6, constant camber of 5 %, constant thickness of 16 %. Illustration of the effects of thickness stagger or camber stagger on the problematic nose region using the initial profile 0-16-5-5-6. These thick profiles require a supercritical flow.

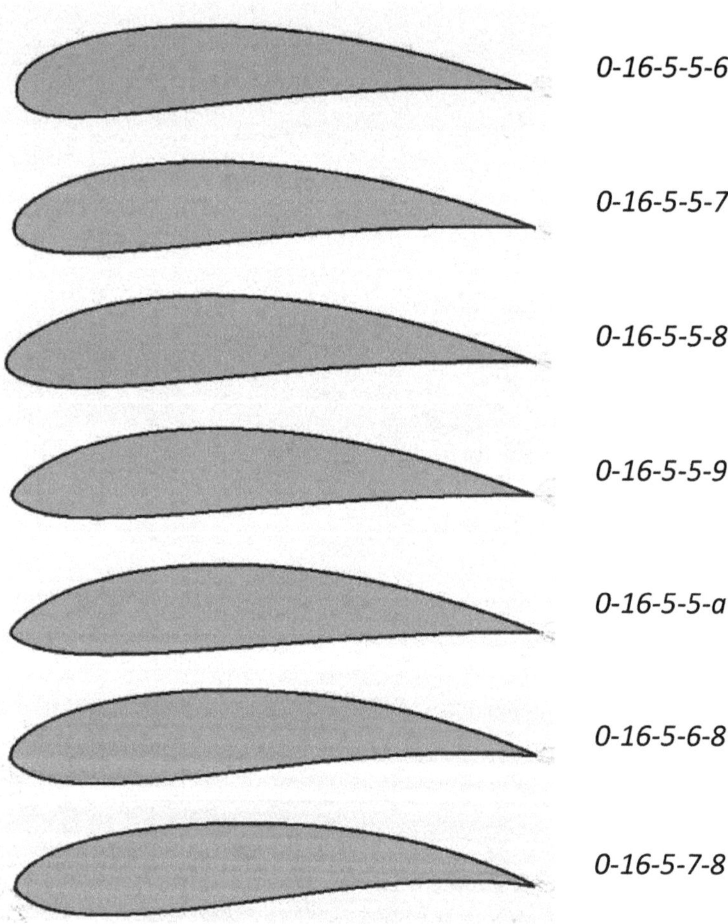

Table VIII

Profiles according to Box 6, constant thickness of 8 %. Effects of different cambers and different k-values for S-shape profiles. Such profiles are typically used in flying wings.

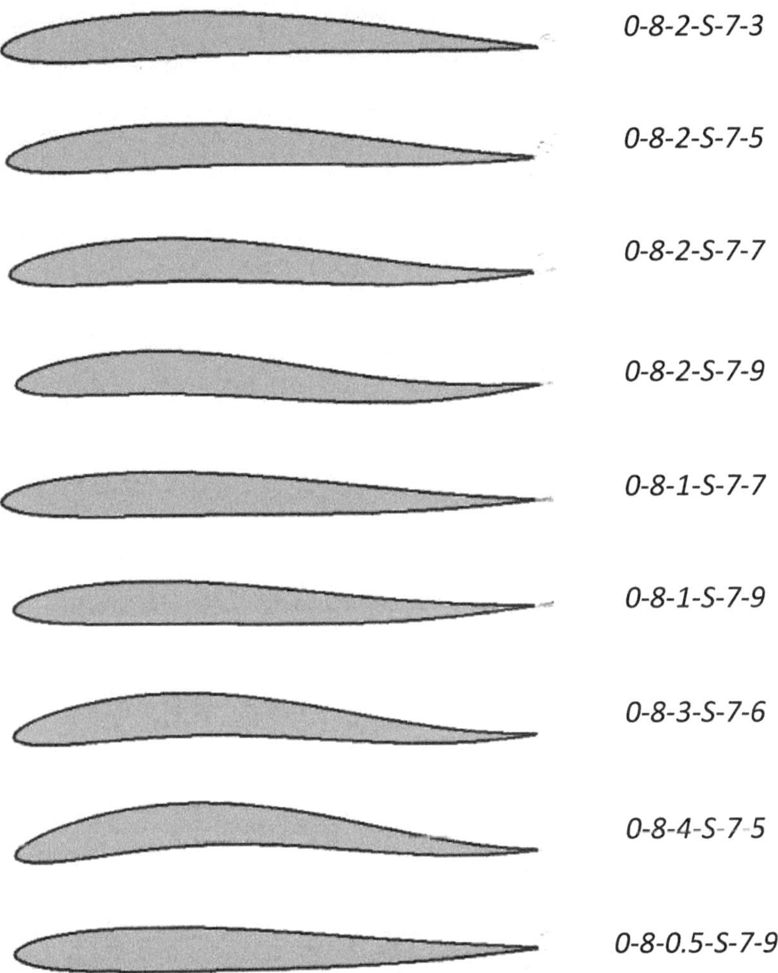

Table IX

"Bird" profiles according to Box 6, constant thickness of 5 % and constant camber of 8 %. Bird-like profiles are thickest in the front part due to the bone structure, and typically, the camber maximum is located there as well. The "corners" in the profile nose are intentional to serve as turbulators during the usually undercritical flows. Birds achieve high lift-to-drag ratios (L/D) while soaring and they possess many unknown tricks to ensure flow attachment.

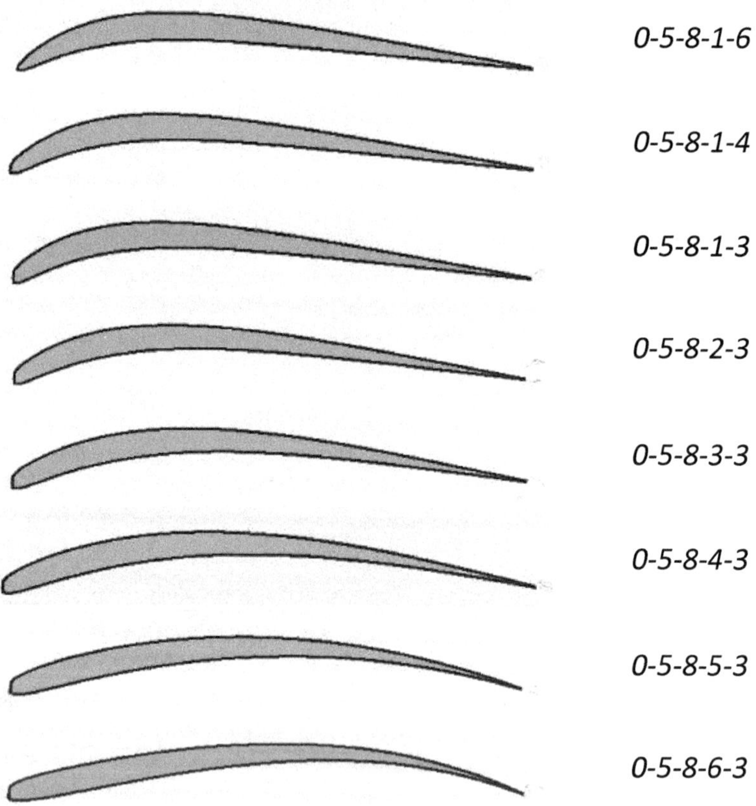

Table X

Profiles with the camber commonly used in modern high-performance glider (or glider model) construction, which is 3.5 %.

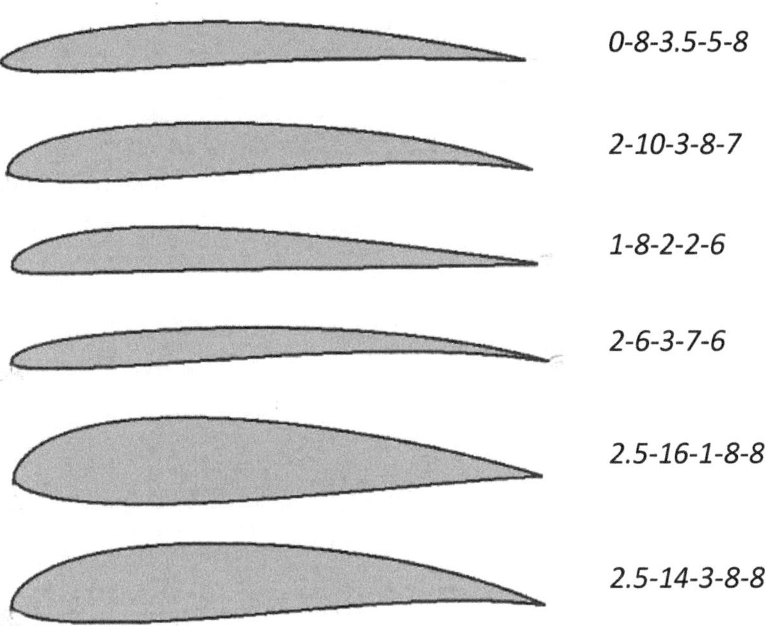

Table XI

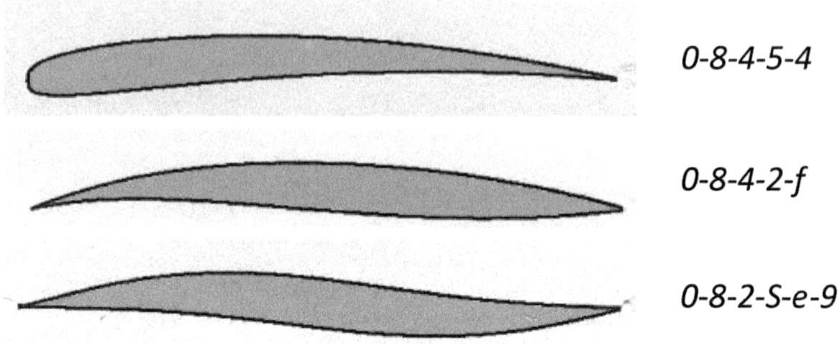

The following are three complete essays on the subject of this book, in which the existing knowledge is applied.

Regarding the Center of Gravity

Lufthansa lässt letzte Reihe frei

Frankfurt/Main. Die Lufthansa lässt in Maschinen des Typs Airbus A320neo aus Sicherheitsgründen die letzte Reihe frei. Die sechs Sitze würden bis auf Weiteres nicht mehr belegt, sagte ein Sprecher der Fluggesellschaft am Freitag. Dadurch, dass ganz hinten keine Passagiere mehr sitzen, wird der Schwerpunkt des Flugzeugs bei Vollbelegung leicht nach vorn verschoben. Die Airline reagiere mit der Maßnahme auf einen Sicherheitshinweis der europäischen Flugaufsichtsbehörde EASA.

Sie hatte Mitte August festgestellt, dass zum Beispiel bei einem sehr forschen Durchstarten nach einem abgebrochenen Landevorgang ein Sicherheitsrisiko bestehen könnte. Zwar sei ein solches Szenario noch nie in der Realität aufgetreten, aber bei Tests im Simulator erkennbar gewesen.

Lufthansa leaves last row empty

Frankfurt/Main. For safety reasons, Lufthansa leaves the last row empty in Airbus A320neo aircraft. The six seats would not be occupied until further notice, an airline spokesperson said on Friday. Because there are no more passengers sitting at the very back, the center of gravity of the aircraft is shifted slightly forward when it is fully occupied. With this measure, the airline is reacting to a safety warning from the European Aviation Safety Authority EASA.

In mid-August, she realized that there could be a safety risk, for example, with a very brisk go-around after an aborted landing procedure. Although such a scenario has never occurred in reality, it was recognizable in tests in the simulator.

For those who are more involved in the construction and flying of model aircraft, the instructions emphasize the importance of adjusting the center of gravity to the "correct" position. As they will experience themselves, if something is not right, the model aircraft becomes difficult to control, or it crashes, or behaves erratically.

However, the explanation for why this is so important is not provided. Naturally, questions arise for which answers have yet to be found: Why is the position of the center of gravity so crucial for flying? Where should the center of gravity be located to prevent the first flight from turning into a disaster? This recently published news article will draw the interest of every air passenger because it concerns their safety. The safety notice issued by the European aviation authority mentioned in this article relates to a problematic center of gravity position in the Airbus A320neo passenger aircraft, which could prove dangerous in the event of an aborted landing maneuver followed by a go-around. Although this safety risk has not yet occurred in actual flight operations, it has been observed in simulations. The landing phase is conducted at a significantly lower flight velocity for various reasons. While a modern passenger aircraft maintains a cruising speed of well over 800 km/h at higher altitudes, the landing speed is much lower, around 250 km/h. The flight condition during landing is generally considered critical because it can lead to flow separation over the aircraft wing, thereby reducing the necessary lift. However, there is another aspect of lift reduction in this context, which is still not well understood.

In the literature, various information can be found regarding the position of the center of gravity. Model pilots are informed, for example, that before the first flight of a new model, the center of gravity should be approximately located at certain positions. For an uncambered wing, it is recommended to place the center of gravity approximately 1/4 of the depth of the reference wing ahead of the leading edge. For a moderately cambered wing, the recommended center of gravity is about 1/3 of the depth of the reference wing ahead of the leading edge. For a lightly cambered wing, the optimal center of gravity lies somewhere in between, while for a highly cambered wing, the center of gravity should be further backwards. These guidelines are considered in the flight direction and assuming that the horizontal stabilizer has a non-lifting profile. However, it is emphasized that the optimal position of the center of gravity will ultimately be determined through practical flying. Model pilots are provided with empirical values for the center of gravity position, and they not only wonder where these values come from but also why they are important.

A logical source of information is the literature on the design of large aircraft. From aviation, calculation methods are derived that can generally be applied to model aircraft as well. An important statement is that the center of gravity must be located a certain distance ahead of the center of pressure when viewed in the flight direction. This distance is known as the stability margin, denoted as Δx, and for conventional aircraft, it is around 6 % of the reference wing depth or slightly more. However, finding an explanation for why this is necessary in the specialized literature is challenging. An answer like "to generate the necessary pitching moment for flight" is not satisfying. Why do we need a pitching moment to fly? If the pitching moment is too small or disappears due to an incorrect center of gravity position, lift performance also deteriorates. Any model pilot who has experimented with shifting the center of gravity backward to reduce drag is familiar with these consequences. But why is this the case?

Regarding the available statements about the center of gravity position, it turns out that precise information is lacking. Let us therefore consider a few known facts to approach the core of the problem. One initial remark concerns the statement: If you have issues with the center of gravity position, ensure sufficient speed. Well, what does "sufficient speed" mean? A commercial aircraft gliding in for landing does not differ significantly from the glide flight of our model aircraft. The flight speed (base speed) of an unpowered glider depends on the wing loading, air density, and lift coefficient of the currently set airfoil. In the practice of model flying, things are even simpler because, in uncontrolled and self-stable flight, the lift coefficient is empirically observed to remain just below 1, regardless of the airfoil used (or must remain so). However, this is different for a powered commercial aircraft. Let us test this fact with a truly large aircraft, the Airbus A380. Its wing loading is about 500 tons per 800 square meters of wing area, or approximately 6250 N/m^2, which is quite high. For it to stay airborne while gliding at a speed of 250 km/h during descent in the lower-altitude air, it requires an airfoil lift coefficient just above 2. Such a high lift coefficient is primarily achieved through significant airfoil camber using deployable leading edge devices and flaps. However, during cruising flight at an altitude of 10 km with the flaps retracted, it flies with a lift coefficient of about 0.5 due to the lower air density at that altitude, at a speed of approximately 850 km/h. Now, this descending A380 needs to go around and perform a go-around maneuver. For this, the nose needs to be pitched up at initially lower flight speed, allowing the lift coefficient to increase to slightly above 2. This not only increases the risk of flow separation over the wing but also, if the center of gravity is at its limit, can lead to additional loss of lift and thus a dangerous flight situation. One reason for this is not mentioned in the press release above.

Let us therefore examine the positions of the center of gravity, center of pressure, and neutral point more closely because it seems that these three points and their respective positions in the aircraft are crucial for flying. First of all, what kind of points are these? The center of gravity and center of pressure are specific fixed points for forces that have similar significance and origins. Unlike a sphere, an aircraft is a highly structured body. All the components of an aircraft have weight. These weights are forces caused by gravity, acting at various points, and directed vertically downwards. According to Newton, all these individual forces can be combined into a single force (the weight of the entire aircraft) that acts at a specific point called the center of gravity. If a body is supported exactly at this point, no torque caused by its weight is present. In the case of a homogeneous sphere, the center of gravity lies at its midpoint. However, the situation is more complicated for an aircraft. For our model aircraft, usually two axes are sufficient to determine the location of the center of gravity: the lateral axis and the longitudinal axis. By observing the balance, the location of the center of gravity in these two directions can be easily determined. The position of the center of gravity in the vertical axis direction is rarely important in model flying, but it can be more significant for larger commercial aircraft.

Similarly, the situation with the center of pressure is analogous, albeit with an unfortunate designation. When a body moves through the air, the point on the body where the so-called aerodynamic force acts is considered as the center of pressure. Again, it can be observed that when the body is "supported" at this point, no torque caused by the airflow is observed. In the case of a sphere in a uniform airflow, it is reasonable to consider a point on the diameter as the center of pressure. However, for an aircraft, the situation is much more complex. All parts of an aircraft generate forces during motion through the air. These forces are typically divided into two categories: the so-called lateral forces, such as lift, which primarily but not exclusively occurs at the wing, and the so-called longitudinal forces, such as drag, which is caused by the displacement work, frictional work, and the generation of vortices in the air. Like the center of gravity, all these individual forces can be combined into a single force, the aerodynamic force, which acts at the center of pressure. Therefore, the center of pressure, like the center of gravity, is a fixed point of forces and not pressures. Let us now stick with the designation "center of pressure." More importantly, where does this center of pressure lie?

In aviation, a third point has gained significant importance: the so-called neutral point. Initially defined as a purely geometrical point within a wing, the neutral point is also related to the sought-after center of pressure, which can be characterized as follows: The neutral point is the anchor at which the center of pressure of an aircraft hangs. The neutral point of any wing is identical to the neutral point of the reference wing. The reference wing is a wing with a rectangular planform that replaces the actual wing in those geometric properties that are relevant for flight: area and location. The neutral point of a reference wing is initially referred to as the point where the symmetry axis and the so-called 1/4-chord of the wing intersect. There is a graphical method by which, for example, the corresponding reference wing and thus the neutral point can be determined for a swept trapezoidal wing (as found in commercial aircraft). However, the most interesting aspect is the concept of the 1/4-chord. When a rectangular wing section is pivotally mounted vertically in a uniform airflow along this line, no torque is observed; the wing section exhibits a neutral behavior. This behavior can be theoretically explained based on aerodynamics, although it is not simple. In the case of a simple glider with a flat plate as the rectangular wing (referred to as a "rectangular wing" here), it is observed that the center of gravity and the center of pressure have specific positions relative to the neutral point for the glider to fly properly: The center of gravity must be placed just ahead of the neutral point when viewed in the flight direction, while the center of pressure is located just behind the neutral point. This is where the aforementioned stability measure comes into play. When using a cambered wing, there is a rearward shift of the center of pressure dependent on the increasing camber. This shift of the center of pressure can be approximated. It is then observed that a certain moment coefficient, specifically the moment coefficient $c_{m0.25}$ (referring back to the 1/4-chord!), remains nearly constant. This moment coefficient results from the torque generated by the component of the aerodynamic force (lift) with respect to the neutral point. This relationship can be used in reverse for the approximate determination of the center of pressure's location. For this reason, the neutral point is also referred to as the aerodynamic center. If the location of the center of pressure is known, the center of gravity must be positioned ahead of it by the stability measure Δx when viewed in the flight direction, for ordinary aircraft.

Everything is wonderful! Models set up in this way usually fly quite well right from the start. Is everything clear now? No, because we still do not know what the interaction between the center of gravity position and the generation of lift entails. So far, only flight mechanical data have played a role. And already there appears a rarely discussed problem on the horizon: A constant nose-down moment caused by the separation of the center of gravity and the center of pressure. However, this does not seem to occur during flight! Therefore, there must be a constant opposing moment during flight that compensates for the nose-down moment. What is this opposing moment? And where in the literature is this phenomenon addressed?

As we contemplate this question, we eventually come across the observed relationship between the magnitude of the nose-down moment, which arises from the position of the center of gravity relative to the center of pressure, and the generation of aerodynamic lift. Therefore, we need to take a closer look at the generation of aerodynamic lift. Regarding the generation of this lift, there are two serious theories to consider. It is assumed that the majority of readers (including the author) see the cause of aerodynamic lift in the formation of a suitable vortex that forms around the wing during flight and remains consistently associated with the wing. This vortex can be referred to as "circulation." It ensures that a certain average pressure difference, corresponding to the wing loading, is created due to the different flow velocities above and below the wing, in accordance with Bernoulli's principle, thus keeping the aircraft airborne. Now, the crucial point is this: if this vortex is actually present and not just a convenient mathematical model used to explain the generation of aerodynamic lift, there must be a physical reason for its existence. In the technical literature, the circulation is attributed to a principle of fluid dynamics known as the vortex theorem, which states that after the aircraft takes off, a closed system of vortices is established: a starting vortex, two trailing vortices, and, of course, the circulation. However, an uncomfortable question arises: how can a rapidly diminishing starting vortex, which disappears shortly after takeoff, sustain a receding vortex like the circulation at the wing continuously? It simply cannot. Trying to resolve this by suggesting that the two trailing vortices sustain the circulation is also futile. The cause and effect are the other way around: only when a circulation vortex is present at the wing does it create a pressure difference, which, due to pressure equalization at the wingtips, then leads to the formation of trailing vortices. Therefore, the question remains: what is responsible for the establishment of a constant circulation?

Given the two questions at hand: What counteracting moment compensates for the nose-down moment? and Who generates the circulation vortex? along with the observation that the magnitude of the nose-down moment and the generation of aerodynamic lift are evidently related, the converging answer becomes apparent. The circulation vortex, or rather the counteracting moment generated by it at the wing, compensates for the nose-down moment. Or, in terms of Newton and his principle of action and reaction: the nose-down moment is the actual mechanical cause of the circulation and thus the generation of aerodynamic lift. The obvious objection that the horizontal tail could be responsible for generating the counteracting moment needs careful consideration. Because the horizontal tail, with its slightly negative setting relative to the wing (in the case of a flying wing, this results in a slight up-cambering of the wing trailing edge), is primarily designed to induce the wing's angle of attack against the airflow. With a cambered wing, this matter is difficult to comprehend, but it becomes easier to understand with a flat plate wing or a wing with a thin symmetric airfoil, as in those cases, the location of the center of pressure is practically independent of small angles of attack. In such cases, an asymmetric flow around the wing, which is a prerequisite for lift generation, can only be achieved by forcing an angle of attack against the direction of the free stream.

Let us assume that the pilot of the Airbus A320neo mentioned in the press release has ensured sufficient speed during landing. Therefore, there is no risk of reduced lift due to flow separation. The pilot expects to be able to control the aircraft safely, and if necessary, perform a go-around. However, the simulator indicates that with the current distribution of weight, specifically with passengers seated up to the last row at the back, a go-around would be too risky. Why? Because during a go-around, the significant change in the aircraft's attitude and the fuel surge back into the tanks could cause the center of gravity to move dangerously close to the aerodynamic center. This would result in a reduced magnitude of the pitching moment, leading to a decrease in the circulation flow and, consequently, a decrease in aerodynamic lift. As a result, the aircraft could sink and contact the ground. To prevent this, the center of gravity should be located sufficiently forward, which is why the last row of seats should remain unoccupied.

Trials and Tribulations

For about 40 years, two serious but fundamentally different views on the cause of aerodynamic lift have been presented: one predominantly European and one predominantly American. What is unusual about this is not only that this situation has remained unchanged for such a lengthy period but also that it seems to continue to persist for the time being. In Scientific American, it was stated in early 2020: "No consensus exists." Here is a brief summary of the two theories: Most Europeans derive dynamic lift from the generation of a pressure difference above and below the wing, while many Americans (and some Europeans as well) attribute it to the reaction of air deflected downwards by the wing. As a result of this controversy, a great deal of confusion has emerged in the applied literature regarding the understanding of flight. One of the most perplexing statements resulting from this is as follows: "By applying Bernoulli's law to the airflow around a wing, one can observe that it leads to a pressure difference between the upper and lower surfaces. The resulting force, due to the conservation of momentum, then necessitates a change in the direction of the airflow downwards. The corresponding change in momentum of the air is precisely equal to the lift force on the wing."

It appears that the author of this quote has boldly and swiftly resolved a persistent problem that has lasted for 40 years: by merging both theories, they have magically achieved consensus! It would be nice, however, if one could actually understand it. Unfortunately, significant problems arise from this approach. Allow me to briefly address the three main statements in the quote.

- "Seeing" how the Bernoulli equation generates a pressure difference in the flow areas above and below the wing based on the observable airflow around the wing with lift is likely only granted to a few. This explanation has been insufficient since the early days of aviation.

- It remains puzzling how a change in the direction of airflow downwards can be derived from the force on the wing resulting from the pressure difference, based on the conservation of momentum. It is the opposite during flight: the pressure gradient on the wing holds the potential for upward airflow. This can be observed at the wingtips, where a potential upward flow transforms into an actual upward flow, forming the two wingtip vortices.

- Finally, it is suggested that the change in momentum resulting from the deflection of air masses by the wing precisely corresponds to the lift force on the wing. Assuming this is true, calculations reveal implausible air masses that would need to be redirected at small deflection angles for weight compensation. Additionally, it becomes incredibly challenging to explain the high glide ratios of aircraft. Redirecting significant air masses requires energy and creates drag that cannot explain the observed glide ratios.

In summary, the provided quote fails to address the complexities and limitations of the explanations it attempts to combine. It highlights the difficulties in fully understanding the mechanisms behind aerodynamic lift and its practical implications.

Let us further delve into the third statement. If the redirection of airflow by the wing is crucial for generating dynamic lift, it is not understandable why flying wings (German Nurflügel) can fly at all. Flying wings have airfoil sections (profiles) that roughly resemble the shape of a lying "S," which is why they are referred to as "S-shaped profiles." With such profiles, the trailing edge of the wing, in relation to the horizontal airflow, is directed upward instead of downward, as in conventional aircraft (see Figure a). Consequently, the flow direction immediately behind the wing does not allow for the necessary downward deflection of airflow and the associated change in momentum required for generating dynamic lift. So, what is the explanation for the flight capability of flying wings?

Figure a: The S-flap airfoil of a tailless wing

Let us continue discussing the flying wing a little longer. The flying wing is likely the first form of a glider developed by nature (example: Zanonia seeds). When examining the flying wing more closely, we can observe the interdependence of conditions that are crucial for its ability to fly. In addition to the problem of generating dynamic lift, there is also the solution to a specific stabilization problem. The S-shaped profile of the wing in a flying wing design is necessary to angle the wing against the airflow and thereby force an asymmetric flow around the wing. This, along with a specific center of gravity position, brings the flying wing into a "flight" attitude that is commonly referred to as longitudinally stable, although the meaning and purpose are usually not explained. Explaining the connections between stabilization measures and the generation of aerodynamic lift is quite complex and requires further elaboration. However, it is worth mentioning the significance of the horizontal stabilizer on a "conventional" aircraft. The horizontal stabilizer is nothing more than the outwardly cambered trailing edge of the flying wing, and due to its much greater distance from the main wing, it is significantly more effective. Therefore, the horizontal stabilizer, with the help of the weathervane effect, forces an upward angle of attack of the main wing against the direction of the free airflow. Consequently, the chord line of the horizontal stabilizer must be slightly negative with respect to the chord line of the main airfoil. Model aircraft enthusiasts refer to this as the incidence angle, while others may call it the incidence angle difference (IAD). (German: "EWD").

Therefore, the following conclusion suggests itself: An aircraft, whether it's a conventional aircraft, tandem configuration, or canard aircraft, can fly longitudinally stable only if the main wing and tail or canard and aft wing, similar to the flying wing, form a flat surface or "pan," and if the center of gravity is positioned in a specific and determinable location. The relationship between "pan formation" and the correct center of gravity position can be studied most intensively in the case of the flying wing. To better understand the conditions that enable flight, one can try something initially seemingly crazy. An inherently stable flying wing, equipped with the usual V-shaped configuration and a vertical stabilizer, is fitted with a wing that is oppositely cambered, i.e., negatively cambered or in a "pan" shape, as shown in Figure b. If one succeeds in gliding such a configuration, it brings us closer to understanding the conditions that make flight possible.

However, the flying wing with a negatively cambered wing glides quite poorly. Its glide ratio of about 5 is, however, slightly higher than that of an optimal forward sinker, which is around 3. In the case of the better-researched flying wing with a flat board-like wing and a cambered trailing edge, the glide ratio is approximately 8. These are all low glide ratios because the respective airfoils are aerodynamically unfavorable. Only the S-shaped profile shown in Figure a is aerodynamically favorable and low in drag, as demonstrated by the designs of the Horten brothers' flying wing gliders with glide ratios well above 25. However, it is a misconception in aviation to conclude that the generation of lift is solely a matter of wing profiling. The profiling of a wing serves solely to reduce certain drags.

In brief, there are several misconceptions and confusions regarding lift generation in aviation that should be mentioned. Those who reject the idea of creating a pressure difference on the wing as the true cause of lift generation must confront two underestimated factors related to the surrounding air pressure. Because we do not usually notice the effects of this pressure in everyday life, it may seem insignificant. However, this perception changes when we consider a few simple numbers. To lift a heavy aircraft like the Airbus A380, which has a wing loading of approximately 6,200 Newtons per square meter, a medium pressure difference of exactly this magnitude is required on the wing. It may appear to be a substantial amount, but when compared to the surrounding air pressure, which is about 100,000 Newtons per square meter, it is relatively small, approximately 6.2 % of it. For a model glider with a wing loading of 12 Newtons per square meter, a pressure difference of about 0.12 ‰ of the air pressure is sufficient to keep the glider airborne. One may question, "How can such a small amount of something I don't even notice be enough to keep an aircraft in the air?" But that is exactly how it works! From a physics standpoint, it is worth examining the amount of work required to create the appropriate pressure difference on the wing during flight and where this work comes from.

In the case of a glider, this work is obtained from the sink rate: When descending, potential energy is released. It can be estimated that roughly half of this energy is used to overcome drags, while the other half is used to create the necessary pressure difference on the wing.

Figure c

An impressive example of the hydrodynamic paradox: In the invertedly attached funnel, air is blown into it from above using a blower. The Styrofoam ball remains suspended in the funnel. Additionally, a lead weight piece is attached to the wooden rod. The instability is caused by a trembling motion of the ball.

A different aspect where the surrounding air pressure has an impact is the observation of the so-called hydrodynamic paradox. If one searches for this paradox in aviation literature, one will usually find nothing, as this observation has not been significant in that context so far. However, upon closer examination, this will have to change, as seen in Figure c. Something astonishing is observed! The Styrofoam ball does not fall off or get blown out of the funnel, but rather gets pulled into it, despite the force of gravity pulling the ball outwards, despite the blower creating an overpressure in the funnel that would push the ball out, and despite the changes in direction of the blown air streams causing impulse changes that would also push the ball out. What is the solution to this puzzle? In the air gap between the ball and the funnel wall, there is a decrease in pressure, leading to a local pressure in the gap that is lower than the surrounding air pressure. And that pushes the ball back into the funnel. Apparently, this alone is sufficient to overcome all other opposing forces! Indeed, this is the aerodynamic lift we are looking for, the lift that pushes the Styrofoam ball upwards and also keeps our airplanes in the air. However, the question of who causes the pressure decrease in the air gap between the ball and the funnel wall is of a specific nature, historically associated with the name Bernoulli, and it is worth discussing it in detail.

Is there a chance of restoring the consensus lost 40 years ago regarding the cause of aerodynamic lift? And thus putting an end to the confusion and misconceptions that have arisen since then? Let us see if what has just been mentioned can convince anyone...

Comments on the "Zeit" Article Page 163

Foreword

Since around 1980, the consensus regarding the explanation of flight and the origin of aerodynamic lift for weight compensation has been lost. Until then, the aviation industry provided an explanation that, while not entirely satisfactory, was generally accepted by all parties involved and even made its way into university and school textbooks. The basis for weight compensation was the creation of a certain average pressure difference on the wing, corresponding to the so-called wing loading. For some reason, a few individuals who noticed the gaps in the aviation industry's explanation came up with a completely different idea: they proposed replacing the pressure difference as the basis for weight compensation with the redirection of airflow caused by an angled wing and the resulting reaction force. When these individuals realized that this idea could reproduce fundamental equations of aerodynamics, an alternative explanation was born. Since then, it has spread in academic circles and textbooks, claiming to be more physically accurate and easier to teach. However, it remains peculiar that the aviation industry and its research institutes have largely ignored and continue to ignore this alternative explanation.

The coexistence of two completely different explanations for the same phenomenon of flight in the field of natural sciences has puzzled and even concerned other thoughtful individuals for the unusual duration of about 40 years. During this period, several questions have arisen that neither of the two explanations can answer, but the answers to these questions determine the direction in which the search for truth should be pursued. Three of these questions and related observations are now being considered to come to a decision.

1. Sinking and Gliding

In all the existing literature, both from proponents of the pressure difference explanation and those proposing the deflection of airflow as the cause of dynamic lift, the following observation has remained unmentioned and therefore has not been considered in discussions regarding the nature of dynamic lift. The observation pertains to the flight characteristics of an uncontrolled model glider, such as those used in the F1A competition class (formerly known as A2), which has been flown in world championships until recently. This glider has a flight speed v_∞ of approximately 4.4 m/s, derived from a wing loading of $F_g/A = 12 \ g/dm^2 \approx 12 \ N/m^2$ and air density ρ, using $v_\infty \approx \sqrt{2F_g/\rho A}$. The glider is launched using a precisely 50-meter-long high-start line. To prevent it from flying away due to possible

242

thermal updrafts, a technique known as "thermal brake" is employed after reaching the maximum flight duration of 180 seconds per flight. This technique involves fully deploying the entire elevator surface, causing the glider to descend in its normal flight attitude more or less vertically downward. During this descent, it descends at such a low speed that no damage occurs upon impact with the ground. Unfortunately, measurements of vertical sink rates after activating the thermal brake for such gliders are not available. However, we now know that these two speeds - the gliding speed v_∞ and the sink speed $v_\perp$ after activating the thermal brake - are approximately equal: $v_\infty \approx \sqrt{2F_l/\rho A c_l}$ and $v_\perp = \sqrt{2F_d/\rho A c_d}$. An unpowered, uncontrolled glider with $F_l \approx F_g$, regardless of other factors, will fly with a lift coefficient c_l slightly below 1, and during steady sinking, $F_d = F_g$, with a drag coefficient c_d of similar magnitude.

During the vertical descent after activating the thermal brake, the glider disrupts a significant amount of air, generating a considerable amount of drag that compensates for its weight (steady sinking). When gliding at approximately the same speed as during vertical descent, the weight also needs to be compensated. Does this mean that during gliding, the specific redirection (turbulence) of air portions, corresponding to the vertical descent, is necessary to compensate for the weight? The answer can only be no. Those who believe otherwise must explain how observed glide ratios of 17 in competition gliders or 50 in modern high-performance sailplanes are achieved under these conditions because the glide ratio is, among other factors, the ratio of the magnitude of lift to the magnitude of drag. And during gliding, the magnitude of drag is much smaller than that of lift.

2. Static and Dynamic Lift

Since the first publications on the so-called Karlsruhe Physics Course (Prof. Falk and Prof. Hermann), processes that were previously described with more static quantities have been replaced by dynamic quantities in our textbooks. In accordance with material flows and electrical currents, energy flows, entropy flows, and even momentum flows should be considered. Although there were clever ideas, this course sparked fierce controversies among physicists and educators. Some observations in mechanics proved to be particularly stubborn. It has not been possible to confine something as static lift into a framework of momentum flow. Based on current knowledge, regardless of how uncomfortable descriptions involving the derived quantity of pressure may be, there seems to be a unanimous understanding: Static lift is a manifestation of pressure in a fluid situated in a gravitational field.

Is the dynamic lift also affected? For proponents of the pressure difference, yes. However, about 40 years ago, Professors Anderson and Eberhardt from the United States (in their book "Understanding Flight: forget Bernoulli, use Newton") and later Professor Weltner and his students in Germany embarked on a quest to find a tangible representation of the desired momentum flow for generating lift during flight: air masses deflected downward from the wing. They found this phenomenon in something that had been known for a long time: the flow downstream of the trailing edge of an ordinary wing has a downward direction. The proponents of the pressure difference theory, who argued that there was an upward-flowing region ahead of the wing generating lift, either ignored or did not believe in the concept of air mass deflection.

Given the incompatibility of the two narratives regarding the origin of dynamic lift, questions naturally arose: What is true? Is dynamic lift a quasi-static pressure phenomenon in a gravitational field, or is it a result of the deflection of air masses by the wing? The crucial question for determining the truth in the natural sciences is: Have resulting deflections of air parcels by a lifting wing on a freely flying aircraft ever been observed? If not, supporters of the concept of air mass deflection may need to reconsider their perspective.

3. "Coandá Effect"?

A significant problem arises when trying to understand the phenomenon of flow attachment to convex surfaces. It is this flow attachment, particularly on the upper surface of a wing, that allows the supporter of the pressure difference concept to draw their conclusions and provides the supporter of air flow deflection with the specific impulse flow required for dynamic lift. The latter group found their answer in the observations made by a Romanian engineer named Coandá in 1910, who noticed oil streaks on the tail of his bulbous fuselage motor aircraft. Subsequently, the term "Coandá effect" was coined to describe the phenomenon of flow attachment to convex surfaces, which was previously unknown in aviation. However, labeling an observation does not provide an explanation. This did not bother most supporters of air flow deflection, but those who wanted to understand why air parcels can follow a convex surface were left with the only option of attributing it to some cohesive properties of the air particles. However, this explanation fails to hold up: Like any other gas or gas mixture at room temperature, air fills any available space provided to it, and cohesion does not play a role. While air parcels can be subjected to pressure, they do not exhibit cohesion. Therefore, the unanswered question remains: What is responsible for the attachment of fluid flow to a convex surface?

Anyone who recognizes that pressure phenomena are solely responsible for force interactions in a gaseous fluid like air will inevitably have to grapple with the unsympathetic pressure problem.

And therein lies the apparent challenge: We do not perceive it due to its omnipresent effect, and therefore, we have no intuitive sense of it. For example, to keep a large and truly heavy aircraft like the Airbus A380 airborne, a moderate pressure difference of approximately $6250\ N/m^2$ is required on the wing. Is that a lot or relatively little? Compared to the atmospheric pressure at the Earth's surface on the order of $10^5\ N/m^2$, it's actually quite small, only about 6.25 % of it. "Wait, such a small amount of something I don't even feel is enough to keep such a heavy aircraft in the air?" a layperson might wonder. However, an expert knows that this air pressure exists and therefore asks: What happens if an airflow along a convex surface refuses, due to its inertia, to follow the curvature of the surface? Imagining the details of how a passing air parcel is pressed against a convex surface by the ambient pressure is certainly not easy, although it becomes easier to visualize with a water film. It is no wonder that a significant part of aviation research is focused on developing an understanding of the conditions under which airflow adheres to surfaces.

Epilogue

The three sets of questions mentioned above are certainly not the only ones to be asked about flying. They were selected because their clarification allows for an answer to the schism in aviation described above: Who is responsible for the necessary dynamic lift? Given the complexity of flying and its conditions, one could apply a method recently known in a completely different fundamental question of the natural sciences: How probable is the emergence of the Homo sapiens species in light of the Darwinian theory of evolution, and alternatively, in light of a "guided design" incorporating the results of modern DNA research? One examines individual sub-questions and assesses the likelihood of the truth of existing, i.e., verifiable answers. For example, a so-called "missing link" that demonstrates the evolutionary transition from primates to modern Homo sapiens in the last 100 to 200,000 years has not yet been found in a cave or excavation (the "missing link" is also missing for the Neanderthal, and even with DNA studies, they are found to have little connection to Cro-Magnon humans). If we had at least one such "missing link," we could answer this sub-question with a certain probability > 0 in favor of Darwinism. Similarly, we proceed with the other sub-questions. Of course, assigning probabilities to each individual question is not free from some degree of arbitrariness. However, in the overall evaluation of all such sub-questions, a tendency usually emerges, allowing for one's own assessment (don't we also know the significance of probabilities for truth in complex systems from modern quantum physics?).

If one engages in such a method of "truth-finding," one comes into conflict with that rigorous evaluation method that determines truth-finding in mathematics and has likely shaped it in the natural sciences as well: Just one verifiable counterexample renders a statement false. Natural phenomena, however, typically prove to be so complex that the mathematical method of truth-finding can hinder an approximation of truth due to our fundamental lack of knowledge about essential connections and conditions. Nevertheless, the mathematically rigorous evaluation method is also indispensable in future sciences of complex systems. If the opposite were to happen, if just one fitting example were to make a statement true, this would require its application. Not only proponents of the diversion of airflow to generate dynamic lift should consider this.

About the Author

The author, born in 1939, has been fascinated by aviation for a long time. As a young boy, he built his first gliders and even then wondered why there was so little explanation about how to adjust a glider so that it could fly at all. Later, he initially wanted to become an archaeologist but ended up studying physics. His academic journey culminated in a Ph.D. in solid-state physics. After years of scientific research, he made the decision to become a secondary school teacher for mathematics, physics, and chemistry. It was there, in school, that he could pass on his experiences in aviation to enthusiastic young minds. He also got acquainted with the controversy surrounding aviation, which became the subject of the book at hand. When it was clear after many years that this controversy could not be resolved amicably, he decided to present his own perspective on flying: "How to Fly".